Praise for *Thunder and Lightning*

'A typically hilarious dive into the early years of Colin Bateman and family in one of N. Ireland's oddest wee towns: Bangor, Co. Down. I loved it!'

Adrian McKinty

'I slipped into a lovely warm epsom salts bath and began reading Mr Bateman's terrific *Thunder and Lightning*. I couldn't put it down, even as my bath got colder! He writes with such truth and deceptive simplicity, always with a smattering of good oul' Ulster humour, even and especially as his early and middle life has the back drop of N. Ireland's 'Troubles' just ten miles up the road from his Bangor home town. Funnily enough, Mr Bateman's autobiography ends with him having a Thunder and Lightning moment as he lies in a bath!'

Liam Neeson

'A beautifully evocative, strangely moving and consistently hilarious portrait of the writer's coming of age in a sleepy Northern Irish seaside town. There's only one Colin Bateman.'

James Nesbitt

'Even at the height of the Troubles, life in Northern Ireland was about more than conflict. Colin Bateman was busy growing up and messing up. This memoir will tickle your ribs while picking your emotional pocket. As mouth-watering as an Ulster Fry, only with fewer calories and a lot more laughs.'

Ian Rankin

T0158715

Colin Bateman is the author of more than thirty novels, including *Divorcing Jack*, *Mystery Man* and *I Predict A Riot*. He wrote the screenplay for the film version of *Divorcing Jack*, and for *Crossmaheart*, *Wild About Harry*, *The Journey* and *Driven*. He also wrote the plays *National Anthem*, *Bag for Life* and *Nutcase*. In 2010 he was made an Honorary Doctor of Letters by the University of Ulster, for his Services to Literature. Yes, seriously. He lives in Bangor, Northern Ireland.

THUNDER
ᴬᴺᴰ LIGHTNING

A Memoir of Life on the
Tough ~~Streets~~ of Bangor
Cul-De-Sacs

COLIN BATEMAN

MERRION
PRESS

First published in 2022 by
Merrion Press
10 George's Street
Newbridge
Co. Kildare
Ireland
www.merrionpress.ie

978 1 78537 435 7 (Paper)
978 1 78537 436 4 (Ebook)

A CIP catalogue record for this book is
available from the British Library.

Typeset in Sabon LT Std 11.5/17 pt

Cover design by Fiachra McCarthy

Merrion Press is a member of Publishing Ireland.

Contents

Preface

I KNOW SOMEONE WHOSE PET parrot whistles our loyalist anthem 'The Sash' every time somebody comes to their front door.

In Belfast, this would be considered vaguely sinister, a reinforcement of historic bigotries channelled through a captive bird with green feathers, the captivity being symbolic and the green being sarcastic.

In Bangor, my home town, it's just funny.

That is essentially the difference between the city and the town, between their Troubles and our troubles. We were always just on the fringes of what went on. Even though there was carnage twelve miles up the road, most of what we experienced, we experienced through the television news. We had a chip on neither shoulder. It was a bit like our football supporting. The clubs we were fervent about were Liverpool and Manchester United – close, but still removed; a sea between us, never to be seen in the living flesh.

Ours was largely a Protestant town. I was eleven years old before I met a Catholic. We were not aware of injustices, of discrimination, of tensions between communities, because there only was one community. If there were Catholics they were scattered around, there wasn't some Papish enclave we had to fear. Nice, safe, mostly middle-class, solidly unionist but still vaguely liberal, sardonic Bangor, with its lovely parks and tennis clubs, where a child pretending to be a paramilitary was something to be encouraged and applauded, as offensive as a Morris Dance.

I love and hate Bangor with equal measure, but what I can never change about it is that it is home. I once yearned to leave, but now know I never will. It is as remarkable and unremarkable as any other town. It used to be a destination, and then planes were invented. Our Victorian seafront is now literally gone, replaced by a fucking marina. A parade that used to feature hotels, bars, chip shops, seagulls and amusement arcades is now a boarded-up eyesore. And yet, once, it was, almost literally, the centre of the world, famous for sending its missionaries abroad. Legend has it that Altus, the Roman Centurion at Golgotha, at Calvary – the soldier who said, 'Truly this man is the son of God' – was an Irish mercenary who fled Bangor because he heard about the plans for the fucking marina.

This is a book about my growing up, about school and small-town journalism. It has the vagaries, and mistakes, that come with memory – but they're still my memories. If there is an occasional embellishment or reordering of events, they are only feeble attempts to make me look fractionally more heroic. Names have occasionally been changed to protect the guilty. If any offence is taken by those still living, well, you were probably asking for it. Never cross me.

1

The Wellington Olympics

I WANT TO TELL YOU about the Olympic Games. You do remember when the Olympic Games were held in Bangor in 1972? More precisely, they were held in Wellington Park. More specifically around the circular block which connected Wellington Park, Wellington Drive and Wellington Gardens. We called it The Block. It had about the same circumference as a 400-metre running track, give or take a hundred metres. The Block is still there, you can go and visit it. The houses it surrounds are much smaller than they used to be. But there is nothing there to commemorate the historic Wellington Olympics of 1972.

The Wellington Olympics were thought up by our gang: The Wellington Boot Boys. Mainly Rodney, Dougie, Terry, Michael and me, though others came and went. Paul was one of those who drifted through. He was Michael's big brother. He had spina bifida. This was before the Paralympics were thought of. He was as enthusiastic as any of us. He could turn, but only awkwardly. He could run, but only slowly. His nickname was Billy Whizz, after the *Beano* character. It was funny then, and it's quite funny now, though possibly cause for a tribunal and my never working in Hollywood again.

My nickname was Bacon. I think it comes from someone not being able to pronounce Bateman. But you never really know. One day it was there, and it stayed. Is Bacon coming out to play? Where's Bacon? It lasted until I was a teenager. Then nobody asked those questions.

I remember the summer of '72 as blazing hot. It may not have been. There's probably a way to check. Summers, then, lasted forever, and there was bugger-all on the TV, apart from the actual Olympics, which were taking place in black and white. Mary Peters was going to win Gold for us in Munich. She was a big woman who looked like a farmer's wife, and she might well have been. There's probably a way to check. She was going to win the Pentathlon. Nobody quite knew what a Pentathlon was, but it sounded like a good thing to win. As part of it, she threw the shot put. You wouldn't mess with Mary Peters. She'd break your back if you messed with her. She sounded Northern Irish, but she was English. We didn't know that then or she wouldn't have had so much support. Besides Mary Peters, the Munich Olympics also had terrorists and many deaths, but we weren't much preoccupied by that as we had our own terrorists and deaths. Our Olympics were taking place in colour, though obviously we didn't actually have any people *of* colour – the first black man didn't arrive in Northern Ireland until 1973 and he thought it was too violent and moved on.

The colours we were concerned with then were Gold, Silver and Bronze, though admittedly we were equally fascinated by Red, White and Blue. Luckily for our Olympics, the Twelfth of July was well over – we had already marched up and down Wellington Park as the Cardboard Memorial Flute Band. We didn't have any instruments – we would play imaginary flutes, and when we got bored with that, we would become Me-Me men – you know, playing the pretend bagpipes. *Me-me, me me me me me me me me.* Rodney always marched at the front of the band because he was the best at throwing the stick. Every band leader had a stick. For us, it was usually a broom handle with a tennis ball taped to one end. Rodney could twirl it behind his back and throw it high in the air and catch it and twirl it again and throw it, all in time to the beat of the drums we didn't have. Rodney came from Lurgan, which for us was quite exotic. He might as well have come from Timbuktu. We had no idea where Timbuktu was either. He lived around the corner in Chippendale. I used to copy his maths answers in P4. His dad might have been a Me-Me man. I think he was. My Uncle Roy was a Me-Me man, though for some reason we didn't talk to that side of the family. You never really know why families divide. You're too shy to ask when you're young, and when you get older, there's no one left to ask.

For three months up to the Twelfth it was the most important thing in our lives. We started collecting for the Eleventh Night bonfire to celebrate it immediately after Easter. This meant knocking on doors and asking for wood. A surprising amount of people had wood. Or made a point of finding wood. It's amazing how many people can find wood when required to by a gang of twenty boys demanding it. There were perfectly good sideboards and wardrobes donated to the cause out of a combination of loyalism and fear. People went out and bought furniture just so they would have something to give us when we called. It wasn't without its dangers. A skelf in the finger was an occupational hazard. You would get rid of the skelf – a small sliver of wood that would embed itself when you were shifting planks – by applying a bread poultice. Yes, I was born in the eighteenth century.

One house we called at consistently was Grumpy McVeigh's. He lived on the corner of the Park and Drive, about four doors away. We called at his house every year, even though he never gave us any wood. We also called at his house at all times of the day and night, ringing his bell and running away.[1] Generations of us rang his doorbell and ran away. He was called Grumpy because he made the mistake of being grumpy about it. He had a long white beard and was very old. He looked like Santa Claus without the red suit, but he didn't act like him. You wouldn't have wanted to sit on Grumpy's knee; he would have throttled you. Do you know what happened to Grumpy? He died. That's what happens to grumpy people. He lived with his sister. She didn't seem bothered by us at all and outlived him because of it. She was easy come, he was easy go.

The Derwents were directly across the road from us. They were English. Their youngest child, Jane, was my best friend for a while, but we also played with her two big brothers, Alan and Roger; there was an older brother we didn't have much to do with. Roger was my brother's age. His nickname was Dibble, after Officer Dibble in TV's *Top Cat* cartoon. Dibble's dad hated him being called Dibble. His dad was an old-school martinet and sometime Scout master. At Hallowe'en my dad invited all the neighbours round to our back garden; it was

---

1   This was called Thunder and Lightning.

probably the last year before fireworks were banned because of the Troubles. The government didn't want Catherine wheels in the hands of terrorists. For many years afterwards we had to make do with sparklers. The terrorists weren't as interested in sparklers. But that last year my dad had all the neighbours round, all the Derwent kids, and their parents too, and many more besides. He placed the fireworks in milk bottles for debatable safety and set them off. Everyone had a good time, i.e. nobody died.

A week later the Derwents had their own firework show in their back garden, because they were still English and were celebrating Guy Fawkes. My brother and I went to watch the fun over their garden fence. Mr Derwent spotted us. We expected him to wave us in. But, instead, he chased us away. Then he went to our front door and complained to Dad that we'd been sneaking a peek. That's the sort of man he was. My dad called him The Duke, and I always thought it was because he was a bit pompous. It was forty years before I finally twigged: The Duke of Wellington.

I can't emphasise enough how everything seemed to revolve around us being Protestants. We had no idea what a Protestant actually was. We went to Sunday School, but, as in most families, that was just so our parents could get us out of the house. My brother was once almost sucked into the Plymouth Brethren. A friend called Uel Kennedy invited him along.[2] My brother went, but soon decided there were limits to friendship. Nevertheless, despite our lack of commitment, the Twelfth was

---

2   He should have known something wasn't right with a name like Uel. That's just weird. If he'd been a Liverpool supporter he could have sung, 'Uel Never Walk Alone'. But he wasn't. Which is just weird as well.

a celebration of being Protestant and it was right up there with Christmas as the high point of the year – although technically it was the Eleventh we loved more than anything, because we could stay up after midnight for the bonfire and were given extra pocket money for sweets. This was before the twin spectres of girls and alcohol altered those nights forever, when Kicking the Pope was still more important than copping a feel. Because there was No Pope Here. Or anywhere, as far as we were concerned, apart from Rome. The Pope was in Rome and he could stay there, while we relaxed in the warm glow of a bonfire on the 'Green Grassy Slopes of the Boyne', though actually the Boyne was across the border where *none* of us had ever been, because why would you?

My dad had been across the border exactly once in his life, and that was on his honeymoon. He grew up in Belfast, first on Lindsay Street and then Ulsterville Avenue. He went to Fane Street Primary School, which was in the shadow of Windsor Park, home of Linfield and the Northern Ireland team. My mum's family was Bangor through and through. She grew up at 100 High Street. There's a beautician's there now, called Breathe, which unfortunately she is no longer able to do. She worked in a shop. My dad's parents, John and Ada, eventually moved to Bangor and lived in the now disappeared Williamson Lane and then on Broadway,[3] right beside Ward Park.

Mum and Dad met at a dance. She was seven years older than him. Today you'd call him a toy boy. Back then he was a toy boy who'd blown up Nazis from his tank. I never saw

---

3   Look Ma, we made it to Broadway!

them dance anywhere else. I was never at a wedding or a funeral my whole childhood. My mum didn't marry until she was well into her thirties. They got married at Bangor Parish Church. The bridal party was conveyed to the wedding in a Daimler limousine, which cost £2.10 to rent from James Russell & Co., 'weddings a speciality'. They also buried people, but that must not have been a speciality. Maybe their burials were rubbish and they left bony hands sticking out of graves. For their honeymoon, Dad put Mum on the back of his motorbike and they headed south. They had seven nights at the Central Hotel in Dublin, and then on to the Metropole Hotel in Cork. In Dublin they went to the Abbey Theatre to see a Terence Rattigan play. I only know about it because long after they were gone I found the theatre programme in the Hat Box of Important Stuff they kept under the stairs. I know that it starred Ray McAnally, who was later in *A Very British Coup* and *The Mission* and then died of a heart attack shortly thereafter.

Although 'the Free State' was right next door, we never officially went south as a family, although we once strayed accidentally into Letterkenny before retreating, horrified. We went to Ballycastle or Portrush on the north coast if we needed a holiday. We never went properly abroad, unless you count the Isle of Man. I wasn't on a plane until I was nineteen. That time we went to Blackpool. I was way too old to be on holiday with my parents. I had just met my first proper girlfriend and spent the week pining for her and thinking she'd be off with someone else by the time I got back. But no, she waited for me, at least for a while. Eventually she was Bad News. I killed time in Blackpool by going to a punk festival in a park, and to the cinema to see a Gary Glitter film, *Remember Me This Way*, which we were destined not to.

My parents lived first in a tiny house in Alfred Street, less than a stone's throw from where my mum grew up. They brought my brother David home there from Bangor Hospital in 1959, but soon moved to the High Donaghadee Road, a twenty-minute walk away from the town centre. That's where they brought me home to. We lived there until shortly after I started primary school in September 1966.

My Auntie Lily lived with us for as long as I knew her. I don't really know what her story was, besides that she was a spinster and my mum's older sister and that she worked in Shorts, the aircraft factory, in Belfast and occasionally brought us home brochures about the plane they were building there, the Shorts Skyvan. She didn't actually build the planes. She was a test pilot. No, a clerk. She smoked like a train and knitted a lot. Eventually she had a stroke. After it she could still smoke, but she couldn't knit, which was a godsend for us all. She could walk, but she was less dextrous than Billy Whizz. We made terrible fun of her.

Michael Caldwell lived next door. He was my age and deaf and dumb. We made fun of him too. We were terrible. When my brother wanted to make fun of me, which was often, he would call me Colin Michael Caldwell – because my middle name is Michael – and I would cry. He still does it sometimes, and he's sixty-two. For the things we said and did, we should have been in the Bad Boys Home. We were occasionally threatened with it. Most children were. But occasionally my dad would drive us past it – it was in Millisle, which is a poor man's Donaghadee – without saying anything, at the same time saying a lot.

We had an Ormo Bread man who had no thumb on his right hand. He told us he'd sucked it off to make us stop sucking our own thumbs. You couldn't say that to kids today, they'd need counselling.

My best friend in P1, Colin Cairns, lived around the corner. He brought me back to his house one day in a state of great excitement because his parents had purchased a fridge. I'd never met anyone who had a fridge. His mum made orange ice lollies in the freezer compartment. I'd never dreamt such a thing was possible. And she gave me one for *nothing*. With that sort of power, she could have brought down capitalism. Once you control the means of production … But she probably didn't think of that. She was too busy making orange ice lollies.

Throughout my childhood I only went to a restaurant once with my parents. That was for my dad's fiftieth birthday. We had minute steaks and Black Forest gateaux in the Skandia on Main Street. We weren't deprived or noticeably poor. I didn't know anyone who went to restaurants. I don't know how restaurants survived. Nor were we ever in a pub. Pubs then didn't serve food. None of them. If we ever did eat out it meant sitting at a table in a chip shop. Usually along Queen's Parade, our seafront before the fucking marina, with its bingo halls and sleazy cinema and seagulls. My dad never went out for a pint with his mates. I'm not sure if he had mates. As an ex-soldier he could go to the Royal British Legion club on Hamilton Road. He went once, perhaps in an effort to meet old friends or foster new ones.[4] He came home and said everyone was drunk, and never went back. He wasn't against drinking and enjoyed the odd whiskey, but he drank infrequently. Mum

---

4   Not *foster* foster. That would have been weird.

hardly drank either. When they had friends round, Mum drank advocaat,⁵ which hardly counts.

I can only remember going once to the pictures with my parents. Bangor had two cinemas, the Tonic on Hamilton Road and the Queen's Cinema on the seafront. The Queen would not have been impressed by the one named after her. It was known locally as the Fleapit. It showed mostly re-runs and X-rated movies,⁶ and specialised in soft-core porn films, which mostly seemed to feature Italian nuns and which we tried to get into but were usually turned away from because we hadn't yet entered puberty. Eventually it burned down under Mysterious Circumstances. My one cinema visit with my parents was to the altogether more salubrious Tonic, which was a 2,000-seater with a massive screen, one of the largest in the UK. It was a birthday treat when I was about five to see *The Sound of Music*. I fell asleep shortly after 'High on a hill lives a lonely goat-herd'. The film seemed to go on forever. I think it was more their birthday treat than mine.

My Auntie Lily took my brother and me to see a double bill of *The Magnificent Seven* and *Ambush Bay*. *The Magnificent Seven* is a classic. But I was even more enthusiastic about *Ambush Bay*, surely the best war movie ever made. When I was all grown up, I set about tracking it down to find out why it had been neglected by film history and discovered it starred Mickey Rooney and was rubbish. I saw various James Bonds

---

5   Hugely popular in the 1970s, a custard-like drink which is 20 per cent alcohol. Originally from Brazil, where it was made with avocados, it was reimagined in Holland as advocaat, but because avocados won't grow in northern Europe they used eggs instead. Boke.

6   Today's 18 certificate. We classified an X-rated movie as one 'with tits'.

at the Tonic, always during someone else's birthday treat. There was always a love for the movies. Around the time of the Wellington Olympics, I would take myself off to the Tonic to watch the Saturday afternoon matinees. I only recently discovered that my brother did the same. Nobody kidnapped us and kept us chained to a radiator in their basement. Very few people had basements. Being chained to a radiator in a living room would have led to early detection. We sat by ourselves and nobody interfered with us. Eventually the Tonic burned down under Mysterious Circumstances. It was owned by the same people who owned the Fleapit. They had bad luck with Mysterious Circumstances.

I mention the plays and the movies only because we were not a family much steeped in culture, although there were occasional flurries. There weren't many books in the house that we actually owned. My dad went to the library every two weeks and took out books about the First World War for himself and about ghosts for my mum, who for some reason was obsessed – or possessed. Later I found out that we had relatives who dabbled in spiritualism and rose quite high up in the Spiritualist Association. Eventually they were Promoted to Glory. Spiritualism grew quite big in the inter-war years because so many lives had been lost in the First, and people were desperate to contact their loved ones. I don't know how seriously my mum was into it. There were no hand-holding sessions around the dining table, and the only voice that ever came from above was my dad trying to fix the TV aerial on the roof.[7]

---

7   That was a dangerous job. It killed Rod Hull. Emu survived, but he was never the same.

I was an early reader and prone to obsessions the way kids are. *The Story of Dr Dolittle* was a favourite. *Dr Dolittle* led to *The Hobbit*. *The Hobbit* led to *The Lord of the Rings*, and *The Lord of the Rings* changed my world. Most of my parents' reading, however, consisted of them perusing lists of houses for sale. Every Saturday morning my dad would go round the various estate agents picking up the new lists and they would spend hours in our kitchen going through them, choosing which houses they wanted to view. They didn't seem to have any real intention of moving. They just liked looking at other people's houses. It was their thing. Maybe they were just nosy. Maybe they were aspirational. They lived in hope of winning the Football Pools, which was a big thing and might finance their big move. Or Spot the Ball in the *Saturday Night*, which was the sports paper published by the *Belfast Telegraph* on – you guessed it – a Saturday night and was often the only way we had of catching up on the football results. It was also, for some reason, known as 'The Ulster'. You had to put an X on a photo from a football match, indicating where you thought the missing ball should be. You put about thirty Xs and then you had to post it in. God knows how it was ever decided. I suspect it was a swiz. They sent theirs in for years and won fuck all.

We occasionally went to the Little Theatre in Bangor, which was a little theatre in Bangor. We went to see *The Prime of Miss Jean Brodie*, which I chiefly remember for the words 'sexual intercourse' being shouted out from the stage – which was mortifying even though I had no idea what they meant. But I suspected. Mostly I remember it being really hot in there and the play going on forever.

We went to see James Young there too. He was a Belfast comedian who sometimes dressed up as a woman as part of his act. He was the biggest star we had in the early '70s, besides footballer Georgie Best. The woman he played was usually no-nonsense and working class, an old Aggie channelled through a camp entertainer. We were raised on Morecambe and Wise, Mike and Bernie Winters and the Goodies on telly, who all did good clean jokes with maybe a touch of innuendo, but a million miles from the political comedy that was to come in the '80s. James Young was doing it in the early '70s, sending up the politicians and the bigotries at a time when it really could have got him shot. He outsold The Beatles at their peak, but only in Northern Ireland (there was a *Very Much Live in Canada* album, but that could have been with two men and a wee lad there for all I know). He was also a *homosexual*, but nobody seemed to hold that against him – which was strange, because at the time you could still be burned at the stake for being one. Often our town centre would be full of burning homosexuals, although on alternate weeks it was Catholics. The *great* thing about James Young being a homosexual was that his lover, Jack Hudson, appeared on stage with him every night, always playing the straight man. The straight man! Oh, how we would have laughed if we'd had any idea.

James Young lived in a bungalow in Ballyhalbert. Ballyhalbert is a tiny village on the Ards Peninsula. It's a hole in the middle of nowhere, though I suppose quite scenic on a good day. When we first got a car, my dad would drive Mum and me and my brother Davie and sometimes my Auntie Lily down past his home and we would gawp in. It was a *bungalow*, and bungalows had only recently been invented. It was a marvel to look at. It had a name too, at a time when we'd never heard of houses having names. It was called 'Camelot'. I drove past it myself in recent years and it's *tiny*. But like Wagon Wheels, it seemed big at the time. I suppose he was having a joke, calling it Camelot. King Arthur would have had a problem squeezing a round table into that living room. Even getting it through the front door would have been a problem. He would have had to take it apart and then reassemble it inside, although he probably had people who would do that for him. We never caught a glimpse of James Young or his straight man, but we didn't mind that.

We'd seen his bungalow.

Maybe we were just blasé about celebrity because we already had one living in our street. Tommy James. He was a Cockney from the Mile End Road in London who came to work in a Belfast music shop, demonstrating and selling pianos, before getting a break playing one on UTV. Pretty soon he had his own show, *Teatime with Tommy*. He was possibly the only musician UTV employed, because he popped up in everything, but we mainly knew him because he played the piano on the children's show *Romper Room*, which we all grew up dreaming about appearing on. Tommy was tall and bald and kind of the antithesis of Liberace in his manner and presentation. We presumed, because he was on TV, that he was a millionaire and we couldn't work out why he would choose to live in our street, just opposite our house then four doors up to the left. He lived next door to the Askews, whose son Peter was my brother's best friend and whose sister was known far and wide as Spaghetti Legs because it was the era of the miniskirt and her legs seemed to go on forever – although she was no Twiggy, more Special Branch.

Whenever we went Hallowe'en Rhyming we always made a beeline for Tommy's front door in the expectation of receiving huge wads of cash. Hallowe'en Rhyming usually started at the tail end of August. Fireworks were banned because of their explosive content and masks seemed to be in short supply; when we knocked on people's doors we merely pulled our anorak hoods down over our faces. In other words, we made the least possible effort.[8] We may as well have just knocked and said, 'Give us your money.' Tommy never gave us cash. He never even gave us fricking *coins*. He gave us nuts. He would hold out a bowl of nuts and encourage us to help ourselves. *Nuts*. Jesus Christ, Tommy man, we want money, not fucking nuts.

Tommy's flame burned brightly for a few years. Sex, drugs, rock'n'roll, none of these played a part in his life – and then he was gone. We didn't mourn his passing, memories of his stellar career always blighted by memories of rock-hard Brazil nuts and almonds we would never suck.

He was lucky he didn't get them back through his windows.

What saved his windows was that we were in Bangor, not Belfast. We were altogether more genteel. And within Bangor, we were in Ballyholme, which was the nicest part. Wellington Park was lower middle class. Or perhaps upper working class. White collar, certainly. Small private houses peopled mostly

---

8   It was legalised begging, but fabulous. We also did the more traditional things at home, like sixpences hidden in silver foil and served up in apple crumble. Lost two teeth that way. And dunking for apples in a metal bath full of cold water. My cousin drowned that way.

with the lower-level civil servants who still make up 98 per cent of the workforce in Northern Ireland. There were no Catholics. We didn't know any Catholics. We were good, hard-working, healthy Prods. Billy Whizz was the only boy with any kind of disability in our neighbourhood, in fact in our entire school, apart from the bloodless boy I'll come to later. There was no asthma, no ADHD, no allergies. Maybe it was something in the water. Maybe it was something not in the water.

Our gang, the Wellington Boot Boys, was the second-toughest gang in Ballyholme, but that wasn't saying much. We talked a good fight, but we made a point of not fighting anyone. There was the Churchill estate just opposite our school, Ballyholme Primary. Churchill had its own gang and its own bonfire, and they were altogether tougher there – or at least we thought they might be because it was a council estate, but we never dared to find out. Rumour had it that there was a tartan gang in Churchill, and when I say tartan gang I mean TARTAN GANG, because that was a thing, being in a tartan gang, and they were reputed to be brutal.

Tartan gangs were loyalist street gangs who gained their name from the tartan scarves and flashes of tartan they wore on their denim jackets and denim bell-bottoms. They'd cut you up, they would. They've largely been forgotten by history, save for their bizarre influence on pop music, their questionable tartan style being adopted or hijacked by Scottish teen sensations the Bay City Rollers. The tartan gangs themselves fizzled out just as quickly as the Rollers, in most cases being absorbed into the newly formed Ulster Defence Association.

The UDA were known by their rivals in the Ulster Volunteer Force as The Wombles because of their habit of wearing fur-trimmed parkas. Sartorial elegance was never the calling card of loyalist paramilitaries, at least until the days of Jim Gray thirty years later. He was the brutal brigadier of the East Belfast Battalion, who was well known for his style and, in particular, for his love of cashmere. He was later shot dead by his own organisation, which just shows what a predilection for cashmere can do for you.

We didn't go anywhere near Churchill and never encountered a tartan gang, because the fear was enough to keep us almost exclusively in the vicinity of The Block and The Field, which was just behind The Block and where the bonfire slowly took shape in the weeks leading up to the big night. The Field had a gentle slope down to a flat base where we played football on rough grass with jumpers for goalposts. The Field belonged to The Farmer, but The Farmer never seemed to use it. There was never a cow in it.

As the donated furniture and discarded tyres arrived for the bonfire, it gradually ate into the area where we could play football, and so instead we switched to building mode, constructing intricate and sturdy forts out of wood and cardboard that could withstand anything but rain and where we would be stationed by the older boys to keep guard over the bonfire materials.

The bonfire itself would not actually be assembled until a couple of days before the Eleventh because we lived in mortal fear that someone, most likely from Churchill, would sneak in during the night and burn it down. It was competitive rivalry, and meanness. That meant some of the older boys – absolutely not us, or not yet – sleeping in the fort overnight. We thought that was pretty brave. Sleeping in the fort was a fairly new thing. Previously boys had slept in a hollowed-out hideout within the bonfire itself, but the practice was discontinued when a Belfast bonfire was burned down with a gang of kids inside it. At least that's what we were told by our parents. You believed everything your parents told you. Now you'd google it and know they were making it up.

On the big night we'd be down to Rankin's shop on the corner of the High Donaghadee Road. It was run by two chirpy sisters, like the Pigeon sisters in *The Odd Couple*. We'd load up on sweets and then hide them somewhere around The Field to be enjoyed later. We'd barely be able to conceal our excitement as midnight and the lighting of the bonfire approached. It was the summer, so it didn't get properly dark until around eleven, and then there was an hour when parents argued with the older boys over getting the fire lit early so that they could go home and there was always a bit of a stand-off until someone lost their temper, emptied a can of petrol over it and threw a match, and there'd be a whoosh and up it would go to a roar from the crowd. There'd be several hundred by this stage – and we'd be singing 'The Sash', and someone who was actually in a band would produce a flute and we'd sing along, and then someone might actually have a drum and we'd sing along some more and march up and down over the smouldering grass in the flickering light, half-choking on the poisonous fumes from the burning tyres and hopped-up on Sukie SunKap orange juice and Football Chums (four for a penny) and Sherbet Dips and Opal Fruits, and it was the best night ever. If we could have signed up with the UDA there and then we would have because we were ready to defend Ulster to our last drop of blood, and of course I had a positive role model in this, because my dad was already in the UDA.

* * *

It had been a bloody year. In January thirteen unarmed civilians were shot dead by British paratroopers in Londonderry. We'd listened to the news bulletins on the TV throughout the evening, with the increasing numbers of the dead and injured being read out in special bulletins like ever-changing football scores. The Northern Ireland Prime Minister, Brian Faulkner, was forced to resign and our parliament was suspended. The IRA announced a ceasefire that somehow managed to make matters worse – and anyway, it lasted less than a month.

In the early hours of Friday 24 March, the Troubles really and properly arrived in Bangor. A woman phoned in a bomb warning shortly after midnight and the police were able to evacuate all residents from the town-centre area. An hour later the first bomb went off in Main Street. Four hours later the army detonated a second. All the shops we knew so well were badly damaged. Nobody was hurt, but it finally felt like we were really in something.

The Wellington Boot Boys were shocked by having our own bomb, but also kind of excited. We understood that it was something bad, but it was also an opportunity. One of the shops that was wrecked was Woolworths. The rumour quickly spread that the company was dumping its smoke-damaged stock on the Mud Hills, which was what we called the long stretch of land where they were constructing a ring road around the town. Our part of it was just a few hundred yards beyond The Field. Incredible to think that back then most of the town was contained within the boundaries of that ring road, whereas nowadays it cuts it in half.

If there was buried treasure on them thar Mud Hills, we were determined to find it. Hundreds of kids, and not a few adults, swarmed around them in a cheap plastic Gold Rush, convinced that there were barely damaged toys just waiting to be reclaimed from the sea of churned-up mud that went on for as far as the eye could see. We became action men looking for Action Men. Fights broke out as prospectors staked claims. Saloons soon opened selling cheap whiskey and cheaper women. We used spades borrowed from our dads. When the spades broke, we used our bare hands. When our hands were scraped and bloody, we swallowed handfuls of Midget Gems to numb the pain and got back to work. We were going to be rich. We were going to live in mansions and buy the best Chopper bikes money could buy. We toiled in the rain, we toiled in the dark, and finally we hit pay dirt and our lives were never the same again.

Or, after all our efforts, we discovered ... a box of wristwatch straps. Not watches – straps. Straps that we were convinced would be the source of our future wealth. Because the world was crying out for mud-covered, smoke-damaged wristwatch straps. All we had to do was get our product to market. Pretty soon people would be queuing round The Block for them. Or in school we could palm them off for cold hard cash or gobstoppers.

But reality soon dawned. We weren't the right product at the wrong time, like Betamax; we were the Sinclair C5s of our generation, the wrong product at the wrong time. Nobody gave a flying fuck about having a wristwatch strap. It was primary school. Nobody had wristwatches. Or if they did, they came with straps. *Of course* they came with straps. Woolworths probably dumped them not because they were smoke-damaged but because they didn't sell. It was most likely part of some complicated fraud, which allowed them to claim they were bomb-damaged in order to get compensation, a deception that ultimately led to the bankruptcy of the company thirty-six years later.

The lacklustre market in insurance-fraud wristwatch straps was what concerned us, not that our fathers were attending a rally in the Bullring close to Bangor Football Club to protest against IRA violence. (It wasn't actually a bullring. It was just a large circle of houses. Though there was an abattoir just up the road.) My dad stood with hundreds of other concerned men – and it was only men – and realised too late that he was at the Ulster equivalent of a Nuremberg rally. He was handed a green hunting cap and handkerchief with which to hide his identity, and everyone had to raise their hands and swear allegiance to God and Ulster in general and the UDA in particular. And so my dad became an accidental paramilitary. He had no choice really. He wasn't about to raise his hand and say, 'I'm not really that interested,' because the atmosphere was febrile. But as soon as he got home the hat and hanky went in the bin and it was never mentioned again.

He'd seen enough violence.

My dad was a civil servant but, before that, a soldier. *Everyone* then was a former soldier. He was a soldier for fifteen years, starting out as a boy soldier until he was old enough to invade Europe. He never passed a driving test. He never *took* a driving test. He didn't have to. He had a driving licence from his days in the army, where he only ever drove a tank. He drove our Ford Anglia like he drove a tank. He didn't take any prisoners and occasionally destroyed other vehicles.

Dad took part in the invasion of Normandy. For most of my life I knew that he'd gone in on D-Day Plus One, i.e. on the day after D-Day. And that was amazing enough. But then, long after he was gone, I bumped into someone in the Mace who asked if I was George Bateman's son, and he said my dad was one of the bravest men he ever met. It turned out that Dad had given him a lift to work every day and I said that that required its own kind of bravery. But he ignored me and said Dad used to tell him stories about the war that would frighten you, and that he'd actually gone in on D-Day itself, in the second wave, not the next day, but the second wave to hit the beaches, and that he'd then fought his way through Normandy and taken part in the Battle of the Bulge and been wounded, and he'd been in a firing squad for a Polish rapist, though he said there was always one rifle which fired a blank so you could convince yourself later that you hadn't executed someone.

He was eighteen when he went ashore on D-Day in Normandy.

Eighteen.

He'd seen enough violence and didn't need to be in the UDA. He knew what war could do.

He had two older brothers, Jack and David, and all three of them were soldiers. There was another brother, Roy, who was too young to serve. It's generally true that most soldiers don't really talk about their exploits in a war. Dad was the same. Even if he had, his stories would have been overshadowed by

Jack's. Jack's heroism made it to the big screen. And he got to play himself.

Jack was a commando. He fought in the desert. Then he became a paratrooper and took part in the Battle of Arnhem. He made it out alive. A year after the war he took part in the battle again. Director Brian Desmond Hurst had decided to make a film about what happened at Arnhem. He had the then-revolutionary idea of shooting it on the still extant battle sites and using as actors the soldiers who fought there and survived. Not as extras, as *actors*. The results saw some of the worst acting ever inflicted on a movie screen but, conversely, it also made for one of the best war movies ever made. *Theirs Is the Glory* was shot in quasi-documentary style, which lent it an urgent realism. It had a script co-written by Terence Young, who would go on to direct *Dr No*. It used to pop up on TV and hasn't aged well. It has one of those newsreel narrators with plums in his mouth. It looks like *A Bridge Too Far* shot on an *Emmerdale* budget.

Uncle Jack was introduced at the beginning of the film in a crowded barracks in England as Sgt Jack Bateman from County Down, Ireland, and it then followed him into battle. When he and his men were surrounded by Nazis they were addressed by megaphone and called on to surrender. My Uncle Jack responded by throwing a grenade and shouting, 'No Surrender!' That wasn't a line from any scriptwriter. That was an ad-lib. He was really method, our Uncle Jack. He went and killed Nazis to get into the part. Apart from King William of Orange, he was the first Superprod.

The only other movie Superprod I can think of is Liam Neeson, who sang 'The Sash' in the Coen Brothers' 2018 movie

The Ballad of Buster Scruggs. And Liam isn't even a Prod. He was at one time going to play another Superprod, the Rev. Ian Paisley, in my 2016 film *The Journey*. Didn't work out in the end. Timothy Spall did it. Paisley was really big and Tim is really small. But that's Hollywood.

At the end of *Theirs Is the Glory* the cameras returned to that barracks in England and showed my uncle again, but this time in a sea of empty beds.

There was a big premiere. It was one of the top ten most successful films at the box office in that year. My uncle went on to become a major Hollywood film star, acting opposite Cary Grant and Sophia Loren. And then he woke up. Scripts did not arrive by the lorryload. We never got to see his Lear. But in our eyes he was a film star. And a hero. So that's two heroes in the family. I, on the other hand, once picked a primary-school fight with Terence McCartney because he was smaller than me.

Still lost.

Money was tight on the home front. Dad was a junior clerk at Stormont, the parliament buildings just outside Belfast, and Mum was mum. My dad's main hobbies were betting on horses and smoking. He was a terrible gambler. And potentially a problem gambler. He didn't bet huge amounts. He bet small amounts, but on dozens of races, and it mounted up. We would go into town on a Saturday morning, and while I raced around every newsagent looking for Marvel comics, he went into the bookie's, usually the one off Bridge Street on Mill Row, in the shadow of the huge gas tanks that used to supply and overshadow the town. (If the IRA had ever thought to target them, the explosion would have flattened the town. Little wonder the powers that be eventually decided it was a good idea to get rid of them.) I'd complete my comics mission and then slip into the bookie's and peer through the clouds of cigarette smoke trying to find him amongst the dozens of other punters, all earnestly studying the betting form in the newspaper pages pinned up on every wall before making their selections and going to the little window to place their bets. I would be impatient to get out of there, mostly so that I could breathe air that wouldn't kill me forty years down the line, to get home and read my comics – but it was always, 'In five minutes,' which seemed to last for hours. Eventually we'd get home and then he'd spend the afternoon with his chair pulled up close to the telly, betting slips in one hand and fag in the other while he watched his money disappear on another donkey. He didn't yell at the screen. There was merely a nod and on to the next one.

My brother and I were allowed to place a bet once a year. Along with Christmas, the Twelfth (Eleventh) and FA Cup Final day, the Grand National was huge. Big horses over sixteen big fences. The fences had names we all knew, like Becher's Brook, The Chair and Canal Turn. We got incredibly excited about it and the prospects of the riches to come from our studied selections, which mostly comprised picking a horse's name that sounded like a winner. We always placed each-way bets, which increased your chances of winning something because they paid out whether your horse came first, second or third. I was convinced that my selection of Fearless Fred for the 1969 Grand National would make me richer than my wildest dreams, and was inconsolable for days when he fell at the first. That put me off gambling for life, together with the blazing rows that broke out when Mum discovered how much Dad had been spending on his precious gee-gees. She needed the money for other things, like food.

When an opportunity came along to earn some of that lost money back, Dad jumped at it. He was transferred into the department that manned the Confidential Telephones. The 'department' turned out to be two men in an office with two phones so that the public could call in to inform on their neighbours and friends if they suspected them to be involved in terrorism. Terrorists could also call in to let you know where they'd left firebombs or bodies, or who they'd murdered and why. It was run by the civil service so it wouldn't look like you were squealing to the police. But you were. My dad was frequently on the night shift. He took some disturbing calls. He would come home shattered, physically from the lack of sleep and mentally from the awful things he had to listen to. He only lasted a few months, though it was a few months longer than he managed in the UDA. He never formally resigned from the UDA. It wasn't like you signed a contract. They weren't offering a pension and job security. This organisation professing to defend Ulster was up to its oxters in terrorism and gangsterism, was involved in around 400 murders, and was legal until 1992. Legal, but you wouldn't put your membership on your CV: 'I served many happy years as a volunteer in the Ulster Defence Association. Mostly I was hunting Catholics and forcing protection money out of shopkeepers. I had my own fur-trimmed parka.' Murderers, but you couldn't have told us that then.

Then, they were heroes.

We formed ourselves into their junior Ballyholme battalion. We wore our anoraks with hoods up, handkerchiefs tied around our faces, and carried broom handles instead of guns. We wore metal UDA badges we bought in Cecil Greenwood's shop on High Street.

Cecil's shop was an odd combination of magic tricks, stink bombs, badges, second-hand books, Marvel comics and nude mags. He had quite an assortment of paramilitary paraphernalia – try saying that when you're drunk – and for many years it was my favourite shop. I was hugely into US Marvel comics and his was the only place I knew of where you could buy back issues. As I got older, I began to notice that he stacked his piles of dirty magazines beside the comics and, being a growing boy, I would wait for his back to be turned before sneaking a peak. I just thought I was in luck – comics and tits, side by side – but there probably wasn't anything accidental about their placement at all.

We bought his badges, pinned them to our denim jackets and stopped cars as they drove down Wellington Park. We'd ask to search the vehicles and then if the drivers could get out and open their boots. Most obliged. We were looking for Fenians. It was a waste of time. We had no idea what Fenians looked like. There were more black men than Fenians in Wellington Park, and there were no black men. Fenians was a derogatory term for Catholics, but none of us had ever met one. By 1971 the town had a population of 35,000. Three thousand were Catholics, but they mustn't have gone out much. We stopped the cars and it was all taken to be in good fun. Even though we had an occasional bomb or terrorist murder, we were really just on the outskirts of it – far enough away that we could play at it without ever being in danger, that we could undertake UDA manoeuvres at night and take part in the Olympics by day.

Our gang fashioned winner's medals out of leftover souvenir coins given away at Esso petrol stations during the 1970 World Cup in Mexico – if you bought enough petrol, that is. We should probably have held onto them instead of drilling holes through them to tie string, because they're probably worth a fortune now. They could have been my pension. Or secured my children's futures. (Actually, I just checked on eBay and a complete set is now worth £9.50. Half a century on and they're basically worth *nothing*. Funny how some things escalate in price and some things don't. Those metal UDA badges we festooned our jackets with are probably worth something, but they're long gone. Actually, I just checked them too, and they're worth £4.50 each. History, it seems, is not valued. That's why that first ever issue of *Superman* is going straight in the bin.)

The Olympics got under way in front of an enthusiastic crowd. I've been living back in Ballyholme for three years and I haven't yet met my neighbours, but back then you knew everyone. The Derwents from across the road, the Andersons on the corner. Grumpy, obviously. The McDonalds on the other corner – their boy Ian went on to become one of the most successful science-fiction authors in the world. Then there were the Cowleys, with their English accents, who were, therefore, snobs and not to be trusted. Toby Cowley, their eldest boy, at the age of twelve was walking past our house when my dad, out doing the garden and being a pleasant sort, remarked on the weather. 'Bit of a nip in the air,' he said. Toby Cowley replied, 'I didn't know the Japanese had launched a space mission.' Snob and Smart Alec and not invited to take part in the Wellington Olympics. My brother read this story and said, yes, that happened, but it wasn't Toby Cowley, it was Michael Trantor, who lived halfway up Wellington Gardens. He's 100 per cent certain of this. He might be right. But it's not how I remember it.

The Olympics lasted for two days. Possibly it started to rain on the third and we stayed in. But that doesn't really matter – because for one brief moment in time they were the most important thing in the world, when we were almost overwhelmed by the excitement of racing against each other in the summer sun. We lived 100 per cent in that moment, a gang of friends with not one single worry in the whole wide world, despite what was going on ten miles up the road. It wasn't about winning, either, it …

Let me stop there. *Of course* it was about winning.

It was about getting my hands on that gold medal.[9]

But I really don't remember if I did. In my dreams I set a new world record for three laps of The Block and took Gold. But perhaps not. What I do remember is that in a frenzy of clipped heels and grazed knees, Billy Whizz stepped sprightly through the carnage to take Bronze. However, sadly, he never got to wear his medal. Never got to shuffle proudly around The Block while the national anthem ('The Sash') played. Billy Whizz's urine tested positive for Brown Lemonade and Dolly Mixtures, and he was disqualified.

Shame on him.

---

9   The Esso coins were silver-coloured. We fashioned gold medals by wrapping the foil from a Mackintosh's Golden Cup bar around them.

2

The Gerbil-Breeding Association

A FEW YEARS AGO, I moved back to live in Ballyholme after the best part of two decades on the other side of town. It seemed like a big move. Although I have travelled, I've always been a bit of a home bird. The only time I've lived away from Bangor for any substantial amount of time was when I lived outside Dublin, thanks to that old rebel Charlie Haughey bringing in tax breaks for artists and writers.

The Irish prime minister had no interest in artists. Or writers. He had an interest in breeding horses, and brought tax breaks in for his horsey friends. He was persuaded at the last moment to invite artists and writers into the scheme. He was told it would make him look good but wouldn't cost much because artists and writers don't make any money. It's true.

Most don't. But some make a fortune, and he lost one for Ireland.

Eejit.

As we have gathered, I grew up a Protestant, in British Ulster, and Ireland was a foreign country full of priests. They played alien sports down there and spoke a different language and had impenetrable accents and they dreamed of invading our lovely wee violent country and stealing it back and then the Pope would dictate our laws and we'd all have to bless ourselves and eat the actual body of Christ – so there was no way I was ever going to live in that Fenian hole, at least until they brought in their tax breaks for artists and writers and then I was across the border like a shot.

We are two different countries, except when it comes to rugby, but you could claim to be Irish no matter what part of the island you originated from; all you had to do to take advantage of the tax ~~dodge~~ free status was to move there.

We settled in a small village close to the Fairyhouse racecourse, and my son enrolled at the local National School and, amongst other things, he started learning Irish, and sometimes at night we couldn't sleep for the sound of my dad spinning in his grave.

We never really fitted in.

Or perhaps we didn't make sufficient effort. We were homesick and soon had a new appreciation of what we had left behind. We missed family and friends and our culture and history, and also they eventually watered down the tax breaks so it wasn't anywhere near as advantageous to continue living there, so we skedaddled back home in time to find that nothing much had changed apart from our perspectives.

We lived in Bangor West and didn't quite fit in there either. Big houses and a lawn-tennis club in the next street. Rumour had it that the tennis club was a gateway to wife-swapping and orgies, but we were never invited. After my divorce, I moved back to Ballyholme. It seems my happy place extends to about

200 yards in every direction from where I grew up. I quite like it like that.

A few days after moving in, there was a knock on the door and an elderly woman from across the road welcomed me to the neighbourhood and began to tell me how lovely it was to live here. I said I already knew that as I grew up in the area and went to Ballyholme Primary and she said that her late husband had been a teacher there and perhaps I remembered Mr Donnan, and a shiver went down my spine.

Now, I have largely pleasant memories of growing up in Ballyholme, and of attending Ballyholme Primary School, but I have to say, there were a lot of fucking weirdos about, and many of them were teachers. I was never in Mr Donnan's class, though occasionally he stood in when our teacher was absent. He was a big man with a bald head and a fearsome reputation, mostly based upon his use of the rezzi-rezzi.

Yes, the *rezzi-rezzi*.

You must remember that back then, in the middle years of the twentieth century, corporal punishment in schools was standard practice. Ballyholme PS wasn't some throwback Jesuit institution, it wasn't a Dickensian poorhouse; it was a nice, largely middle-class school in a pleasant leafy area, where the routine punishment for children who stepped out of line just happened to be a caning, usually with a bamboo stick, which was often slightly splayed at one end for greater effect.

That was bad enough, but the rezzi-rezzi was something else. The rezzi-rezzi was a piece of wood much thicker than a bamboo cane, almost like a block of wood, with which Mr Donnan used to beat children who misbehaved. They would be sent to him from other classes because he was so good at it. Sometimes from other schools. Once, from Belgium.

Some remember it as a very thick ruler. Others have told me it was a walking stick with nobbled bits on it. One even recalled there being a nail in the end of it. The rezzi-rezzi, it appears, was whatever you wanted it not to be. Mr Donnan was The Enforcer and the rezzi-rezzi was his instrument of torture. He had either inherited the rezzi-rezzi or created it himself. With the former, you could at least respect the tradition of it being handed down from generation to generation, of teachers tasked with making men out of boys who were still boys. Nobody dared ask where it came from, and in the not-knowing, it became myth and legend. Tales abounded of boys who were beaten to death. Of bones that were smashed and heads that were crushed. I can't even begin to imagine what its true provenance was. I've tried sourcing its very name in ancient languages, including Latin and Elvish, without success.

It was what it was: the rezzi-rezzi.

I got the rezzi-rezzi once once. On the hand. It was like being struck with a mallet. Little old Miss Martin was the headmistress when I joined school. She used to go from class to class with a jewellery box full of Dolly Mixtures, which she would dispense if you did well. But then she retired. Mr Cummings came from outside and became headmaster and he employed his bog-standard cane liberally. Perhaps it was something taught at teacher-training college. Corporal Punishment 101. It was ingrained. It was normal. The police could give you a kick in the arse. Your parents would routinely give you a slap round the back of the head. But they rarely took out a bamboo stick and whipped you with it. Today,

33

teachers would be up on charges; back then, you sucked it up and displayed your wounds like a red badge of courage.

Mr Cummings only caned me once, for telling Karen McClean to 'fuck off' in P7, and she squealed to the teacher, Mrs Geddis, who sent me for punishment without a fair trial, which was all the rage at the time. I was duly caned and it hurt like hell and I burst into tears but recovered enough bravado by the time I returned to class to act the big lad, like it hadn't hurt at all, only for Mr Cummings' secretary, Miss Carson, to inform her son Willy in the class below mine that I had been crying and thus the story quickly made its way back that I was a big cry-baby. That was a much worse punishment than getting caned. I denied it of course, but *they knew*. And it affects me to this day. I still like getting caned.

For nigh on half a century I've thought about Mr Cummings as some kind of a monster. Not as bad as Mr Donnan, perhaps, but still up there. Not quite Himmler, more of an Albert Speer. He would come into our P7 class on a Friday afternoon to teach us rudimentary geometry, to give us a taste of what was awaiting us in big school. I couldn't make head nor tail of it, and I was terrified of him picking me out to give an answer. Before his class, for the first time in my life, I suffered sleepless nights. My brother was in his final year at Ballyholme when Mr Cummings arrived. He and another boy would often be called to his office at the end of the school week and presented with two large bags of coins, probably dinner money, to take to be deposited in the bank on the Groomsport Road. They had to walk the half mile, by themselves, carrying hundreds of pounds' worth of coins.

Mr Cummings died just a few months ago. I went on to the school's Facebook site to enjoy, with the privilege of time passed, other pupils' horror stories about him, and was astonished to discover how much he was loved. Post after post of fond memories, including how he dispensed sweets as he went from class to class, and the school assembly where he took out his cane and snapped it in half and promised that no child would ever be struck again, and how that action had stayed with so many boys and girls through the years, and I wondered if I had gotten him completely wrong, that he had only been doing what he had been compelled to do by his superiors. He was 'only following orders'. I don't know if the theatrical cane-breaking was inspired by a road-to-Damascus moment or because thrashing children was suddenly made illegal, but it certainly made an impact on those who came after I did. However, it's hard to shift those early impressions. A well-trained crocodile is still a crocodile.[1]

Curiously enough, I don't recall that female teachers ever did any caning. Respect. They would punch and slap, but no caning. Mrs Geddis would thump you in the back, and she always did it with her ring hand so that her engagement ring jabbed into you like a knife. She was a big woman, and fierce. She would also throw the hard wooden blackboard dusters at you, and they would hone in like artillery shells and with similar results. Sometimes it was like the first day of the Somme in our class. Nearly all of us eventually passed our Eleven-Plus though, so there was method in her madness. It was the carrot-and-stick approach, without the carrot.

Back then, the teachers invariably lived close to school, so you soon knew where their homes were and, bit by bit, learned

---

1   See Martin McGuinness' autobiography, *I Haven't Gone Away, You Know*.

little details about their lives – not to humanise or empathise with their difficult jobs, but for gossip and ammunition. Mrs Geddis' house was about a hundred yards from where I now live. Half a century on, it's still painted the same colour. She's long gone, of course. Rumour had it that the source of her anger was that her husband had died prematurely. Rumour also had it that she had killed and eaten him. You can't always believe rumours, but I was prepared to go with that one. When I walk past her house now, on Windmill Road – the windmill isn't actually on Windmill Road, it's on the next street up – I always pause for a moment and think back to my primary-school days and the year I spent in her class, and now that so many years have passed I think, what a cunt, and walk on.

My first teacher was Miss Swan, young and beautiful and teaching us more French than I ever learned at Bangor Grammar. *Ouvre la fenêtre.* There you go. P2 was Miss McCrory, she would yell and scream and slap. P3 was Mrs King, an elderly woman who would teach us Scottish dancing, which was like Irish dancing – but Scottish. Irish dancing was for Catholics. What we were really doing was Plantation of Ulster dancing. Miss Morris for P4. She was my first crush. She wore a miniskirt. She was known as Mini Morris. P5 was Mrs Pow, who had hair like an explosion in a mattress factory and a beak nose like mine would become. P6 was Mr Whittle, a nice man with greased-back hair and horn-rimmed glasses, and a heavy smoker who seemed mostly concerned with the school football team. I was a decent enough player but was never picked. One of my friends, Dougie Armstrong, went to him and complained about it. I still wasn't picked, but I appreciated the support.

Dougie had a small field beside his house in Chippendale, just around the corner from Wellington, with football posts in it, so we'd play there all the time. He knew how good I could be, but I was only good when I was playing with a small group of friends. Once on the bigger stage I tended to freeze.[2] We played massive games in the playground with great herds of boys following the ball around the pitch. Then there were inter-class matches held at the Shankhill football pitch a few hundred yards along the High Donaghadee Road from my house. There was an abandoned white cottage at the far end of the pitch, which everyone said was haunted by the Blue Lady. Years later they built an old people's home over the pitch, so it's probably haunted now by dozens of Blue Ladies. We sometimes played there on summer's evenings, forgetting what time it was until it began to grow dark and our eyes would dart towards the cottage and someone would always say, 'What's that?' and we'd wonder if it was the Blue Lady and we'd all laugh and then go home before it got any darker.

Mr Whittle would keep an eagle eye on these games at Shankhill, but not so eagle that he spotted my talents. The best player I remember was Derek Larmour. He was certainly the fastest. Mr Whittle would constantly shout at us to stay clear of one of our classmates because he was a haemophiliac and might bleed to death if tackled. I think he was rubbish at

---

2   The same is true today – I play five-a-side twice a week, but I'm still better playing against people I'm familiar with than against strangers. I'm a goal-scorer – or, as my teammates prefer to think of me, that greedy bastard up front – and I can sometimes convince myself that I'm an excellent player, until I realise that I'm playing against overweight, middle-aged men, and am, in fact, rubbish.

football anyway and haemophilia was a convenient excuse. Billy Whizz could run rings round him.

Seven years of primary school. You start off playing with a broken fire engine on your first day and crying because you can't have the toy you really want because Colin Cairns had it: the little shit had everything, including a fridge which could make ice lollies and bring down capitalism. I remember Mum coming to pick me up, and wearing a big red coat, like something Santa would wear. I don't remember my dad ever being at the school. Of course, he was working. I don't know if parent–teacher meetings had yet been invented. You got a report sent home with you every year, which usually climaxed with 'Could do better' – which is probably true of everyone, with maybe the exception of Einstein. Or maybe he got it as well. Maybe it said his adding up was reasonable, but he was rubbish at Scottish dancing or football. You never heard about Einstein cutting a rug or his Theory of the Flat Back Four. So, he wasn't perfect, though I'd still rather have him on my team than a fucking haemophiliac you couldn't touch, no disrespect intended.

One of the perks of being in P7 was that you were theoretically more mature and thus you could get chosen to get out of class to escort Mr Flannagan, the school caretaker, as he transported crates of milk from class to class. Everyone was entitled to free milk, which came in half-pint glass bottles. Mr Flanagan was quite content to exploit this free child labour while raking in his fat salary. The only actual job I ever saw him do was mopping up puddles of vomit in the school canteen. This happened regularly, usually on a Monday, when the staff served what became known as Monday Muck. Traditionally you had to sprinkle sawdust on the sick before you cleared it up. I suppose the sawdust helped it congeal.

Mr Flannagan never spoke to us as we trundled from class to class. We never learned his backstory. He might have been an ace fighter pilot during the war. Maybe he was just dulled by fifty years of delivering milk to small people and wiping up sick. Maybe proper milkmen looked down on him and called him 'Half Pint'. Perhaps, coming from generations of milk folk, he carried the shame of never progressing to full pints. He certainly never had his own float. Perhaps he dreamed of becoming 'Ernie, the Fastest Milkman in the West',[3] and forever regretted digging his heels in, making a courageous stand for half pints, little knowing that in just a few years Maggie Thatcher, 'Milk Snatcher', would make the greatest part of his job redundant.

Helping to deliver the milk was the first job I ever had. It was great training if I wanted to be a milkman when I left school. Never rule anything out. I usually got to do it with Michael, my fellow Wellington Boot Boy, who lived across the road and whose dad was the area rep for Riley's Toffee Rolls, which had to be the greatest job on the planet. Apart from Adrian Anette's dad's job. Adrian lived about six doors up. His dad was a chocolate sales rep and had access to huge numbers of Easter Eggs.[4] Maybe we were actually all living in tied housing provided by Willy Wonka. It would explain why I have very few teeth left.

---

3   A big hit in 1971 for comedian Benny Hill. It's a fabulous song. Benny was massively popular before falling victim to Stalinist revisionism.

4   My brother has just said that Adrian's dad worked in a bank. My chocolate addiction may be causing brain damage. Or he's just plain wrong. Write your own fucking memoir.

Our reward for helping out with the milk deliveries was that we got to drink whatever milk was left over at the end. In summer term it might by then be warm and curdling. We still drank it anyway.

The second job I ever had was newspaper-delivery boy. Harry Walsh's shop at the end of the Groomsport Road was one of those stores you don't see any more: the corner shop (but not on a corner) that sold literally everything. (Though not literally, of course. Within reason. Food. Nails. Armalite rifles.) In those days it was normal to get your newspapers delivered to your home, either first thing in the morning, or in the evening – and sometimes both if you were well off, which most of Ballyholme was. Harry employed a small army of boys (again, always boys) to deliver the papers, and I was recruited in the summer between P6 and P7. You got paid a couple of pounds, which seemed like a fortune. Harry was smart though – he allowed his boys to open a tab in his shop, so that you could have as many 'free' sweets as you wanted, but every Mars Bar or Football Chum you ate was set against what you were due to be paid. Often, by the end of the week, you'd end up owing Harry money.

There was something marvellous about those morning runs. It was the summer, and summers then were warmer and brighter, and my delivery route took me along Ballyholme Esplanade and into the big expensive houses facing the beach. You see in American movies kids delivering papers by just chucking them on the lawn: there was none of that – you had to jam them into the letter box and try to do it before the dog took your fingers off.

Sometimes I would stop on my bike and just look out at the water and disappear off into a fantasy world, losing track of time, and then Harry sacked me for losing track of time and because there was a steady stream of complaints about me delivering papers to the wrong houses. I never was great with numbers, or directions. But it wasn't such a hard knock. It wasn't as if my family depended on it. We didn't go without food because of my absent-mindedness. Anyway, school was starting again.

Michael and I would run home at lunchtime. Literally run. It was about half a mile. I can't remember what I had for lunch, except for my mum mixing up huge bowls of gloopy strawberry Angel Delight for afters. Then we would run back. Michael and I would discuss what we were going to do when we grew up. We agreed that joining the army was probably the best bet. There was an advert in my dad's *Daily Mail*: join the Commandos and earn £40 a week. That was a fortune, plus you got to shoot people. It sounded fantastic. Neither of us joined the army as it turned out, though we did join the Boys' Brigade, which was much the same thing. (Of this, more later.)

On our runs back to school we would often stop to chat to Eddie White, who was simple. Legend had it that Eddie had been knocked down by a car when he was a child and suffered brain damage, and now he was in his thirties or forties and wore a black leather blouson jacket and a black beret and spent his days noting down the licence plates of all the cars that passed his house. And it was possible. There wasn't anything like the same number of cars on the road. He had notebooks filled with thousands of numbers.

We didn't get our first car until I was halfway through primary school. An Austin 1100. Then there was a white Ford Anglia, affectionately known as Rocky because it shook orgasmically every time Dad changed gear. My mum never drove. There was a green Cortina with the number plate RLC216L. Nothing funny about that, apart from the fact that I remember it when there are cousins I can't recall. There were no seatbelts. Ashtrays full of Dad's fags. You had to try and look after your car because even the best would routinely break down, but it was always a losing battle.

When we got our first car, the whole family would pile in and Dad would just start driving without any plan at all. It meant countless meandering country lanes, and the question 'Where's he taking us now?' became our mantra. Going to Belfast, ten miles away, was like going to a different world. We went Christmas shopping. We would go to Robb's, which was *the* big department store, and Father Christmas would be there, and it would be incredibly exciting. Then the IRA firebombed it and Santa stopped coming. He still came to our house, though, which was decent of him.

I doubted sometimes that Santa actually existed, having stayed awake long enough to see Dad tiptoeing into our bedroom and leaving the presents at the foot of our bed. We were never a family that left presents around the tree. Family friends would visit on Christmas Eve and get pissed downstairs. These were our pretend uncles and aunties. Our real uncles lived in England and wouldn't send actual presents – they sent postal orders made out for five pounds, which was a fortune. Pretend Uncle Andrew and Pretend Uncle John, diminutive twins, kept gundogs and owned a fishing boat, the *Catherine*, named after John's daughter, which was tied up in the Long Hole, a safe mooring on Seacliff Road. The Long Hole is now sadly disused since they built the fucking marina. The Pretend

Uncles took us deep-sea fishing once – or, as they described it, fishing. I caught a fish. Full of bones, as it turns out, and no fingers at all. And that was the end of my seagoing years. Pretend Uncle Andrew and Pretend Uncle John didn't fight in the war – because of their small stature they were employed usefully in the shipyard going into parts of the ships they were building that other workers could hardly reach. But there was always a feeling that they should have gone. *Someone* had to build the ships, but the feeling persisted.

Starting from some time in September, you would begin fantasising about what your Big Christmas Present would be and dropping hints. The presents left in the bedroom were the Little Presents, but what you were really excited about was the Big Present. You'd flick endlessly through the toy section of the big Kays catalogue that Mum and every other house got in the months leading up to Christmas. The Kays catalogue was like the internet before there was an internet. It was Amazon in one book. It weighed half a tonne, but we didn't mind because it contained Paradise. Every toy you could imagine. And when we were older, women in bras.

Pretend Uncle Andrew and Pretend Uncle John would help Dad assemble whatever the Big Present was. One year it was a wooden fort from the Wild West, which came with cavalry and Indian figures, and I remember being really annoyed that they'd put the Indians inside the fort and the US 7th Cavalry outside, and that made *no sense whatsoever*. Were they mental or something?

Western movies, Western TV series, they were the MCU of their day. By the late '60s, Westerns had probably had their day as a force in the cinema, but they were ubiquitous

43

on the telly. There were shows like *Bonanza* and *The High Chaparral* and *The Virginian*, which we adored. One of my abiding memories is of Dad drawing me a picture of Big Hoss from *Bonanza* and me thinking how fantastic it was. They say you don't remember much of what happens to you before the age of six, so I may have it entirely wrong – but I don't remember my dad ever drawing anything else. I remember him playing football with us. I remember him taking us to see the Highland Games at the Valentine Playing Fields in Bangor. And once to see Northern Ireland play. George Best, who would have been the big draw, was suspended. It was a very boring game. I did see Best play once, long after he retired from proper football, when he turned out for an exhibition game at Bangor's Clandeboye Park. Everyone conspired to let him score a goal, and that was kind of sad. Anfield has the Kop, Manchester United has the Stretford End; I wonder if George Best ever told his famous friends that he once played in front of the Abattoir End?

For some reason, Big Hoss sticks. Sitting in the front room, telly on, Dad producing this remarkable likeness in a matter of seconds. *Custer of the West* (1967) was my favourite film, *Custer* was my favourite TV show. The Battle of the Little Bighorn was the most important battle in history. You say to kids today, what about what happened to Colonel Custer at the Battle of the Little Bighorn in 1876? And they do not give one fuck. But for me it might have happened only the day before. Just so as you know, Colonel Custer and his men were massacred by Sitting Bull and his Red Indians. It was a major shock to the American psyche that 'savages' could inflict such a defeat on one of their army's most decorated and celebrated leaders. Of course, they had their revenge – and continue to have their revenge. But I was devastated by his death. With his flowing locks and handsome face, Custer looked like Jesus Christ in a buckskin jacket. When people made fun of him, generally by referring to him as Colonel Custard, I got very annoyed. I later discovered that *Custer of the West*, far from being basically a documentary, was a makey-uppy version of what happened, and that rather than being shot on the plains of Montana, it was made in Spain, with the climactic battle filmed on the Costa del Sol. The company's only other big picture was *Krakatoa, East of Java*, which apparently it wasn't, so they had makey-uppy form. Those Hollywood tricksters! I would never sink so low![5]

Westerns were huge. Wee Soldiers were also huge. But also small. That's what I called the little plastic soldiers you got in boxes of forty-eight or so, all drawn from various wars in history. I favoured the American Civil War, the Second World War and the Napoleonic Wars. Quite often I would have them all fight in one mad, confusing battle. I would occasionally get Airfix models of Spitfires to fly overhead, but I never truly had the patience or dexterity to build them. The real Battle of Britain would have been lost if I'd been involved. The Nazis would have won because I couldn't be bothered. But I had thousands of Wee Soldiers. I'd paint them and re-enact the Battle of Waterloo (inspired by *Waterloo*, the 1970 movie I went by myself to see

---

5   *Driven*, my 2018 film, set in southern California, was filmed in Puerto Rico. *Divorcing Jack*, my 1997 film, substituted Donaghadee for Bangor, because being able to see the sea made it more visually striking, whereas in Bangor you can't see the sea because of the aforementioned fucking marina. My film *Wild About Harry*, set in Belfast, was also filmed in Donaghadee. I *am* the Donaghadee film industry.

at the Tonic.[6] Dull movie until the battle started, and then it was epic. The British soldiers looked even better than the Churchill Tartan, though probably weren't as tough).

I saved up my pocket money to buy a model Howitzer artillery piece from McCulloughs, which fired metal shells which decimated opposing table-top forces. For years McCulloughs was Bangor's main toy shop. It sold Wee Soldiers and Big Soldiers, and Scalextric and model trains. I built forts for my soldiers to defend/attack out of the polystyrene packing material. It was deliciously grooved and shaped so that you could use it to create a kind of *Grand Designs* military fort. And because I was a boy, I also tried to set fire to it, just to add some realism to the battle. Unfortunately, polystyrene doesn't so much burn as melt, and releases noxious fumes in the process, which ultimately killed my granny.

Fortunately, we weren't close.

I whiled away thousands of hours playing with my Wee Soldiers. It was mostly a solo endeavour, because finding someone on your own wavelength was nearly impossible. I tried Michael across the road, inviting him over and dividing up the armies. We painstakingly laid all of them out in battle formations, and then I said, 'Will we get started?', expecting that we would spend further hours discussing the finer points of military strategy, only for him to reach out and sweep his arm across all of my soldiers, knocking them all down and saying, 'I win' before going off to do something more interesting.

Wee Soldiers were my big thing, but they went hand in hand with Subbuteo, which appeared from nowhere and

---

6   I just checked; it was filmed in Ukraine!

quickly took over our world. Within months of its arrival, it seemed like every boy played Subbuteo. Or table-top football. A box came with a green pitch about the size and consistency of a tablecloth. You had to iron it before you put it down. There were small plastic nets. Then two teams – initially one red and one blue, but you could soon buy new teams, which came in plain green boxes. As Subbuteo took off you could get virtually every team in the world, including Bangor and local rivals Ards. You could also buy Linfield, and they even came with a small paramilitary unit.

You played the game by flicking the players with your fingers. There was an art to it. The players sat on a smooth, round base about the size of half a Malteser. Their design allowed you to not only move them directly forward but also, with a certain amount of practice and natural talent, to swerve them around your opponents. You took turns – the only time you played at the same time was when you took a shot and your opponent was able to use his goalkeeper, who was the only player that came with a long plastic lever attached to him so that you could manoeuvre him to try to make the save. The only surreal thing about Subbuteo initially was the ball, which was about three times the size of the player. This was later scaled down to make it more realistic, though *realistic* was stretching things. We all began to accumulate more teams, until everyone had at least half a dozen. The remarkable thing about the players was that they weren't made of the same kind of durable plastic as, for example, my Wee Soldiers, which could withstand all kinds of warfare. Subbuteo players were fragile and stiff, which meant that their little bodies routinely snapped off when you knelt on them – and you knelt on them all the time, because even though it was called table football, you quite often played on the floor with your cloth pitch pinned to a large wooden base. Decapitation or dismemberment was one of the hazards of the game. Imagine if some giant routinely knelt on Premier League players. It would cause havoc in the transfer market. But there was no transfer market in Subbuteo. You couldn't just go out and buy a new player every time you broke one. You had to fix him. The glue of choice was Bostik. And not just a drop. You had to squeeze out a small anthill of Bostik in order to make your player stick properly to the base, and then leave him to dry. As the months rolled by, more and more players got injured. Many teams became half man, half Bostik. You'd put your team out on the pitch and it would look like *The Walking Dead*. Quite often your fingers would also be stuck together.

We formed Subbuteo leagues. Someone with the desired skills drew up the fixtures, and you'd go from house to house playing your games. This could go on for weeks or months. Sometimes the leagues were completed. More often they were abandoned because someone 'accidentally' knelt on your favourite player and tempers flared. The only referee was common sense and good manners, neither of which is conspicuously present in primary-school children.

Subbuteo had been around since the late '40s, but hit its peak in the '60s and early '70s. Emboldened, the company began to branch out – you could soon buy Subbuteo World Cup, then Subbuteo Express (their version of indoor football), then Subbuteo Cricket and Subbuteo Rugby. But they expanded too quickly. Subbuteo Camogie didn't sell any copies at all. By the late '70s Subbuteo was in decline. Rudimentary computer games and video recorders became the entertainment of choice for a new generation of children. From selling hundreds of thousands of sets and millions of accessories, by 2003 they were down to selling just 500 sets a year. I don't think Bostik ever recovered either.[7]

Sports-related toys were a bit of a thing. Besides Subbuteo, the other big one in our house was Arnold Palmer's Pro-Shot Golf. Arnold Palmer was one of the top golfers in the world, and in an early Beckham-style cash-in released APPSG through the game makers Louis Marx. (Louis Marx was the biggest toy company in the world in the '50s. Louis Marx – 'the businessman with the mind of a child'.) What you got was a toy golf club at the end of which was a miniature Arnold Palmer figure, into which you inserted any one of a half a dozen tiny golf clubs chosen from your scaled-down golf bag. Using a switch on the larger club you were able to control your swing. You then attempted to strike one of two golf balls – a soft polystyrene one for driving and a harder marble-like ball for putting. The box also came with a length of green felt to use as a green, and a piece of plastic with a hole in it and a flag to aim at. The box said you got a realistic Arnold Palmer – doubtful, unless he was very small – and you could play eighteen holes of golf indoors. I think what they meant was that you could play the same hole eighteen times. It hung around in our house for a couple of years, wheeled out as a distraction on a rainy day, and there were a few exciting competitions

---

7   According to legend, horses used to be boiled up to make glue. There was a famous Irish horse in the '60s, Arkle, winner of the Cheltenham Gold Cup for three years running. But he got injured and had to be put down. For years afterwards the expression 'Arkle for Bostik' was commonplace. Bostik has a lot to answer for. It was also invented in the '40s, which begs the question, which came first, the Subbuteo or the Bostik?

with my brother, including one where I was leading by several holes and closing in on victory – which doesn't happen very often against an older brother – when one of my pet gerbils, having been given the freedom of the living room, grabbed the polystyrene ball and disappeared with it under the sofa. We're still arguing about whether that invalidated the result.

Ah, my gerbils.

I always wanted a pet. Really, I wanted a dog. We tried that. After much cajoling we got Rusty, a fox terrier, from the Whitespots USPCA pound at Conlig, between Bangor and Newtownards. Rusty was lovely. He was lively. He was going to be my best pal. On the first night we all settled into our little living room: Mum, Dad, Davie, Auntie Lily, me and Rusty lying contentedly beside me, watching something on our black-and-white TV. And then Rusty began to growl and snap, and we all quietly moved away from him, and it quickly became clear that all was not well with Rusty. My dad said he probably had distemper. Or *a* temper, as I heard it. He slept in his new basket in the kitchen. When I say slept, he barked for most of the night. My Auntie Lily, who was always the first to leave for work and was perpetually late, came rushing into the kitchen as usual the next morning, completely forgetting about Rusty, and went flying up in the air as she slipped on the first of half a dozen small lakes of diarrhoea. She landed in another. As she scrambled to get up, she slid and fell into yet another. Auntie Lily was literally covered in shit, screaming and yelling, and Rusty's days were numbered.

In ones.

One, in fact.

When we got home from school Rusty was gone. My dad said he escaped. I think 'let him out' might be closer to the truth. I recruited the Boot Boys to go looking for him, and we spent the rest of the day and evening searching all around Wellington and the rest of Ballyholme without success. I was devastated. Someone at school the next day said they thought they saw him riding on the back of a milk float, and for a while I clung to the hope that he might have found a happier and more fulfilling life somewhere else – and perhaps a cure for his temper.

By way of compensation, we got two guinea pigs.

They escaped too.

They probably ended up on a dairy farm with Rusty.

Finally, I got gerbils.

My brother was never really into pets, but it was important to me to have one. Rusty was a disaster, but my two gerbils, Whiskey and Lightning, were a delight. You couldn't go too wrong with gerbils. You could let them out of their cage for a run around the living room as long as you kept the door closed. They were friendly – and didn't bite like hamsters. They ate sunflower seeds in a very cute fashion. They drank from their water bottle. They had a lovely little cage with a wheel. They had babies. Then they ate their babies. That was disgusting but apparently quite normal if faced with a stressful situation. Being confronted by a tiny man with a golf club might do that to you. Their logic must have gone something like this: 'Quick, you cause a distraction by stealing the golf ball, I'll eat the kids.' I mean, Catholics have been eating their children for years, but this was in my own home.

Gerbil cannibalism didn't put me off. In fact, the fact that they were breeding was quite inspirational. Noel Coop lived opposite Ballyholme Primary and was in my class. And he also had gerbils. Though it would have been more poetic if he'd kept chickens. But he had gerbils, and together we formed the Gerbil-Breeding Association, aiming to make my next fortune by bringing our pets together to have unstressed sex and so produce non-edible children, which we could then sell on, taking advantage of the business acumen I had accrued through selling bomb-damaged watch straps.

Unfortunately, before we could get properly started, we suffered an unexpected business reversal when I knelt on Lightning, who proved not to be as quick as her name. I broke her spine, and with that her ability to reproduce – or indeed, breathe. Unlike Subbuteo men, she could not be restored with a liberal application of Bostik. Her death sucked the life out of our business venture. I just couldn't face all that gerbil sex without her. Lightning was buried with full military honours in the back garden, nestled softly in a wooden domino box lined with sawdust from her cage. The death of a pet is always hard, but not so hard that it stopped me from digging her up six months later to see what she looked like. Not good, was the answer. Her poor partner Whiskey lived alone in his cage for several further months, moping about, pining for his lost love, playing aimlessly with his purloined Arnold Palmer's Pro-Shot Golf ball. And then his time was up too. A passing cat sneaked into the garage where we kept his cage. It smashed in the door and dragged Whiskey out and ate him; or ate most of him. Cats are such bastards. They leave bits of what they've caught and eaten just to try and impress you. I've news, cats. *Not impressed.*

It seemed then that we were done with pets. All we had left was street football, knocking doors and running away, and raiding orkies. Orkies being orchards, of the apple variety.

Raiding orkies was a rite of passage: a delicious mixture of high adventure, risk, fear, climbing ability and theft. You took your life in your hands when you raided orkies because raiding was followed by fighting between rival gangs, and if you've never suffered a direct hit to the head from an apple launched from several hundred yards away, then you haven't lived – but if you have, you've nearly died. They'd come in at you like mortar shells. And they generally weren't the nice sweet little red apples you get in the Co-Op; they were massive fucking cooking apples that would take your head off. There are more than a few still walking around town who suffered brain damage from partaking in mass apple fights, and several of them went into politics.

The only *organised* thing we went in for after dark – apart from being in the UDA – was the Boys' Brigade. These days it styles itself as 'an international interdenominational Christian youth organisation'. When we were in it, it was the paramilitary wing of the Presbyterian Church.

Up until 1926 the Boys' Brigade drilled with dummy rifles. It's a worldwide organisation. In Nigeria, they still use dummy rifles. Unfortunately, we didn't have that option.

The BB has been around since the later years of the nineteenth century, having been formed in Glasgow. It's like a tougher version of the Scouts. Not so much *dib-dib-dib, dob-dob-dob* as *what the fuck are you looking at?* Our 'theme tune', sung at the start of every session, was 'Give Me Oil in My Lamp'. The lyrics went:

> Give me oil in my lamp, keep me burning,
> Give me oil in my lamp I pray,

Give me oil in my lamp keep me burning,
Keep me burning till the break of day.

It's a traditional Christian hymn. But given that we were growing up in the Troubles, where petrol bombs were handed out like cooking apples, it might be considered problematical, or even inspirational. It's one of those tunes that gets stuck in your head. To this day I sometimes burst into it when I'm doing the shopping in Tesco or out scoring nails down the sides of cars with personalised number plates. The hymn was a hit single for Jamaican Eric 'Monty' Morris in the '60s. It also appears on The Byrds' album *Ballad of Easy Rider* and is rubbish.

The 7th Bangor BB met in the church hall opposite Ballyholme Primary every Friday night. We wore a dark-blue uniform with an anchor crest and a pill-box hat. Later, the pill-box hat was replaced with something like they used to wear in *Thunderbirds*, a nod to modernity which didn't sit well with everything else they were selling. There was also a brown leather belt with a metal clasp which you had to polish with Brasso. Our motto was 'sure and steadfast'. Our purpose was 'the advancement of Christ's kingdom and the promotion of habits of Obedience, Reverence, Discipline, Self-respect, and all that tends towards a true Christian manliness'. Or we marched up and down a lot and played crab-football. They did try to drill Jesus into us, but it didn't really stick.

On Saturdays we played proper football matches against other local BB companies. There were fourteen other companies in Bangor, which shows how Presbyterian the culture was and is. I was brought up in the Church of Ireland, which is just on the right side of not being Catholic. But you could mix and match your Protestantism, so going there on a Friday night wasn't a problem. I'd go with my friends by calling at their houses at about the right time and hoping they were still there, because we had no phone.

My family may have been slightly late getting a car, but we were really late in getting a phone. Phones had been around since the 1920s but were far from standard until the 1960s. Why would you need one anyway? Everyone you knew lived across the road or around the corner. But change was coming on almost every front.

One summer's evening my dad arrived home from playing cricket for his civil service team and collapsed by the front door. Thankfully, it wasn't anything major – but it was a wake-up call. Too many fags and a diet that regularly featured the traditional Ulster fry. Then, most everyone was in the same boat, and it was sinking. A change of lifestyle was required. Out went the cigarettes and in came months of muggins having to run to the shop twice a day for packets of Wrigley's Spearmint chewing gum to help take away the cravings. Instead of *bread* bread, Dad ate Nimble, which was advertised on telly by a pretty girl literally hanging from a hot-air balloon, thus banging home the message that it was lighter than air and therefore good for you. It was also too light to slather butter on. You ended up slathering the plate, or the table, or your knee.

One night there was a knock on the door, and it was the police, there to tell my dad that his brother Jack had died in England. Film-star Jack. War-hero Jack. They were at the door because we had no phone and there was no other way for his family to contact us.

No phone, black-and-white TV, no fridge, no washing machine – we were living a 1950s lifestyle in the 1970s.

There was another death, too – a neighbourhood chum, a year younger, little Jackie Courtney, who marched back and forth with us in the BB. He was knocked off his bike by a car. I stood quietly watching with the other Wellington Boot Boys at the bottom of Chippendale as his funeral cortège moved slowly past, and then we shrugged and continued playing. We didn't know how to articulate anything then. And maybe we still don't.

The Wellington Boot Boys were coming to the end of their time. We were entering P7, the final year of primary school, and that meant every waking minute was devoted to studying for the Quallie, a test to separate the wheat from the chaff. My brother had already made it to Bangor Grammar, so the pressure was on me to follow in his footsteps. If I failed it, I'd end up in the secondary school, which, at least in my parents' heads, really was secondary. Maybe they felt that that study also needed a change of environment, or perhaps that the Boot Boys were too distracting, but after all those years of doing their own studying of those lists of houses for sale, they finally found one they really liked: a brand-new bungalow in Ballymacormick Avenue about a mile away for just over £7,000.

A mile, but it felt like twenty.

But we were moving up in the world.

We got a phone.

We got a colour TV.

We got a dog.

Our bungalow was bigger than James Young's, but still smaller than an American fridge.

Also, we got our first fridge.

3

The Age of Crimplene

I AM MECHANICALLY ILLITERATE – or, to put it another way, I struggle with shapes and assembly instructions or anything that might resemble DIY. I have wired exactly one plug in my life, and after the resulting fire I swore never to attempt it again.

I have never painted a wall or attempted to hang wallpaper. If my car gets a flat tyre, I have to sell the car. Some might say that all of these so-called faults could be summed up with one word: *lazy*. They may have a point. But I've never seen the point in even attempting any of these things. That's why tradesmen were invented. They are experts, some of them. Joiners join things together so that I don't have to. My brother is the same. He got around the problem of having to change a flat tyre by never getting a car. He never learned to drive. I don't think he can swim. At least I can do that. I learned at Bangor Swimming Pool. The pool was fairly new. Before this the only way to learn to swim was at Pickie Pool, which was an outdoor pool at the seafront. It had a big fancy exterior that made it look like you were going into somewhere nice, but what you were actually going into was the sea with a wall around it. Somehow, via magical science, they were able to take the cold sea water and make it many degrees colder. Learning to swim at Pickie was like learning to swim in an ice bath, with added urine.

At least there were no jellyfish. In the sea at Ballyholme there were jellyfish. We lost many children to jellyfish. 1973 was a terrible year for that. There's a memorial to them on the seafront.

To all the jelly babies lost in the summer of '73.

My generation was the first to graduate from Pickie to the heated pool. For a while they co-existed, until the council realised that nobody was using Pickie any longer because it was freezing. They knocked it down and built a playground with an artificial lake about a foot deep, full of gigantic swans. They aren't real swans. Real swans don't have pedals. Also, real swans can break your arm if they choose to and only the Queen can eat them.

Nobody ever froze to death at Bangor swimming pool, although Tufty McDade nearly drowned. Tufty wasn't his real name. He was Glen McDade. He had about twelve brothers and sisters, all crushed into a small house in Thornleigh Gardens. His original nickname was Smelly McDade. Even then he was aware that nicknames could stick for life. (Only the other day someone called me Bacon, and I'm fifty-*fucking*-eight.) He came to me and said that from now on he wanted people to call him Toughy McDade. I don't know why he came to me. Maybe I appeared open, or malleable. Toughy was, altogether, a better nickname. By osmosis he would become Tough and people would respect him, plus he had a dozen siblings to back him up. Except, either because I misheard or because I am bad to the bone, I said, 'Tufty?', thinking of the little red squirrel who was the symbol of our road-safety lessons – we could all join the Tufty Club and learn how not to get knocked down – and he said, 'No, Toughy,' but it was too late.

It didn't quite catch on at first. People were used to calling him Smelly. Even his parents. At least until The Incident at the Swimming Pool.

Tufty thought it would be a good idea to put the inflatable armbands on his ankles. Perhaps he was encouraged. Either way, he jumped into the deep end and his feet rose to the top and his head went to the bottom and he couldn't do anything about it. Nobody noticed for a long time, apart from those of us who did and were laughing hysterically because it was funny to see him flailing around dying. We were not yet acquainted with the reality of death, seeing it only on the news in Belfast and in Westerns, and Jackie Courtney not yet having come off his bike. But a teacher eventually noticed, dived in and he was saved, though not without a lot of panicked screaming and yelling from those few who showed concern. He went into the pool Smelly but emerged Tufty, having proved he was at least worthy of a better nickname by managing to survive underwater for so long, and he's still known as Tufty to this day. He was able to grow up and get into teeth. Not as a dentist. But teeth. That's all I know. There's probably a way to find out more.

My dad was never really into DIY either. He participated on a needs-must basis. He didn't have a workshop in the garage. He didn't have a tool belt, or, indeed, tools, beyond the usual. The new bungalow at Ballymacormick needed painting inside, so he did that. Davie and I shared a bedroom. Dad painted it a bright blue. Within a few months black patches of damp began to show through. There was no central heating.

Eventually we got some. It was coal-fired. The boiler was in the garage. You had to light it in the morning. It was very difficult to light. It was dirty, smelly and it huffed and puffed; it was the Billy Whizz of boilers, partially disabled but prepared to give it a go. Eventually it gave a semblance of heat, but it went out all the time. The heat that did arrive was fed into storage heaters. They weren't very good at storing. Or they were very good at storing but very poor at releasing. It seemed always to be cold in the house. Eventually we bought a SuperSer gas heater to supplement the coal heating. They were all the rage. You would wheel it from room to room. On freezing school mornings my brother and I would jostle and push and pull to get closest to it in the kitchen, and we lived in fear of the gas bottle running out of puff.

Once, on a Sunday evening, with the rest of the family watching telly, I sat in the kitchen on a stool in front of the SuperSer, with my feet up on top of it, reading a book, luxuriating in the warmth and solitude. And then I felt something strange and painful, and realised that my crimplene trousers were melting onto my leg.

For it was The Age of Crimplene.

Everything was made from it. Shirts, trousers, jackets, underwear, condoms. It was ubiquitous. Items made from crimplene were soft, they were stretchy, they were comfortable, they could be washed and folded easily and, above all, they were cheap. They dominated the late '60s and early '70s. Crimplene's inventor, Mario Nava, got an OBE. It was produced originally in the Yorkshire town of Harrogate. More specifically in the Crimple Valley. The fact that it was highly flammable hardly seemed to matter. I had a lucky escape with my melting trousers. Others weren't so lucky. Most recorded cases of spontaneous combustion can be traced back to Crimplene. Eventually the authorities became aware of the high death toll. Crimplene was outlawed. You can still buy it on the black market or Dark Web, along with child porn and heroin, but why would you?

The SuperSer changed my life, and not just because of the burns. On one cold winter's morning, with the central heating failing to fire, my brother and I again clashed over who should stand closest to it. There was pushing and pulling and shouting and complaining, and that was just from me. Eventually he snapped and headbutted me. By this stage he was already at Bangor Grammar School, so he must have learned how to do it there. He headbutted me square on the nose, breaking it.

Blood everywhere.

Now, babies all look the same. Toddlers are hard to tell apart. But as you grow older and your features begin to spread and elongate, you become more distinctive, more individual. It became noticeable (to me) that my left ear was small and neat, while my right ear was large and bent slightly out. Then there was space, the final front ear. (Sorry, '70s *Star Trek* joke. I was really into *Star Trek*. It led to many fights with my brother, because it was repeated on BBC2 on Monday evenings at the same time as *Coronation Street* went out on ITV, and we only had the one TV, and it was before video recorders, so you either saw a programme or missed it. He was a big fan of the *Street*. He was clearly a loser. While I was a geek, before geeks were invented.)[1] But nobody ever commented on my mismatched ears. Apparently, it's quite common.

---

1   Davy Crockett had three ears – a left ear, a right ear and a wild front ear.

The part of me which grew faster than any other – ladies, please – was my nose. My mum had a long, straight, pointed nose, so I guess it came from her. My brother never got it. But mine was big. A big nose. But for the headbutt I might just have gotten away with the odd comment. But now it was no longer a fine Roman nose: a Roman nose which might have inspired men to follow me into battle, or at least raiding orkies. The break affected one side of the bridge, so that depending on your point of view I had a different profile. This might have been useful if I was Clark Kent or Zorro, but I wasn't. I was Bacon. From one side my nose looked long but relatively normal – from the other hawk-shaped and striking, but not in a good way. It was a nose you remarked upon. A nose where if someone didn't know your name they would say to a friend, who's that with the big nose? Going to see Steve Martin in *Roxanne* in the '80s was the longest ninety minutes of my life. There were no references to my nose in primary school. But by the time I was a teenager it was routinely commented upon – and I when I say commented upon, I mean, 'What're you looking at, you big-nosed cunt?' You'd hear variations of that a dozen times a day, and it had an effect. That's how you begin to see yourself. I became very shy. And what girl is going to want to look at someone like me? It ushered in many years of torment, and all from an argument over who could stand closest to a SuperSer.

You might say, but why didn't you get your nose fixed? And I might say, I was too shy – then and now. And too vain, because people would surely say, look at him, he used to have a really big, crooked nose and now he doesn't, still a cunt though. And it's made me who I am, good and bad. Perhaps it even made me a writer. All those nights I could have been out with beautiful women I was inside writing stories. Also, I could have played for Liverpool, if I'd been any good.

Back then there wasn't even a thought about getting my nose fixed. I sometimes wonder if my parents even noticed that my entire face had changed. It was never mentioned. That day I cleaned myself up and went into school, unaware that the course of my life had swerved off the main road.

The course of my dad's life was also changing. As I said, he wasn't hugely into DIY, but for some reason he decided to crazy-pave the front garden. And not content with that, he decided to crazy-pave part of the back garden as well. That part of the garden was referred to as 'the patio', and perhaps Mum and Dad dreamed of barbecues there and lying on floral-patterned sunloungers sipping advocaat, but we never had a barbecue in our whole lives, and the patio was built in the shadow of the house, so it very rarely saw any sunlight. Still, the thought was there, and he did a good job, though he couldn't have foreseen at what expense.

Dad had been working quite happily in Stormont following the aberration of his time on the Confidential Telephones. On returning to his car after a day's work he noticed a pile of weed-strewn broken paving stones lying dumped in a corner of the car park. As they were clearly abandoned, he decided there wouldn't be any harm in putting a few in the boot of his car to help with the crazy paving. Except one of his colleagues spotted him and reported him. In hindsight he probably should have asked someone if he could take them. He was hauled up in front of a board and, although there was clearly no criminal intent or investigation, it was a black mark against him. Any chance of further promotion or even a pay rise was effectively blocked for years to come, which was a big price to pay for a fucking patio that rarely saw sunlight. If he'd stuck with the UDA, they could have sorted it out – but it was too late.

Dad laboured away at the front and back gardens, watched by curious neighbours. The Jacksons, a retired couple, lived in the corner bungalow on our right, with their dog Sweep, who we looked after when they went on holidays. They then all moved to Canada, but not entirely because of us. An assistant bank manager moved in with his beautiful young wife. We soon fell out with them. There was an argument over a garden fence. Also, they were Catholics. I don't know if that had anything to do with it, but it always seemed to be mentioned, as if that was a genuine factor in the fight over who would pay for the erection of the fence. When I later brought my first girlfriend home, she was Catholic, and that did not go down well. My parents weren't bigots, exactly. I think it was fear of the unknown. There are people who think being a Muslim is the same as being a terrorist. That's what it was like. Being a Catholic was like being in the IRA. Her black beret and sunglasses didn't help.

On the other side there were the Reids. They ran a catering company by day and performed as a showband at night. They were all in it. Parents, three children. Like *The Partridge Family*. We could now watch the actual *Partridge Family* in colour because we had a new TV. It was rented, through Rediffusion on Main Street. That was the done thing, renting a TV. The technology was coming on in leaps and bounds, but they never updated the model you had. Over the years we probably paid thousands for our rented TV. Eventually we wised up and bought one. Then we went back to Rediffusion and rented a video recorder.

We had our new house, our new fridge, our new TV. We even upgraded our car, and Dad no long drove it like he was driving a tank. There seemed to be more money around despite, or perhaps because of, the shenanigans with the paving stones. Maybe Dad, far from being weighed down by his mistreatment, had discovered a gap in the market and was selling purloined crazy-paving stones on the side. When life gives you lemons, etc. Perhaps he was selling them to rioters, because there was still a lot of rioting going on, and for that you needed a good and reliable source of missiles. Most of his sales must have been in Belfast, where riots were a daily hazard. Bangorians tended to keep their riots for special occasions, probably thinking that you can have too much of a good thing.

In 1973 everyone was wearing flares. Long hair and flares. My brother took a photo of Slade drummer Don Powell into a hairdresser's and asked them to give him a big poodle-boy hairstyle like his. It was revolutionary for a boy to go into *any* hairdresser. Boys went to a barber. Bangor boys mainly went to Psyche's. Psyche's was a barbershop in The Vennel, a narrow alley off Queen's Parade. His real name was Mario 'Siki' Togneri, but he was always Psyche to us. He would give you a short back and sides and could also sell you 'something for the weekend' before Boots muscled him out of that business.[2] My brother could only get his ridiculous haircut because Bangor Grammar School pupils had finally rebelled

---

2   As we have observed, nicknames are easy to come by and hard to lose. But it is known that shortly after visiting Psyche's for a short back and sides in 1978, Stephen Sondheim was inspired to write *Sweeney Todd: The Demon Barber of Fleet Street*. The experience left Psyche bitter and broken and pricking holes in the French letters he sold. A generation of Bangorians have him to thank for being a generation of Bangorians.

against headmaster Randall Clarke's edict that hair had to be above the shirt collar.

Hair had been getting gradually longer since The Beatles in the early '60s, but not at BGS. Clarke managed to maintain his ban right through the hippy era, but by 1973 he was fighting a losing battle. Prog rock and glam rock were on the rise, so he should have been grateful that hair was his only issue, because mascara and suits made out of Bacofoil were all the rage. Clarke was bald himself, so maybe there was something else going on. But the older boys finally had enough and, perhaps inspired by the recently televised Lindsay Anderson movie *If*, in which Malcolm McDowell led an armed insurrection at his private boarding school, they walked out on strike. I suppose it says something about the pace of life in Bangor, and how little the Troubles really affected us, that the hair strike became a big story, and in otherwise traumatic times attracted national television coverage. A classic political compromise was eventually reached in which the school adamantly refused to budge in public while quietly allowing hair to inch down over its collars in private.

Our rioting in 1973, however, wasn't hair-related. It occurred during a twenty-four-hour period in early February following the arrest of two loyalists in Belfast in connection with the murder of a Catholic. They became the first Protestants to suffer internment without trial (it had been fine for Catholics up to that point). In response, the recently formed United Loyalist Council called for a one-day general strike, which began on 6 February with power cuts affecting the whole country. Factories, shops and schools were all forced to close. It was a short strike, but it demonstrated that, if they wanted to, loyalist workers could control the economy and shut it down at will. The strike was accompanied by violence, with five people killed and many injured, with explosions and arson giving us a taste of what was to come in the following years.

In Bangor, police were stoned in Main Street. Petrol bombs were hurled at Catholic homes. Hundreds of tartan-gang members, some from Churchill, besieged the police station. At home we all sat around the radio listening to the 'Police Messages' – incredibly you could still tune in to listen to the police radio channel to find out where they were being sent and what was going on. It was like reality TV. On the radio.

Of course, it wasn't the first violence visited on the town. Several years before, our university was burned down and all of the students massacred. By several I mean more than a thousand. And it wasn't called a university then, it was a monastery, and the lecturers were monks, and the hallions running amok weren't rioters but Vikings. It was a long time ago, but not long enough for us not to still hold it against all Scandinavians, those bloodthirsty bastards.

The monastery, or Bangor Abbey as it became, was exactly where it is now, though there's not much of it left. A wall, in fact. It was founded by St Comgall in AD 555. He was a former soldier who took monastic vows and initially became a hermit on Lough Erne. His rules were so demanding that seven of his fellow monks died. He was tough, but also didn't quite understand the concept of being a hermit. He was 'persuaded to leave' and pitched up in Bangor to start again. This time, though, his policies of incessant prayer and fasting attracted thousands. He became fashionable. When he died in AD 602, thousands of monks attended his funeral. By then Bangor had become the greatest monastic school in Ulster and one of the three leading lights of Celtic Christianity. It became famous for its choral psalmody, a kind of continuous singing that went on for hours, though it was still slightly shorter than a Snow Patrol album. The area was originally called Inver Beg, after the stream which ran past the abbey. The town that grew up around the monastery became known as Beannchor, from the old Irish word meaning a horned or peaked curve, as the shape of our bay apparently resembles the horns of a bull, if you squint and have a healthy imagination and can ignore the fucking marina. The area was also known as the Vale of Angels because St Patrick once rested there, and, having been at the magic mushrooms growing on Bangor Golf Course, had a vision filled with angels.

The monastery had such influence that the town was one of only four places in Ireland to be named in the famous Hereford Mappa Mundi in AD 1300. It says famous, here on Wikipedia, but all fame is relative. I'm sure it was a bestseller in its day, but it wasn't exactly *The Bridges of Madison County*. The only printing they could do was potato printing, and it's hard to turn a profit at that. The Mappa Mundi is the largest medieval map still in existence. The Mappa Tuesday has been lost. An even larger one, the Ebstorf Map, was bombed out of existence in northern Germany by the Allies during the Second World War in a handy piece of tourism forward planning. I've looked at the Hereford Map, and I have to say it doesn't reflect the real world at all – it's difficult to decipher and the scale is all wrong: it's almost as if they were too lazy to use satellites.

Bangor Abbey's subsequent suffering at the hands of the Vikings was sadly predictable. You can't blame them, really – they were just looking for treasure and knew then, as now, that the Church has more treasure than anyone. They raided in AD 823 and 824, which is barely a minute between raids. In the 824 raid they plundered the monastery, destroyed the oratory and killed scholars and students.

The Vikings couldn't all have been violent marauders, because some of them stayed and settled. Or perhaps they were so busy killing and stealing that they completely lost track of time, missed the last boat home and decided, fuck it, let's make the best of it. But let's not set up too close to the monastery, they're still a little sore about what happened. They moved out to the rather well-heeled Ballyholme. That's where a Viking burial mound was found in 1903. It contained a pair of bronze brooches, a bowl, a fragment of chain and a note saying they only ended up in Bangor because someone sold them a really dodgy map.

* * *

In Wellington we had lived within a few hundred yards of The Field.

With the new bungalow we had a field almost literally at our back door. It also became known as The Field. This Field was destined for more bungalows, and some initial digging had taken place, but there must have been a problem with the development, because nothing else happened for the next few years. The Field was thus dominated by several large mounds of excavated earth, which had solidified into The

Mountains. At their base was the hole they had emerged from, which quickly filled with rainwater and never drained away. It became known as The Lake. Beside The Lake was The Forest, though it was more of a small wood. There were well-worn trails through The Forest, made by dog-walkers, wild bears and dwarves. So, we had The Field, The Mountains, The Lake and The Forest. It was almost as if someone had taken a quick glance at the maps in what had become my favourite book, *The Lord of the Rings*, and decided to build an adventure playground based upon them. The Field, the Mountains, The Lake and The Forest became my Middle Earth.

I was obsessed with the book. My brother's class had been read *The Hobbit* in Ballyholme Primary and he thought I would like it. Unusually, I took his advice, because most of the time we were like chalk and cheese. He liked Slade and I liked The Sweet. He became a Black Man and I did not.[3] He supported Man Utd. I supported a better team: Liverpool. He mentioned there was another book set in the same world called *The Lord of the Rings*, and I nearly had a heart attack when I saw the size of it. Over a thousand pages. But I devoured it whole. I lived in Middle Earth. Maybe the reason I fell for it so hard had to do with leaving Wellington. Even though it was only a mile away, I still found myself increasingly isolated from my old friends. I saw them at school, but then we walked home in different directions. So much happens on walks to and from school. And they were too far away for me to just call round unannounced at their houses on the off-chance they might be in.

---

3   A member of the Black Preceptory – the senior branch of the Orange Order. In theory it is extremely religious, in practice less so. You routinely hear about someone being a member of 'the Black'. Given the times, it should really think about rebranding. They're pretty safe with Orange.

Richard Mason hadn't been in the Boot Boys but he at least was prepared to cycle up to my new house, so he became my new best friend. We played games based around hobbits and dwarves and orcs and trolls. We made swords out of wood and spears out of brush-shafts, and we charged through The Forest and splashed through The Lake – except on Frog Sex Day, when it was too dangerous to enter – and fell down The Mountains with arrows stuck in our backs and got home dripping with mud to bowls of Angel Delight newly cooled in our new fridge. When we played in The Field I would wear my mother's leather boots, because you couldn't be a sword-wielding hero like Aragorn wearing fucking wellington boots; you needed boots like a swashbuckling horseman might wear, and my mum's knee-high boots were just perfect. Today, I'd be asked about gender reassignment.

Richard was game, despite the fact that he hadn't read either of the books. He relied entirely on my descriptions of Middle Earth and its history and tribes and characters. Maybe that's where my storytelling started; it must have been good enough for Richard to make sense of the complex world Tolkien had created and I had interpreted, usually to my advantage – at least in The Field, The Lake, The Mountains and The Forest. Richard's dad was the Methodist minister in Ballyholme, so he must have been used to elaborate fantasy worlds.

Every Wednesday in school we'd have a guest minister at morning assembly. The Church of Ireland sent the dour Rev. Mercer. The Presbyterians sent Rev. Willie Erskine, a spindly little old man who once staggered us by shinning his way up a rope in the school hall to prove he was more agile than he looked. He had a stroke afterwards. The Methodists had Richard's dad, the Rev. Mason, and everyone loved him, especially the lady teachers. He was tall, tanned and handsome. He smoked cigars and could make everyone laugh. He was a groovy minister all right, and he lived with his beautiful wife, Rosemary, in a church house, which was all dark-wood panelling inside and smelled of cigars and pipe tobacco, on the Groomsport Road.

Smoking was huge. Everything everywhere must have stunk of it. But you weren't aware of it then. It was only when most people quit that you started to notice it. My mum never smoked, my dad had recently given up, but most everyone else was still at it – and if you weren't, you were a bit odd. By the '70s it was generally accepted that it was bad for you. The healthy option was cutting down from forty a day to thirty. Fags were still advertised everywhere. Every sports competition was sponsored by Big Tobacco. Your teachers, when they weren't thumping you with blocks of wood, smoked in front of you. Every car, and some bicycles, had an overflowing ashtray. There was simultaneously tremendous pressure to start smoking and a terrible fear of getting caught. Most shops would sell them to you. All you had to do was say they were for your dad. There were six-year-olds with a twenty-a-day habit.

Getting them wasn't a problem. Next you had to find somewhere to smoke. We, that is the Wellington Boot Boys and Richard, got on our bikes and cycled to Groomsport, a lovely little village about a mile out of town. We found somewhere secluded down near the beach and opened up our box of Embassy Regal, the brand my auntie smoked. There was a coupon inside. I knew that if I started with the smoking now, and quickly built it up to forty a day, I would soon accumulate enough coupons to trade them in for another box of Wee Soldiers.

But the truth is, I never inhaled.

I smoked my first cigarette by sucking in and blowing out so quickly that I was down to the butt in thirty seconds flat. And because I didn't inhale – I didn't know you had to – there was no 'hit', so I couldn't see what all the fuss was about. But, like sex, if you keep at it long enough, you're bound to improve, or get worse. Like sex, as time wore on, we got a little bolder. We no longer felt the need to cycle to Groomsport. Instead, we went into Richard's dad's garage, and that's where the Rev. Mason found us not-inhaling and yelled at us so loudly that he literally put the fear of God into us, and I've never touched a cigarette since. Heroin is still a bit of a problem, but I never smoked again.

It's funny though, how, as you grow older, 'being naughty' changes from something largely born of innocent curiosity into the active knowledge that what you are doing is wrong, but you do it all the same. We knew instinctively that the smoking was wrong. One of our Wellington Boot Boys knew it was wrong to write 'UDA' on the corridor wall in school, but he did it anyway. It was an act of rebellion, it was an act of solidarity, it was in letters no more than half an inch tall. It was minute. But it stood out like a Belisha beacon because the walls were otherwise pristine. It soon attracted the attention of Mr Cummings. He dealt with it by ordering every pupil in each of the classrooms along that corridor to line up outside their room with their pencil cases. He then went along the line of close to a hundred children demanding that each one produce their black felt-tip pens so that he could compare and contrast, and by those means, he told us, he would deduce who was responsible for such a scandalous act of vandalism. Better that the culprit step forward now and prevent the possibility of some poor innocent soul being punished. And Rodney stepped forward clutching his black felt-tip pen and took one for Ulster. His fellow pupils, his *friends*, uninspired by a weekend TV showing of *Spartacus*, as one, failed to step forward in a collegiate show of support, and so he sacrificed himself on the altar of paramilitary loyalism and was dragged off to his punishment. He was caned to within an inch of his life. He wasn't expelled, but in the months to come, vital months leading up to our Eleven-Plus exams, his sad, shuffling figure could often be seen traversing the school corridors in an eternal quest to find his classroom, such were the psychological and physical scars of his beating. The school had a very high pass rate for the Quallie, and when I sat beside him I used to copy his answers because he was a smart kid, but Rodney didn't pass and he went to secondary school. However, he later became a World Bowling Champion – so fuck you, Mr Cummings.

Of course, you say Belisha beacon to kids today and they've no idea what you're talking about. Let me put them out of their misery. A Belisha beacon is the amber-coloured globe on top of the poles on either side of a pedestrian crossing.

Ah, now you get it.

Belisha beacons were named after Leslie Hore-Belisha, the Minister of Transport who, in 1934, added beacons to pedestrian crossings. It could have been worse, but 'lit up like a Hore' is just … wrong. Later the crossings were painted with black and white stripes and became known as zebra crossings. During the Second World War a study was made into the cost-effectiveness of melting down the 64,000 Belisha beacon posts to make munitions. A fellow MP, Mr Cocks, speaking in the House of Commons, decried the suggestion, claiming that it would 'deprive Mr Hore-Belisha of his last chance of immortality'.

Ouch.

Mr Cocks was the Labour MP for Broxtowe in Nottinghamshire. After the war it was revealed that he had been placed on the special search list of prominent subjects to be arrested by the Nazis if they succeeded in invading Britain.

But that's not what's memorable about Seymour.

Yes, his first name was Seymour.

Seymour Cocks.

I used to know someone called Mary Christmas.

But Seymour Cocks takes the biscuit and swallows it whole.

They were, undoubtedly, more innocent times, but still. His parents must have been *lunatics*.

My parents weren't lunatics, but they were drug-pushers.

The Quallie was fast approaching. It was actually two verbal reasoning tests, administered a fortnight apart in November and December, and then the agonising wait for the results until June. I did okay in school, but my parents were obviously worried. On the day of the first exam they gave me drugs to settle my nerves and up my brain function. Not speed or cocaine, unfortunately. They gave me Pro Plus. Caffeine pills. Not exactly at the top end of the spectrum, but on a body that had hardly previously been exposed to it – I didn't drink tea or coffee and Coke was an occasional luxury – they were like rocket fuel. These days you have to be over sixteen to buy them. Some countries have banned them – try buying Pro Plus in the South. But it gave a wonderful buzz and fired me through my exams. Before long I was taking it constantly, and then dealing it at the school gates, and this soon led to a falling out with the Sinola Cartel and me spending time in a Mexican prison. However, I passed the Eleven-Plus and Bangor Grammar School was soon looming into view.

All I had to do was pass the interview.

Because Bangor Grammar School didn't just want every drugged-up child who'd managed to somehow pass the Quallie, they wanted the *right* type of drugged-up child who'd somehow managed to pass his Quallie. It was partially a postcode thing, it was partially a religious thing, but mostly it was to see the cut of your jib and, if they liked it, to assign you to your house.

House. Think Gryffindor. Come to think of it, the school magazine was called *The Gryphon,* so one of them could easily have become Gryffindor. The interview was the equivalent of the sorting hat. Bangor Grammar had School House, Crosby House, Ward House and Dufferin House. I don't know of anyone who passed their Quallie and was then rejected because of a poor interview. But I didn't know that then.

We knew from my brother's experience that it was good to have a specialist subject, something you could talk about when the interviewer asked if you had any hobbies. Well, that was easy. I was going to talk about birdwatching.

I was fascinated by birds. I had a pair of binoculars to watch them with. My Auntie Lily took me to Castle Park so I could study them. I became quite an expert, the way my youngest son is on *Star Wars* Lego. I even bought an LP of *birdsong.* You couldn't dance to it, but it had its own charms. I liked chaffinches. And pied wagtails. We had house martins nesting in the eaves of our house in Wellington. Occasionally a chick would just fall out and splat on our tarmac drive. Itinerant Travellers made our drive. It was never quite right. It was uneven. They had a spirit level, but they drank it.

I was well armed for my interview. I was going to impress the fuck out of Mr Bonnar with my knowledge of ornithology and my ability to pronounce it.

But when it came to it, I froze.

He asked if I had any hobbies. I said birdwatching, chickening out of ornithology. He asked me to name a few of my favourite birds.

I said, 'Blackbird.'

I literally saw his eyes glaze over.

I was consigned to Crosby House, where losers went to die.

But my days at Ballyholme Primary were finally over.[4]

It had been a perfect little cocoon for me and my friends to grow up in, where the worst that could happen was a severe beating with a large block of wood or a caning with a sharpened bamboo, where young paramilitaries roamed the corridors drinking half-bottles of warm milk while trying to sell bomb-damaged wristwatch straps to unsuspecting dupes while high on Pro Plus.

But we still felt safe.

There was a bigger, dirtier, scarier more violent world waiting for me out there, and I for one couldn't wait to join it.

---

4   Sadly, Ballyholme Primary was knocked down just a couple of years later, following the Great Verruca Epidemic of 1975.

4

Pogles' Wood

THERE WAS A BOOK LIST they sent out. The titles you'd be studying in English during your first year at grammar school. I was so excited. I was such a vociferous reader. I haunted Hugh Greer's bookshop on Hamilton Road. They had a fine selection of science fiction. It was always as quiet as a library in there. There was a second-hand bookshop at the bottom of Gray's Hill. Ditto, science fiction. Virtually every church had a summer fête, and there were always book stalls there. It wasn't unknown for me to stagger home under the weight of science-fiction books I'd pick up at one of those. You're getting the picture – avid reader, but generally only of books where the action took place in different galaxies. But I knew that I would have to widen, or indeed, narrow, my horizons. The titles I needed for school would be English Literature, not Martian.

The books would be supplied by the school once we started, but I wanted to get ahead of the pack. I'd heard about Shakespeare but didn't know what he'd written or where he lived. His name stuck out from the list. I bought a copy of *The Merchant of Venice* from a shelf of used books in the Boulevard Café on Bridge Street. The volume was small with a heavy red cover and its pages were slightly yellowed and the print was dense. It smelled like Shakespeare himself might once have tapped out his pipe on it, if he had lived in the 1940s when it was printed. I couldn't wait to get it home and get started; and then I got home and got started and immediately thought, 'What the fuck is this gibberish?' Didn't understand a word. More to the point, still don't. Ditto poetry. I may be a philistine.

Prior to starting, the prospective first-year boys were invited at the tail end of August to a week-long stay in a youth hostel outside Ballycastle on the north coast. Not everybody went, but my parents signed me up. I'd never spent a night away from home before with people I didn't know. But it seemed like a good idea. My parents knew that grammar school was big and scary, and this was a way to break me in gently. I'd existed in such a bubble in Ballyholme Primary, going through seven years with the same friends. The fact that the grammar was an all-boys school wasn't an issue – though our primary was mixed, the concept of playing with girls hadn't entered our heads. Boys played together, girls played together, there was no common ground. The frightening part was going to be boys I didn't know, and older boys who could punch my lights out. As it turned out for all of us, getting away to Ballycastle, living in a dorm, playing team games on the beach, exploring dark forests together, and killing and roasting wild pigs with spears, all helped smooth our entry to big school.

Also, I became A Christian.

That was what it was really all about. The teacher in charge was called Lindsay Brown. He was lovely and friendly and charismatic. A big, balding man with glasses who taught geology and ran the Scripture Union. He was always patting you on the back and ruffling your hair and asking if you were okay. There were older boys who helped him run the camp. They were also lovely and friendly and charismatic. They all talked about Jesus and played guitar and sang songs about Jesus – but not the sort you'd hear in church, not the dour hymns Rev. Mercer had led in Assembly, none of that 'Away in a Manger' nonsense. Even those hymns we'd loved when trendy Rev. Mason sang them now seemed archaic and, by comparison, he himself seemed incredibly old and dull. These were actual songs with choruses we could all join in with and clap our hands to; and the Bible stories they read were all in modern English and seemed to make more sense. Mr Brown and his disciples made us boys, just feeling our way into a Brave New World, feel good about ourselves.

Mr Brown wasn't like our parents. He was more like a pal. When was the last time Dad had led a crowd of us up to a hidden lake deep in a forest and allowed us to dive in just in our underpants? Never! And who wouldn't want to live a better life? Who wouldn't want to repent for his sins and be Born Again? And I did have sins. I had stolen apples from an orchard and pressurised old folk into handing over furniture we could burn. I had sung about kicking the Pope and searched for Fenians in the boots of cars and knelt on a gerbil and then dug up his corpse. I had had impure thoughts, though largely about Victoria sponges and Jaffa Cakes. I had smoked, but not inhaled. I was swept up in Christian fever and committed my soul to the Lord for all eternity, which turned out to be just over a week. Then I thought, what a lot of fucking superstitious nonsense and binned my New Testament. Then, fearing I might be struck down by lightning, I hoked it out again and hid it under some Marvel comics, which featured superheroes with more believable powers.

At least there were a few newly familiar faces from Christian camp when I turned up for my first day of school. Of the Wellington Boot Boys only Dougie Armstrong had made it, and because we were divided alphabetically rather than academically or financially, he was in my class. Gavin Martin was there – not a Boot Boy, living as he did on Windmill Road, which was just outside our catchment area, but a chum all the same. But it still wasn't easy. It probably wasn't easy for any one of us. We were all thrust into this massive sea of uniforms, twisting and turning in unison, seemingly as assured as a giant black murmuration, while we first years struggled with tattered, crumpled timetable cards telling us what class we should be in next but not where it was, and we only had a couple of minutes to get there or we'd face the wrath of the teacher and possible detention. It would have made much more sense for us all to have stayed put and have the teachers move from class to class. Instead, at the end of each forty-minute period, up to a thousand boys, many of them with the dimensions and aggressions of men, spilled into narrow corridors fighting and kicking and punching their way to French-language labs and basketball courts and English teachers with beards and lunchtime drinking habits.

Like most grammar schools, it was all about tradition. The house system. The importance of rugby. Soccer was something played by poor people. By the terms of his will, made in 1828, the Right Honourable Robert Ward ordained that a sum of £1,000 should be expended in building and endowing a school for the education of boys in mathematics, astronomy and navigation. Well, they ignored that and instead opened Bangor Endowed School in 1856,[1] on what is now the site of the old Bank of Ireland building at the corner of Central Avenue. Following another bequest, it moved to College Avenue in 1905 and remained there until it was eventually bulldozed by Formula One driver Eddie Irvine in 2013. Eddie was educated at Regent House in Newtownards. There has always been an intense rivalry between the schools – and indeed, the towns. Eddie had millions to spend from his erratic but hugely rewarding driving career. He bought the old school. He knocked it down. He built houses on the site. He drove the bulldozer himself and was heard to be sarcastically singing the Bangor Grammar School song 'Comgall noster, Columbanus' as he did it.[2]

Randall Clarke was still the headmaster. He was old and austere, and the author of a tedious book on Irish history which he insisted we studied. The vice principal was Bertie Styles. Anyone with a first name of Bertie – well, you get the picture. Kind of bumbling but kindly. Sergeant Wilson to Captain Mainwaring. Then a procession of teachers with nicknames handed down through the generations. Stringer McCord in History. Voodoo in Maths. Mr Big in Physics. Willy the Worm. Jimmy Drip. Big H. Hook. Even Lindsay Brown, the inspiring teacher from our Christian indoctrination camp, was affectionately known as Pogle, after the children's stop-motion animation show of the late '60s, *Pogles' Wood*.

---

1   If he had left more money, it could have been called Bangor Well Endowed School. But he didn't.

2   A dance mix of 'Comgall noster, Columbanus' was released by Kylie Minogue in 1992. It was not a hit.

These were all *Mr Chips*-style nicknames bestowed through a mixture of affection and loathing. They were undoubtedly a bunch of oddballs, some of them lovely, some out-and-out cunts. They were obliged to wear cloaks or gowns, and you'd see them crossing the playgrounds with them billowing out behind them. The cloaks were designed to be intimidating. Without them, they were mere adults and fallible – just like our parents. With them, they were vampires on day release. But the cloaks were overused. Familiarity breeds contempt. By the time we were through to Third Form it was routine for the ballsier boys to spit on the back of their cloaks as the teachers swept past in the corridors.[3]

My year was the first that wasn't obliged to study Latin. The only Latin we actually learned was 'Dulce et decorum est, Pro patria mori', from the Wilfred Owen poem, roughly translated as 'It is sweet and fitting to die for one's country', which plenty of nutters were putting into practice up in Belfast but not noticeably in Bangor, which was generally above that kind of thing.

You had to play rugby in first year. There were freezing cold days at Ballymacormick Playing Fields when you couldn't feel your fingers, when your spindly frame was at risk of snapping in two from the attentions of fat boys, when you had to go into showers afterwards and you were NAKED and your already minuscule testicles would shrink into your body and your willy would lie twisting and turning like a little white maggot.

The one advantage of taking the bus to the playing fields was that while most of my classmates were compelled to go

---

3   The actual term was *grotting*. To grot. I *grotted* on the teacher.

through with the rugby in order to get the bus back to school at the end, I was able to slip away over the hill opposite and down the muddy track beyond, to skirt The Lake, meander through The Forest and be home in time to feed the gerbils and snuggle up to the SuperSer while everyone else was still queuing for their bus.

Mum was always there waiting for me. She was just always there. I don't know if she ever really went out. I don't remember her ever going to the shop by herself. I just don't. I remember once, when we still lived in Wellington, Michael Graham's mum inviting her to go with a group of her friends to the pictures to see *Hello, Dolly!* and being shocked that she went, and that she wasn't in the house, and then that she seemed to have such a very good time. But it never happened again. She was sick quite a lot. She had her gallbladder removed. She spent a lot of time lying on the couch with pains in her stomach. She would get migraine headaches. She used to get me to brush her hair. She baked fabulous cakes. I can smell them now. Because of this I will shortly go out and buy a cake from the bakery a couple of doors down from where I now live. It's a good bakery. Dad used to go to the same bakery on a Saturday morning and buy a box of cream buns, six of them, of different types, including a chocolate eclair and a cream horn. A cardboard box tied with string. But they were never as nice as Mum's. Whatever I buy, it won't smell or taste the same as the cakes she made. Whatever the afterlife brings us, I hope she's there waiting with a cake. Or buns. Buns that are still warm and the icing still soft.

Our town, like most small towns then, was made up mostly of sole traders. No chains or franchises. There were a couple of department stores – the Co-Op at the bottom of Main Street, and Robinson and Cleaver at the top, but the concept of doing 'the Big Shop' hadn't been invented. When Bangor's first out-of-town shopping centre, at Springhill, opened in the early '70s, it revolutionised grocery shopping with its anchor store, Crazy Prices. Mum and Dad would go on a Thursday night, because there was Late Night Opening, which was an alien concept. Late Night Opening traditionally only happened at Christmas and was wildly exciting. Shopping when it was dark outside! Going for the Big Shop was like Christmas all over again. And your parents arrived home with foods you had never heard of before. Like pizza. Little pizzas. About six inches in diameter. Which we microwaved.[4] It was like eating a discus. And sometimes we were literally eating cardboard if we forgot to remove all of the packaging.

Not being used to real pizza was not unusual. There were literally no pizza restaurants. You could not phone up and order one. There was no Domino's or Pizza Hut. No Chinese or Indian, for that matter. Carry-out food meant only one thing – fish and chips. You went and queued for it. And, actually, we weren't entirely convinced by fish, because back then fish still had bones. These days fish don't have bones. I suppose it's evolution. Back then, they had loads of bones and you would never really know if the fish you bit into had a bone in it until you were in the back of the ambulance on the way to hospital. Fish were tracheotomies in the making. Hardly a lunchtime at

---

4   Microwave ovens were invented in 1946 but didn't become generally available in the UK until the 1970s. Watching food rotate through the glass door of a microwave oven was a popular pastime in many homes, and more entertaining than *Crossroads*.

Bangor Grammar would go by without someone being carried out on a stretcher gasping for breath. The fish they served was 75 per cent bones. The bones were cannily hidden in a white sauce. The white sauce had the consistency of Tippex. At least the fish was fresh. Fresh when they were landed at Bangor harbour thirty years before and then frozen.

Here's how dull school dinners were – a wave of excitement would go through the school when news broke that Christmas dinner was going to be served. It wasn't that we were being served turkey that made it exciting, it was because we were being served roast potatoes. Roast potatoes were in the same ballpark as chips, and we were never served chips in much the same way that we weren't allowed to play football. Football and chips were for poor people. Nine months of the year we were served scoops of lukewarm mashed potato. I've had an aversion to scoops of anything ever since.

Scoop, on the other hand, was one of the books on that first reading list. *Scoop* was sold to us as a great novel about journalism and class. *Scoop* by Evelyn Waugh. He was one of the great English satirists. Hold on, hold on – *Evelyn* is a man? Why does he have a woman's name? Is *that* satire? And, Sir, Sir – I thought you said it was one of the funniest books ever written? Morecambe and Wise are funny. This is just shit, Sir.

I couldn't make head nor tail of it. None of us could. It seemed to be mainly about a lot of upper-class twats having a jolly time while reporting a war in Ishmaelia, which didn't even exist. Did I get that it was a devastating takedown of Lord Beaverbrook? That it skewered pre-war society? We learned it, but we didn't get it. It could have put me off journalism for life. Forcing children to read books at too young an age can alienate them – at best from those particular books, at worst from reading in general. But you never can tell when the right age is to read a book, because there is no right age. It's more about when your brain is open to it, and it was another twenty years before I reread *Scoop* and discovered that it was, indeed, fabulous. I had already read *Catch-22* and thought it fantastic; it was and continues to be a huge inspiration. Maybe it has more to do with the pressure to read that comes with school. Similarly, I recently reread *The Merchant of Venice*.[5]

For her whole life, when she wasn't reading books about ghosts, Mum read Mills & Boon novels, formulaic romances churned out at the rate of dozens every month. Nothing wrong with that. Whatever floats your boat. It just never crossed her mind to try any other type of fiction. Or maybe she thought she wasn't smart enough. When she was on her Death Bed,[6] she picked up a copy of a book I had studied for my A Level at the Tech: *Tess of the D'Urbervilles* by Thomas Hardy. She read it in one sitting (she kind of had to) and absolutely adored it, and then within a few days she was gone, and I have often thought since about how much she missed out on in terms of books. But that was The Way It Was.

English literature I could cope with. History I could manage. My French was abysmal. My maths, appalling. Music – there has never been a musical Bateman. I could not play the triangle without somehow fucking it up. There was a reason my flute in the Cardboard Memorial Flute Band was imaginary. I could play a mean tennis racquet while bouncing on my bed to 'Ballroom Blitz' by The Sweet, but when I

---

5   Still shit.

6   Don't buy a Death Bed at Ikea, they're a nightmare to put together.

played the recorder at Ballyholme Primary I was asked to stop because I was putting everyone else off. If I had been the Pied Piper of Hamelin those kids would have been absolutely fine. Music at Bangor Grammar was a lost cause from day one. A lot of effort seemed to be put into learning how to read it. I just couldn't grasp the concept. They say if you understand maths, you can understand music. I could not understand maths. What prevented me from becoming a rock star during the punk era of Three Chords and The Truth was that I could not master even one of the three chords required. In the '80s I bought a synthesiser, hoping that would simplify things, but I could only ever get it to make a sound like a car alarm.

I wasn't even good at geology, despite the encouragement of Mr Brown. He wasn't just responsible for geology though – he was also entrusted to deliver our sex education. This was a good move, as he was popular and friendly with his pupils, and he could give a healthy Christian slant on it without demonising the dirty deeds we were by then all thinking about but not fully understanding. There was then no twenty-four hours a day of porn on tap with which to badly educate yourself. Sex was all in your head, occasionally on the top shelf of a newsagent's or in an abandoned copy of *Mayfair* found rolled up in the undergrowth. Most importantly, Mr Brown said there was nothing wrong with masturbation, which was a relief in more ways than one. I was of course squirming with embarrassment while he told us this, but I often think now about how much more mortifying it must have been for some of the other boys, given that our lovely Christian Mr Brown had so recently wanked some of them off.

For there was a monster stalking the corridors of Bangor Grammar, and his name was Lindsay Brown. He was a paedophile and everyone knew it, even if we didn't know the correct word for it. The boys knew it. The teachers knew it. Yet he was allowed to get away with it. For decades. His nickname Pogle was not an affectionate one; it was awarded as a kind of warning: don't go with Pogle into the woods. He had been at it since before I joined the school, he was at it while I was there and he was allowed to continue it long after I left. His activities were reported on numerous occasions, but somehow he always talked his way out of it. Nice Mr Brown wouldn't do that. Nice Christian Mr Brown couldn't do that. They knew about it and they still allowed him to take children away to camps. (I went twice more to his camps – both to Auchen Castle at Moffat in Scotland. It was a perfect hunting ground for him – miles from anywhere, surrounded by woods, nowhere to run to, no means of contacting your parents or anyone. He didn't come anywhere near me. I was lucky.) When he wasn't called Pogle, he was called Fruity Mr Brown. It was a sign of the times that what he was up to was largely thought of as harmless. Harmless unless you were a victim of it and nobody believed you, or, more likely, you were too scared to say. But enough people said it quietly and it became known, which makes it all the more appalling that nothing was done about it for decades. In fact, he was promoted to vice principal after Bertie retired. And here's something that's barely believable: not the fact that after he was eventually investigated he was totally exonerated, but that he was then named as the designated teacher for child-abuse issues. Let me just repeat that: *a teacher widely suspected of being a paedophile was put in charge of child-abuse issues.* They put the fox in charge of the chicken coop.

The boys got him, finally, not the school, and he went to prison.

Later, after he was released, he fled to France. Later still, he made the mistake of returning home for a family event and was rearrested and charged with further historic sex crimes – and sent back to prison.

I saw him a few years ago hurrying through Bloomfield Shopping Centre in Bangor. This would have been after his first stint in prison. There was a moment of eye contact, a slight nod of recognition, and then he was gone before I quite realised who he was.

Actually, that's a lie. I knew exactly who he was. And that sums it all up really. I didn't say anything. I didn't stop for a chat and ask what he'd been up to. I didn't trip him up or call him a cunt. He was clearly moving fast to reduce the possibility of anyone confronting him. His very presence was both defiant and oddly foolish given that he hadn't changed much physically and would thus be easily recognised by any former pupil, while those pupils themselves would have changed out of all recognition and thus have the advantage of surprise. He remembered them only in – or out – of school uniform. He knew them as smooth-faced boys fresh to puberty, not as the scarred men many had become: men he wouldn't recognise until they were upon him.

I suppose I was lucky that he never found me attractive, or I never found myself in a position where he could take advantage of me. And he probably could have, because I was floundering during those first few years at big school. I was quiet and sensitive and didn't make friends easily. It seemed like everyone else did make those friends, but I was not a boy to whom other boys gravitated. I was still in the thrall of Marvel comics and science fiction, and that made me the exception rather than today's rule. I didn't fit in. I spent lunchtimes that seemed to last forever wandering about looking lost. I wasn't bullied, exactly, I was just alone. And quite frightened. I'd been used to my Wellington gang, and now they were nearly all at a different school and making their own new friends.

The newest fad was Bruce Lee and kung fu. For a while I lived in fear of one boy who'd go around kicking and chopping anyone who got in his way, and I always seemed to be in his way. He claimed to be taking kung fu classes. Then another boy in the class invited him into the toilets and punched his lights out, and he didn't talk about kung fu much after that. There was another boy in the class who had tiny little arms. His mum had taken thalidomide, prescribed in the '60s to combat sickness during pregnancy, which led to a generation of children with malformed limbs. Mum told me she'd taken thalidomide. It was all a lottery. The boy in my class was called Richard Gledhill. You don't want to have tiny little arms in a class of teenage boys because they're ruthless. I thought I had it rough with my nose, but he was destroyed. Eventually the worst perpetrators were expelled. Bullies weren't tolerated, but a blind eye was turned to paedophiles.

If I wasn't reading science fiction, I was watching it. Science fiction was largely ill-served by television – the special effects just weren't good enough. But I was a little obsessed by *Planet of the Apes* – initially through the Marvel adaptations of the films, then the TV series, because it wasn't easy to see the actual movies. There were five of them in all. Along with James Bond they were one of the few franchises that were around at the time. It's hard now to say it without melting into the ground, but I enthusiastically joined the *Planet of the Apes* Fan Club.

As I grew older, the books I read became more sophisticated – Frank Herbert's *Dune*, Robert Heinlein's *Stranger in a Strange Land*, but it was still science fiction and somehow something I instinctively knew to keep to myself. I joined the British Science Fiction Association and got their newsletter and lists of new books and magazines I could order, and I discovered fanzines and fandom. There was this great community 'out there' that I became a part of, even if it was also completely removed from me: it was all done by letter, by little mimeographed magazines full of in-jokes and mostly run by men at least ten years older than me and mostly in their forties. There were no meetings I could attend. There was no fraternal clubhouse to hang out in. Once, in a fanzine, I discovered a letter from someone who seemed to be of a similar age and who lived in Dundonald. That was about ten miles away. Somehow, that frightened me. I didn't actually want to meet someone who shared my interests. I imagined our encounters would be embarrassingly silent. There are things about science fiction that are best kept internal: you can convince yourself that it's really for intellectuals, that it's all about the science and grand theories and the quest for knowledge – and then you start trying to explain it to someone and they point out the impossibility of travelling to other galaxies, and you try to argue that lightspeed travel just hasn't been invented yet and then they ask, how do Daleks get upstairs? And suddenly you've lost the argument.

My science-fiction obsession was also beginning to overlap with something new and altogether more grounded in reality. I found myself caught in a weird world between nerdiness and rock'n'roll rebellion, between the *Planet of the Apes* Fan Club and 'Anarchy in the UK'.

Gavin Martin sowed the seeds. Prog rock was then big – Genesis and Yes and Pink Floyd[7] – hair was long and flares were wide. Pop was what you mainly heard on *Top of the Pops*. Rock with lots of twiddly guitar breaks was what you heard on *The Old Grey Whistle Test* if you could keep your eyes open long enough, both because it was on late and because it was extremely boring. My brother listened to Slade and Queen, and Mott the Hoople and David Bowie. He was a member of a record club in England, which sent him a new album on approval every month – if you didn't send it back quickly enough then you had to pay for it; inevitably he forgot, which meant he quickly built up a collection of records he didn't like very much. Bachman–Turner Overdrive arrived singing 'You Ain't Seen Nothing Yet'. The problem was, we had. Rick Wakeman arrived wearing a cape and looking like a wizard or a grammar-school teacher with his rock-opera version of *Journey to the Centre of the Earth*.

There was also a record library, which was briefly established in a small shop inside Bangor Railway Station,

---

7   There was a local prog rock band called Fruup, who looked for a while like they might be on the verge of stardom. They had support slots in England with Genesis and Queen. They may have fallen for some of their own hype – they optimistically booked our own 2,000-seat Tonic cinema for a show. My brother went. They only sold out the front row. That gig can't have been easy. It was my brother's first live-band experience. He said they were too loud, 'and crap'.

where you could pay a small amount to borrow a record, then you could immediately tape it when you got home and return it so you didn't need to borrow it again. I'm not sure the record library thought their business model through. It lasted about a month.

I'm sure my brother would have gone to see his favourite bands in concert, but that wasn't a possibility. It was the height of the Troubles and nobody would risk their lives coming here. It was also the era of the showband, groups who played cover versions of popular hits – jukebox bands whose hair might have been long, and their suits may have boasted fashionably wide lapels, but they were steeped in tedious tradition, didn't play any original music and only succeeded because there was no alternative. One of the most popular was the Miami Showband. They toured all over Ireland. Then the UVF stopped their van one night and tried to plant a bomb under it. It went off prematurely, killing two of the bombers and setting the others off into a blind panic, during which they shot dead three band members and seriously wounded two others. As a result, live music, even by locals for locals, all but stopped.

Even if my brother had ever felt inclined to go and see a showband, he'd just missed that boat. Instead, he had to take his flared trousers, his platform heels and his poodle perm onto the disco dance floor.

We have established that I had a nickname. Bacon. In the grand scheme of things it wasn't so bad, and these days it's hardly ever used. Smelly McDade graduated from a poor nickname to something altogether better and fluffier with Tufty. My brother has never quite lost his, though. He was, and is, known as Boker. Boker Bateman. It is not unusual to still hear someone shout, 'Hey, Boker, how's it going?' as they pass. If you don't know what a boker is, it is not a reference to the nineteenth-century American poet George Henry Boker. Nor indeed to John G. Boker, creator of Boker's Bitters, a crucial ingredient of nearly every cocktail that called for bitters as listed in Jerry Thomas' revered 1862 book, *How to Mix Drinks or The Bon Vivant's Companion*, and a product which was hugely successful until Prohibition led to its demise in the 1920s. No, 'Boker' refers to the ancient Northern Irish art of The Boke, of Boking, of Boking Up – that is, to be sick, to vomit and, in the context of youth, to boke up after drinking too much alcohol. Boker Bateman was Boker Bateman because he had a nasty habit of boking up when he was drinking. He was actually quite lucky with the nickname. Shit Your Pants Lennon hasn't been out of his house since a Blue Lamp disco in 1975.[8] Boker didn't just get his nickname for boking up, however. Because everyone in those drinking years boked up. Boker got his name for boking up down the back of a girl he was dancing with in the Savoy disco, and more than forty years later he's still being reminded of it. Think of that poor girl carrying that *Carrie*-like horror around with her for decades. Boker Bateman survived and thrived, but whatever happened to that poor girl who went out that night to dance under the mirror ball of romance, to shake her stuff to the smooth rations of passion provided by

---

8   Blue Lamp discos were discos organised by the RUC for teenagers and manned by police DJs. They were a bizarre attempt to foster love between the communities, and for the police. They were hugely popular in towns like Bangor, where there wasn't much trouble (or many Catholics, so there were no real communities to bring together). If they'd tried organising them in Belfast, the DJ would have been shot and there would have been full-scale rioting.

resident DJ Jon Anthony (who only had one eye), but instead suffered the public humiliation of having someone boke down her back?

Reader, he didn't marry her.

So fuck knows.

The thing was, even though there were some of my brother's records I liked, the problem was exactly that, it was his taste in music. And you can't just ape your brother. It's not what you do. If anything, you go in the opposite direction. Just as with football, if someone supports United, then you support Liverpool. I desperately needed some music of my own. But you cannot just manufacture that. You have to explore. You have to try things out. You need something new and fresh. The problem was you couldn't actually hear what was new and fresh, because there were only a handful of radio stations. BBC Radio 1 was already a prisoner of its unadventurous playlist. There was scratchy Radio Luxembourg, which sold itself on being one small step removed from pirate radio but actually wasn't much better than the BBC. And there was the newly minted Downtown Radio, Northern Ireland's first commercial radio station, which launched in 1976 but seemed to play mostly country and western and American adult-oriented rock. There was no Spotify. You can listen to everything on Spotify, which actually often means you listen to nothing new because there's too much choice and there's no useful way to navigate it, so you listen to the same songs you've always listened to. There's no barrier to appearing on it either, no quality control. If I was still in the Cardboard Memorial Flute Band, we would have a life on Spotify. I know this because its real-life equivalent, the Pride of Whitehill Flute Band, is on Spotify. That shouldn't be allowed. It's just not right. But 28,000 people have listened to their most popular track. Or one person has listened to it 28,000 times.

Then, there was no way to find new music, unless you knew someone who *did* know how to find new music.

And luckily, we did.

That someone was Gavin Martin. He was always into his music. He was reading the *New Musical Express* and *Record Mirror* from an early age. He knew what was happening. He began enthusing in school about bands we'd never heard of. Eddie and the Hot Rods, Johnny Moped and Dr Feelgood. They were part of what became known as pub rock, and still not quite what we were looking for. That scene couldn't have existed here because bands rarely played in pubs following the Miami Showband massacre. But it was leading us somewhere. Gavin was soon raving about Richard Hell and Television and The Ramones – bands coming out of America with a new, harsher sound that people were starting to call punk rock.

And then we began to hear whispers about a band called the Sex Pistols, who were leading an English version of this punk rock. There was a steady stream of articles about them and their wild front man, Johnny Rotten, and we were soon caught up the excitement: they looked extraordinary and were talking revolution, about getting rid of the dinosaurs of rock and actually changing society not just through their music but their attitude. Through anarchy. This was all incredibly exciting to a withdrawn teenage boy who until then had existed mainly on other planets. And the strangest thing was it was exciting despite the fact that we hadn't heard a single note by the Sex Pistols because they hadn't yet released anything.

We fell for them on faith alone. We knew that what they eventually released would be incredible.

The knowledge that they weren't alone either was also exciting: there were other bands following in their wake, and in some cases preceding them – The Damned released what was arguably the first British punk single, 'New Rose', in October 1976. I bought it in the recently opened Record and Tape Centre in Abbey Street. It was an instant classic. And if *that* was a classic, how much better would the Sex Pistols' first release be? We were, of course, potentially heading for disappointment. News spread that they would be interviewed, and their first single played, on Radio Luxembourg on a Sunday evening at the start of November. I was impatiently pacing up in down in the kitchen waiting for it, the SuperSer blasting. And then the first chords of 'Anarchy in the UK' rang out. It was a road-to-Damascus moment.[9] The DJ played it, then he interviewed the band. Then he played the B-side, 'I Wanna Be Me'. Then he played the A-side again. That just didn't happen. But there it was. 'Anarchy in the UK' was the greatest song ever released by any band ever anywhere in the universe.

A year before, my mum had bought me a new pair of drainpipe jeans. I looked at them in disgust and demanded she hide them away. You couldn't go out in those. You'd look like a freak. Trousers had to be flared. And the wider and baggier the better. Overnight, those flares became a symbol of everything I despised. Long hair was disgusting. Permed hair was an abomination. Men striding about in platform shoes was ridiculous. My brother wore massive flares, had long permed

---

9   I wonder if people living near Damascus have a road-to-Damascus moment? Maybe they just have 'a moment'.

hair and staggered about on platform heels boking on girls. He became the enemy. The drainpipe jeans were fished out of the wardrobe. Mum 'took in' my other flares, transforming them into punky drainpipes.

Three weeks after the radio interview, 'Anarchy in the UK' was released. I rushed down after school to buy it in Aquarius Records on Queen's Parade. I asked for the new record by the Sex Pistols. My face was very red because it was the first time I said the word 'sex' out loud. One of my friends misheard the title and went into the same shop and asked for 'Archery in the UK'.

It came in a plain sleeve and on the EMI label. It went straight on the record player in our living room as soon as I chased everyone else out. Volume up full. Wow. Just wow. It was revolutionary and it was loud. Even when my parents banged on the door and I turned it down, it was still loud. It is still one of the most powerful records ever released. And it mentioned us, the troublesome Northern Irish with our UDA and IRA. No one had ever done that before. We'd heard Bob Dylan, but his protest songs were oblique and full of symbolism; Johnny Rotten's lyrics were a grot right in the face.

And it was all still essentially our secret – punk bands weren't on TV, the music wasn't played on the radio with the exception of the John Peel show on Radio 1, squirrelled away after ten at night. But we didn't care, because it was perfect and pure. Punks were against big corporations. They were against the system. The Pistols were signed to a big corporation and relied on the system to get their record out to their fans.

But still. Punk was about doing things for yourself. Punk was about rejecting the normal and the average. It was about wanting to boke when you saw the faux Irish Nolan sisters on *Top of the Pops* with their bland cabaret disco.[10] It was about releasing your own records, it was about publishing your own fanzines, it was about doing anything you wanted to do ('Do Anything You Wanna Do', Eddie and the Hot Rods).[11] A lot of it was bollocks, but it was our bollocks. And it was ours for about a week – and then the Sex Pistols appeared live on the *Thames Today* show on ITV in early December as a last-minute replacement for pomp-rocking Queen. A drunk presenter, Bill Grundy, goaded them into some effusive swearing. A nation was shocked, the Pistols were on the front page of every newspaper and they were booted off their record label. Punks were soon being picked on in the street for being punks, but, despite this, in fact *because* of all of this, punk entered the mainstream, because nothing succeeds like excess.

Of course, we couldn't see the TV interview ourselves – and wouldn't for years – because we were stuck with the UTV news and mere trivia about who had been blown up or murdered here, and we were bored with that. It didn't really matter that we didn't see it. It was all about the impact it had.

---

10 The Nolan sisters would come back to haunt me. Not literally. Spectral Nolan sisters weren't hanging about at the bottom of my bed; they had better things to do, like releasing rubbish records. But, much to my shame, they would appear on the soundtrack of my film *Divorcing Jack*, while the producers rejected a song by Joe Strummer of The Clash.

11 Many years later Eddie and the Hot Rods played at a pub in Bangor. Except lead singer Barrie Masters, the Eddie in Eddie and the Hot Rods, who was in prison. We didn't know that before we went to see them. That was a disappointment. We also went to see Dr Feelgood with *no* original members. It's not a new phenomenon. There have been about fifteen versions of the Four Tops touring for years, one of them entirely white.

The Pistols briefly became Public Enemies Number One – and, by association, we did too. And it was *great*.

Even though punk was now taking off as a youth movement, and bands were springing up everywhere, we were still in the minority – most of the population remained in flares, and mindless disco continued to clog up the charts. We wore our drainpipes, we sported badges promoting our favourite bands, we scoured the music papers for new releases, we gathered in corners of the Bangor Grammar schoolyard to swap news and records and badges and eat crisps with new-found attitude. The Damned's single had come out in October 1976. The Clash, who would become my favourite band, didn't release their first single until March 1977; that's half a year later, but back then it seemed like it came out in the blink of an eye.

We were young enough to still be getting pocket money. For a while you could just about afford to keep up with the new releases, but soon there were just too many. Some of us were better off than others, of course. With one boy, Geordie, as soon as the name of the latest band was mentioned he had their record the next day. Money was clearly no object. This started to piss people off. We were part of the oppressed working class, albeit from our lower-middle-class homes and we were all at nice Bangor Grammar, so no one was supposed to have that much surplus cash. But Geordie had no qualms. Every day he had something new. Every day he rubbed the faces of the proletariat in the dirt with his ill-gotten bourgeois gains. A conspiracy was launched to put him back in his place. Next time we gathered the name of a cool new singer-songwriter was on everyone's lips. It could have been the then emerging Elvis Costello or the recently converted pub rocker

Graham Parker. But no, this new star was even better: he was going to change the face of popular music, and we were all devastated that we couldn't afford his acclaimed new album. Geordie went straight out and bought it that day and returned to school the next morning puzzled by how enthusiastic we all were about middle-aged folk singer and beardy whistler Roger Whittaker.[12]

It has been argued that in Northern Ireland we needed punk rock more than anyone. It brought the youth of a divided society together. It didn't matter if you were a Protestant or a Catholic, it was all about the music. That's how the story goes anyway, and as the newspaper editor Maxwell Scott said in *The Man Who Shot Liberty Valance*, 'This is the West, sir. When the legend becomes fact, print the legend.' There was some truth in this. But what is undoubtedly true is that punk eventually took off spectacularly here because we were actually already living in anarchy, so desperately needed a soundtrack. We were on a permanent pandemic lockdown, without the pandemic. We were searched on the way into shops, instead of on the way out, in case we were carrying hidden firebombs. Gates at the top of our Main Street, and every Main Street, were closed at night to prevent car-bombers. There was no curfew, but there may as well have been. And when the politicians and the paramilitaries weren't fucking things up for us, crazies like the Lord's Day Observance Society revelled in their achievement of making sure everything stayed closed on a Sunday – swings were even chained up in children's playgrounds – while managing

---

12   The alternative plan had been to persuade him to go in and ask for Ian Dury's 'Sex and Drugs and Arctic Roll'.

to get the whole world simultaneously laughing and shaking their heads at us.

Punk rock was important the way skiffle wasn't, vital the way beat music or jazz wasn't – or the way the New Romantics or ska, which would soon follow on, never could be. Or maybe it wasn't. Maybe it was just pop music in different trousers, trousers held together with safety-pins, with a little bit of canny marketing thrown in. Perhaps it was just an interesting blip in rock'n'roll history, destined to be quickly forgotten. Like most teen movements, in hindsight it can all look quite silly and irrelevant. But if you were there, if you were part of it, it was the most important thing in your whole fucking world.[13]

---

13 Also, Mummy wouldn't let me get my hair spiked.

5

The Story of The Blues

I HAD *TEENAGE DEPRESSION*.[1] OF course I had. I had a nose like Concorde and people weren't afraid to point it out, including the friends I didn't have. I was remarkably skinny. And increasingly spotty. I couldn't speak to a girl without going red in the face and melting into a small puddle. Despite the growing camaraderie of punk rock, I was still living largely outside of the known universe – but increasingly there wasn't even comfort there because science fiction was also moving into the mainstream, and I Did Not Like It.

My friend Richard had moved to America after the first year at Bangor Grammar. Ministers are routinely moved around different parishes, but this was a bit extreme. They sent his dad to Vermont, where they must have been short of Methodists. Richard had inherited his dad's good looks. In some photos he looks a bit like Paul McCartney. He played ice hockey. He quickly became an all-American boy. And he saw *Star Wars* in 1977, six months before anyone on this side

---

1 The first album by Eddie and The Hot Rods. My friend Phil has a copy of it with a photo of The Damned mistakenly placed on the back cover. This might be worth a fortune. But probably not.

of the Atlantic, because that was the way films were released; there was always a time lag. He knew I loved science fiction, so he sent me a copy of the novelisation and, as soon as I jumped into it, I knew the gig was up. It was great, the film would be great and, if the photos in the book were to be believed, the special effects would be amazing, but I didn't want it to be great or amazing. I didn't want the rest of the world to know about science fiction, I wanted it to all be mine, I didn't want to have to compete for it with millions of others. I didn't want it reduced to something popular.

I was depressed about *Star Wars*. I was angry because I was a punk rocker and we were supposed to be angry. And I was chippy because I was a teenager. I was also suffering from post-traumatic stress disorder because of my exposure to the Troubles.

No, wait, that's bollocks.

We were at best on the very fringes of it all. Ours was a very safe and idyllic town to grow up in. Part of the reason for this was the geography of Bangor, where it actually was on the map. It was ten plus miles from Belfast, where merry hell continued to be played out, but there were no easy escape routes from it. That was our saving grace. There was one main road going to Belfast. If terrorists wanted to launch attacks and still get home in time for bed, then they had to be sure of an escape route, and that main artery could be closed down too easily by the security forces to often take that risk. This is why we escaped with so few bombs and murders. It's also worth noting that there are zero instances of suicide bombers in the history of the Troubles – they wanted to get away with it, and then gloat. There were plenty of unintentional suicide bombers, because both sides were a bit rubbish at putting their explosive devices together, but no actual suicide bombers. You've got to hand it to Islamic terrorists – they're certainly committed. They pilot planes into tall buildings. IRA terrorists wouldn't pilot a bread van into a soft-play area if they thought there was a danger of hurting themselves.

Bangor was thought of as fairly safe for police officers and prison officers to live in. It was already largely Protestant and, because of the escape routes, there was always going to be loads of them about, in or out of uniform, which made it even more unattractive to terrorists. In the early '70s soldiers were also able to come out of their barracks up the road in Holywood and go to pubs and clubs in the town, in particular The Helmsman in High Street. The local girls flocked there, and why not? They were fit young men with steady jobs, unusual accents and money to burn, but of course this didn't go down well with the local boys. After a while there was so much post-disco fighting that the army stopped letting them out. Now our young men had no one but themselves to fight with, so they did.

We were so close to Belfast, but also on the margins. Our Troubles were small. *Big* if you lived in Surrey, but otherwise small. The bombers went for months without considering us, and then they probably had a meeting and said, let's have a day trip to Bangor, and down they came again.

In March 1974 they left incendiary devices in a dozen shops on Main Street. Woolworths, Wellworths and the Co-Op, our three biggest stores, were all gutted by fire. We watched the black clouds over our town from afar. We went back into town a few days later and the big stores had found alternative premises or rebuilding was well under way.

In July, a teenage Catholic then living in the loyalist Whitehill Estate made the mistake of attending the Eleventh Night bonfire there and was shot dead for his trouble. Our Resident Magistrate was shot dead at his home in Belfast. The following March, Mildred Harrison became the first serving female police officer to be killed during the Troubles when a bomb left on the windowsill of the Ormeau Arms in High Street blew up as she was passing. Shrapnel pierced her chest and she died in the arms of a colleague. Like I say, we had it easy.

Maybe the Troubles had a cumulative effect. We were exposed to some aspect of them twenty-four hours a day. It seeped into your system, like dry rot. But I really can't blame the Troubles for more than a smidgen of what was making me depressed. Maybe depressed itself is too strong. I was *a bit down*. I was *blue*. I was frustrated for the usual reasons, but also because I already wanted to be a writer, but it's very hard to be a writer at thirteen, fourteen, fifteen, sixteen – any age, really. But particularly when you're young, unless you're a frickin' genius.[2]

I was writing short stories. Science-fiction short stories. I knew little science, and not enough about life. I had asked for a typewriter for Christmas when I was twelve and my parents, thinking of it still in terms of toys, bought me a Chad Valley effort with a hideous blue ribbon, which only ever made ugly smudgy letters and was largely useless. Eventually they gave in to my whining and got me a proper portable typewriter. I'd sit at the dinner table in our living room typing away, typing away. At the end of each line a little bell rang and you'd have

---

2   S.E. Hinton wrote *The Outsiders* when she was in high school. It still sells half a million copies a year.

to push the carriage return back to the other side to start again. It was a very easy manual labour. Once the bell rang there was also another sound, that of my brother going, 'Shut up, shut up, shut up, you little shit,' because he was trying to watch *Coronation Street*. I would refuse and there would be angry words. But I only had one nose to break and a writing career to get on with, so I persevered. I also kept a diary. For six months. Every night, writing a full page. Oh Lord, let's not go there. At least there wasn't any poetry.[3]

I kept at the short stories. Eventually one was accepted for *Tangent*, the magazine for amateur writers run by the British Science Fiction Association, and I was elated. I thought I was on the road to the Nobel Prize or at least the Nebula. The magazine folded before it came out. Undeterred, I sent another story off to a brand-new science-fiction magazine I'd spotted in the newsagent's, *Vortex*. It was all glossy and lavishly illustrated – if I could get something published there, I'd be off and running with my writing career, and probably rich too. I sent it off to the editor, Keith Seddon. Never heard back. The magazine lasted for four issues before disappearing. There was no way then to find out what happened to it.

It started to get me down. Everything started to get me down. Writing. Girls. Writing about girls. Friends. Falling out with friends. The way I looked. Oh, the way I looked, and sounded, or didn't sound. My inability to engage in idle chit-

---

3   That's a lie. I had a poem published in *The Gryphon*, the school magazine. I stole the poem from a science-fiction novel. I have no morals. Or scruples. Nobody noticed. I don't know what the statute of limitations is on purloined poetry, but I suspect I'm in the clear. For years I thought it was the Statue of Limitations. I'd like to see that.

chat. These were the days before therapy, before self-help, before mindfulness. Mindfulness would have been hurled out of the window in our house for being wanky nonsense. I could not have talked about my issues to *anyone*, not in a thousand years.[4] It was the era of *catch yourself on*. But my parents could see I was down, so they paid for the best kind of therapy there is.

Got me a dog.

A Jack Russell called Patch.

Because he had a patch over one eye.

Patch came home in a straw-filled wooden crate. He crawled up into my arms and that was it. Hook, line and sinker. I loved him. He loved me; hated everyone else. He really did. Perhaps hate is a bit strong. But he was snappy. He bit my brother on the lip and I didn't even order him to. He started out cute. When he was a tiny pup, he performed little handstands as he tried to drink milk from a saucer. He became my constant companion. My confidant. My *consigliere*. I walked him for miles. Then, you didn't even have to pick the shit up. If you had picked the shit up, people would have looked at you like you were mental. There are still people locked up in secure units whose only crime was to pick the shit up, though admittedly some of them also ate it. Sometimes my dad would take him to Castle Park and Patch would disappear down rabbit holes and badger setts for hours at a time. More than once, Dad would be standing in the bushes waiting for Patch to emerge or whistling to attract his attention when he would be hesitantly approached by wary men and asked if they could lend a hand, without his realising it was a gay cruising ground.

---

4   Still wouldn't.

In August 1977 The Boomtown Rats became the first punk band to appear on *Top of the Pops*. They were Irish too, but Southern, which *kind of* resonated. Only punk bands were brave enough to travel to Northern Ireland to play. The Clash came in October '77 – but their gig was cancelled at the last moment due to insurance problems, with Belfast punks already lined up outside the Ulster Hall. A mini riot ensued, with the police wading in heavy-handed. By local standards it barely qualified as a riot, but it has been awarded mythical status, up there with Altamont as one of those cathartic moments when *everything* changed. I wasn't there, of course. I was probably on one of Saturn's moons. I was just a little bit young. It was a few more months before I got to experience rock'n'roll first-hand, punk rock live. But it was a beauty.

I went up with Dougie Armstrong and Gavin Martin. Gavin's dad gave us a lift. We went to see the Buzzcocks. They were actually more punk than either The Clash or the Pistols, because they'd released their first EP, *Spiral Scratch*, on their own label. DIY punks. But then they got rid of idiosyncratic lead singer Howard Devoto and shifted guitarist Pete Shelley onto vocals, and suddenly they were having hit singles. And they were going to play them for us.

We joined an excited queue outside the McMordie Hall at Queen's University in Belfast. Dougie showed me a bottle hidden in his jacket – Olde English cider. Have a taste of this. I had a taste. I thought it was horrible. Never touching that again. Why would you want to drink that shit? Why would you want to get drunk anyway? In a few months I'd be drinking litres of it. But not that night. That night I just wanted to see the band.

As we waited impatiently to get in out of the autumn chill, rumours began to swirl that the gig was off – that the Buzzcocks, like The Clash before them, couldn't get insurance. Or that they'd missed the ferry from England. Then it was official, gig cancelled.

Or was it?

Word came – the show goes on with the local punk band who were supposed to be supporting them playing instead. Their name was Rudi. Well, that didn't sound punk. Expectations were low. Gavin knew all about them. He pointed at someone standing beside us in the audience, someone in a paint-splashed boiler suit, like he'd just come from decorating a house – that's the guitarist in the band. And I thought, what's he doing here, instead of backstage? And then he disappeared and a few minutes later the lights went down and an old-fashioned police siren began to sound, and then big tom-tom drums kicked in, and then that same guy and another fella came to their mikes and began to pump their fists and chant, 'SS/RUC! SS RUC!' and I could scarcely believe it and the whole audience was chanting it with them and punching the air and bouncing up and down, and they were singing a song called 'The Cops' and it was all about the riot outside the Ulster Hall and it was the second-greatest song I'd ever heard and it was being performed by guys just a couple of years older than me, from where we lived, and they were sensational.

We didn't hate the police. They were helping to protect us from the IRA, but in the narrow confines of punk, they were the enemy. I had been a convert to the music before, but now I was a zealot. We were used to everything here being negative – we couldn't do this, we couldn't do that, we weren't allowed to do this, it was too dangerous to do that or go there – and suddenly here was a band showing us how to do it. It was like an old Hollywood musical – let's do the show right here!

It was a coming-of-age night – first rock'n'roll, first mouthful of alcohol, then sniffing up speed on the way home. Well, at least, a spoonful of Calpol before bed because my ears were still ringing.

But there was a definite shift.

There'd been further inklings of that shift during the summer. I'd gone off with Rodney and Michael and a new friend, Willy, to Boys' Brigade camp in a field on the outskirts of Douglas on the Isle of Man. There was a Girls' Brigade camp next door to us, but interaction wasn't encouraged. It was a glorious summer, the summer that Virginia Wade won Wimbledon. For the past few years we'd been content to follow orders from our BB leaders, but now we were beginning to push back. We were punks, after all. Our gang arrived back late at the campsite after hanging around the centre of Douglas all afternoon – and the officer in charge smelled alcohol on our breath. We hadn't actually been drinking, unless you count Top Deck shandy.

Top Deck looked like beer, smelled like beer, but wasn't actually beer. There might have been a tiny smidgen of alcohol in it, but not enough to prevent it being marketed primarily at children. It was the drinking equivalent of the sweetie cigarettes they used to sell. Nowadays you call them candy sticks. You would have to drink about 5,000 cans of Top Deck to get drunk. But that wasn't the point. The point was that you could act drunk, and you would smell like it. You could pretend you were a grown-up. It was bizarre, but it was hugely popular all through the '60s, '70s and '80s, and in fact was only discontinued in 2012.

On our way back to camp that afternoon we shared a cold can of Top Deck. We were horsing around as we arrived and were admonished for being late, but then the whiff of alcohol was detected and we were accused of being drunk. We were put on trial. It wasn't even a mock trial. It was a real trial. And the whole camp was assembled for it. Evidence was presented. We tried to explain, but we didn't even have the assistance of a barrack-room lawyer. We were found guilty as charged, and for our punishment Rodney and Michael had to peel potatoes, but for some reason – me being a cheeky little shit, possibly – I was singled out for extra punishment. I was sentenced to having my clothes stripped from me down to my underpants. I was then held down while dozens of hands daubed boot polish on my lily-white skin. Then I was grabbed by the older boys and officers and dragged mostly naked around the Girls' Brigade camp next door. I can still remember the horrified screams, and that was just from me.

We never went back to BB after that camp. But at least the Wellington Boot Boys were together again and intent on creating our own entertainment on a Friday night, and very soon this meant going to The Whites.

The Whites were stone shelters built along the promenade above Ballyholme Beach. Adjoining them was a row of wooden bathing boxes, which people used to get changed in before going for a swim. So far, so Edwardian. But it was the '70s, a time when everything seemed to be run down and in constant need of repair, and the bathing boxes were no exception. They were still used during those rare days when we had some sunshine, but otherwise they just sat there quietly rotting away. When it came to the dark nights of autumn and winter, they were easy enough to break in to, and that where we conducted our first experiments with the Devil's Vomit.

You'd think I might have steered clear of alcohol, having spent so many sleepless nights listening to Boker boke up, but it doesn't work like that. We just had to find our own way into it. We were too young to get served, and too new to it to get older boys to buy it for us. We did what every generation does, and what every generation always forgets when it comes to their own children: that is, to hide the alcohol properly. We stole from home. In this first case we had a bottle of Bacardi between four of us. It could have been worse; it could have been advocaat six years past its sell-by date. We wouldn't have got drunk, but we might have ended up with salmonella. But Bacardi it was. We mixed it with Coke. I think I handled it pretty well, right up to the point where my mates had to carry me home. Luckily, the Boker nickname was already taken. They laid me down in the garage while they debated how best to get me into the house, as my parents were semi-permanently camped out in the kitchen and there was no other way to get me to my bedroom. I lay with one ear listening to my friends argue, the other to the sounds of a new generation of gerbils, over-excited by this unexpected night-time visit, eating their children, and my third ear, the final front ear, listening to the sounds of my own dry-heaving while all around the world spun out of control.

Fortunately, after a little spying, my friends established that my parents had vacated the kitchen and were now in the living room with friends, and they were able to sneak me through the house and into my bedroom before flopping me down on the bed and sneaking away – all the while silently praying that I wouldn't die during the night. That was unlikely. I was already dead.

Later I discovered that while my head was swimming, my parents had invited their friends round to watch *Emmanuelle* on our newly rented video machine.[5]

I swore I'd never drink again, and meant it – at least until the following weekend, when we began the process all over again. But it was a hard no to the spirits. And I never drank them again. One bad experience and I was off them for life. I can be like that with drinks, and foodstuffs and women. But I gave cider another try. I still wasn't crazy about the Olde English, but one of the boys had access to Strongbow, which had a different, sweeter taste, and pretty soon I was hooked.

We all were.

It was great.

We turned up at The Whites every weekend, somehow managing to get hold of supplies of cider. There was just the four of us, initially – occasionally there was a girl or two from the youth club held in the hall adjacent to the Church of Ireland, my church, on the Groomsport Road. Michael hadn't made it to the Grammar, but he was a rugby boy anyway, joining Bangor Rugby Club as soon as he could. He was blond and handsome and well built, and we weren't.

---

5   *Emmanuelle* was a 1974 soft-porn movie – it was the first of its kind to truly enter the mainstream. It played at the Fleapit in Bangor. My parents wouldn't have been seen dead there. It became a huge success when released as one of the first movies available on home video. My parents weren't particularly into soft porn. It was just the curiosity factor. I ~~think~~ hope.

He had his pick of the girls. Occasionally we'd be in the shelter, drinking Strongbow and cans of Harp, and he'd be snogging away with his girlfriend Jane, the only light coming from a candle we'd thought to bring[6] and we'd stand there awkwardly trying not to watch. When occasionally Michael couldn't join us because he was away somewhere playing rugby, I thoughtfully stepped into his shoes and snogged her instead. I'm good that way. She didn't seem to mind. Michael didn't seem to mind either, at least until he found out. There was a bit of a falling out. We made up. He wasn't that fussed about her and I couldn't afford not to be fussed about anyone. I got on very well with her, we'd laugh a lot. The cider helped me out of my shell. There is a school of thought that girls like boys with a sense of humour and that good looks aren't that important. I'm sure they do like a sense of humour. Why wouldn't you? But they'll stick with the handsome rugby-playing guy with the muscles every time. You get your hopes up, and then they're dashed. That's what being a teenager is all about.[7]

After our carry-out and snogging, we'd be drunk enough for the youth club. There was a bit of a disco. There was a pool table. A dartboard. One night, I nearly killed someone.

We were playing darts. I was, almost literally, blind drunk. I threw a dart at the board and missed it completely. The dart flew straight through an open doorway where two girls were standing chatting intensely, their heads almost pressed together. It flew between their faces and harmlessly embedded itself in

---

6   Just a standard white candle, not the perfumed variety. They weren't invented until 1985.

7   And being an adult.

a wall. Half an inch to either side and there would have been an eye out.

It was a sobering moment.

I swore never to drink, etc., etc.

Lasted until the following Friday. The lesson was don't throw darts when you're drunk, not don't get drunk.

All those nights in the boxes, in The Whites, there was always music drifting on the sea breeze from just farther along the promenade at Ballyholme Park. There were much bigger shelters there – The Blues. Because they were blue. An older generation of drinkers met there, though just by a couple of years. My brother had drunk there but had since moved on to a better class of shelter. Because we knew some of them – from Wellington, and even from Churchill – we gradually began to move up there, until we became part of a much bigger crowd. Most weekends there'd be twenty or thirty of us, all drinking cider, all throwing our finished bottles onto the roof of the shelter, where they rolled down into an inaccessible little alley known as The Pit. When it was eventually cleared, many years later, there were 10,000 bottles in there, and a dead alcoholic.

Thirty drinkers, and barely a girl between us. We weren't *all* spectacularly unattractive. Occasionally one of us would indeed hook up with someone, and then you'd never see them again. That was young love. Or young sex. Once you found someone, or someone found you, you were gone. No girl wanted to hang out at The Blues. It wasn't the testosterone. It was the shame.

We were there, rain or shine. If you've ever seen footage of penguins crowding together for warmth in the Antarctic winter, that was us, except instead of insulated plumage we were fortified by cider and the raw heat of a single cigarette lighter. Occasionally we resorted to setting fire to something to keep us warm, or for badness. There was a wooden bandstand opposite the shelter. Didn't last long. I think Nigel and his brother Neal did for that. We knew them from primary school – one younger than us, one older. Nigel also famously painted the Ward Park cannon pink. Sometimes we'd drink there as well, just for variety. The cannon is still there. It was taken from a German U-boat at the end of the First World War and installed on a small plinth in the middle of Ward Park. It's directly in front of the Cenotaph. To this day the cannon points at the Presbyterian church on the other side of Hamilton Road. Generations of kids have pretend-blown it up. I don't know what inspired Nigel to paint the cannon pink, but the police found out he was responsible and went looking for him. Nigel panicked, fled the country, and joined the Foreign Legion.

Seriously, he joined the Foreign Legion.

The Foreign Legion was and is a seriously tough outfit.[8] We only knew about it through *Beau Geste*, the book by P.C. Wren and the movie versions of it, one in black and white and one in colour, which were repeated endlessly on TV. We weren't sure that it really existed until Nigel joined up. It is and was a French army regiment supposedly made up of murderers and felons on the run. You didn't have to be French. In fact, it helped if you weren't. They didn't really want to know where you were from or what your crime was, they just wanted to turn you into lethal fighting machines and send you to outposts of colonial France to kill people. I'm not sure if

---

8   Though not that tough – Laurel and Hardy managed it.

Nigel ever admitted to them what his crime was. Probably not. He would have been drummed out for not being sufficiently evil. But fair play to him, he made a real go of it and eventually ended up working as a deep-sea diver in Vietnam. Me, I was too cowardly to join the British Legion.

I don't know when my parents discovered I was drinking. And I say drinking as if it was a problem. It wasn't a problem. It was the norm. A natural progression. It was expected. We drank at the weekends. Friday-night drinking became Friday- and Saturday-night drinking at The Blues. Some of the older boys could get served at the Esplanade off-licence, which was immediately above The Whites, and then, as the months went by, we would chance our own arms. The Esplanade, like most off-licences then, was lax about who they would serve. You could look twelve years old, but if you could memorise a false date of birth you were usually fine. They made a huge profit on selling cider to underage kids. And good for them. That didn't mean that we weren't routinely barred. Because once you drink one bottle, you need another. But this time you had to buy it drunk. If you were all slurry and staggering, they were less likely to sell it to you, and you were more likely to kick up a fuss because they wouldn't. You'd get barred and then you faced the desolation of a ruined night, or at least a tramp of several hundred yards in the opposite direction where the Sefton Bar also had an off-licence. They were slightly warier about selling you drink, but you usually got there in the end.

A couple of weeks would go by and the Esplanade would forget you were barred, which was convenient for both parties – unless, of course, you did something more deserving of a lifetime ban. In the end, most of us did that something. My major offence was refusing to accept being barred and demanding to see the owner, who worked out of an office at the very top of what was a large three-storey building. I stormed up the stairs into his office and gave him a piece of my mind, which was stupid, because I didn't have that much to give away. He listened patiently to this fifteen-year-old drunk punk, then threw me out and banned me for life.

That was going to be a problem, because you couldn't always rely on the kindness of strangers – or friends – to get you alcohol. The Esplanade was only a few hundred yards from where we drank, but it was still a big ask for someone when they might already be well into their own drink. There was no schedule to our drinking, you just turned up hoping someone else would be there. The solution to my being barred for life was to recruit someone I could rely on to never get barred himself, who wouldn't be asked to prove his age, who was prepared to take on the illegality of supplying minors and not give one fuck about the consequences.

Thanks, Dad.

My parents knew I drank – how could they not? My hangovers were and are legendary, and there's nothing worse than a cider hangover. They couldn't *not* know. And Boker had been there before me. Dad listened patiently while I pleaded my case and railed against the injustice of being banned when I Had Done Nothing Wrong. Being cheeky isn't a crime! Except, of course, it is. I suppose he figured that it was better for him to buy me the drink than risk me getting into further trouble trying to get it by other means. He didn't want a black mark on my CV because there was nothing else on my CV, apart from delivering newspapers for Harry Walsh and the job Dad had just lined up for me at the *County Down Spectator*.

Dad knew I was in love with writing. And he understood that I wasn't likely to become the Great American Novelist at the age of fifteen, and that no Bateman had ever gone to university and that I was showing no inclination for it anyway, despite me being at a grammar school where it was the expected thing.

My brother had left school at sixteen with a handful of O Levels and managed to get into the civil service, just like Dad. He was in the Department of Education at Rathgael on the outskirts of town. He would get the bus there every day for forty years. And then he would get it home.

Dad knew that wasn't for me.

I was like an inverse James Stewart in *It's A Wonderful Life*. I wanted to do incredible things, but I had no particular desire to leave Bedford Falls. I liked my home town. I wasn't happy in myself, but I was happy in Bangor. I had no idea what I wanted to do when I grew up, but the dream was to be a writer. But there was no tradition of writers, not from my kind of background, unless you counted Belfast's Jack Higgins, then riding high with *The Eagle Has Landed*, but he was half English and didn't live here any more, or Brian Moore, who lived in Canada when he wasn't commentating on *The Big Match*. Our heroes weren't writers, they were sporting champions like George Best or 'Hurricane' Higgins, each of them almost better known for being alcoholic narcissists. And they didn't live here either. It seemed as if to be successful, you had to get out. But I didn't want out. I couldn't imagine being out.

Dad told me he'd arranged for me to go in and have a chat with the editor of the *Speccy*. He was canny. He didn't tell me it was a job interview. I would have refused to go. I had no desire to be a journalist. I read the papers, but I didn't want to be in the papers, unless they were reporting on me getting the Nobel Prize. Even then, I would get a day return to Sweden.

The *Spectator* was a fixture in our house. It was a fixture in every house. It was the source of all local information. Who died. Who was born. Who stole minced meat from the Co-Op and hid it in his underpants. What James Bond movie was on in the Tonic. What movie about Swedish nuns was on in the Fleapit. How Bangor were doing at the football. It was the ultimate arbiter of justice. It even published an annual directory listing who lived in every house in the town. That was called *The Directory*. Every house had one. The most popular single feature in the *Spectator* was 'Rat of the Week'. It was usually only a paragraph long. Rat of the Week is the man who stole a pensioner's Zimmer frame. Rat of the Week is the boy who set fire to a charity collection box. Rat of the Week is the teenager who pushed a boy off the sea wall into the sea.[9] My brother, Boker, was the boy who got pushed. He survived. And he probably deserved to be pushed. The problem was that Rat of the Week was so popular that evil people began to compete to get into it.

The worst Rat of the Week, which ultimately caused the feature to be discontinued, happened to a *Spectator* columnist. Lolita Alexander was the mother of the managing director of the paper, David Alexander. She might have been one of

---

9   Before the fucking marina was built.

the last women ever to have been christened Lolita. She went to boarding school in Spain. She was an elderly woman who wrote a column about art and culture every week. She was an artist herself, and occasionally illustrated her articles with her own paintings, which also hung on every wall of the editorial office. They were, should I say – and being no scholar of art myself, though I know what I like – an acquired taste. Another word might be God-awful. Lolita had cataracts, which might explain a lot. She lived in a large house on the edge of town, with fields and woods behind it. By some means she became the custodian of a badger cub. She christened it Snooky. She raised it and it became part of her family. She tried not to separate it from its natural surroundings, so that as it grew older it spent time both in the house and out in the woods. Lolita chronicled Snooky's progress in her column every week and also, later, in a self-published book called *Snooky's Progress*. It was a heart-warming story, somewhere between *Tarka the Otter* and *Marley & Me*, which the readers loved.

Well, not all of them loved it.

Someone trapped Snooky, bludgeoned him and left his corpse on Lolita's back doorstep.

People are capable of terrible things. Luckily her family discovered the body before Lolita did and were able to spirit it away. She never found out what happened to Snooky. She supposed he'd finally answered the call of the wild. The killer might have had an axe to grind against the paper, or just been bad to the bone, but Rat of the Week disappeared soon after. It was gone before I even went for my chat with the editor, but if you mention the *Spectator* in adult company today, someone will always say, 'Do you remember Rat of the Week?'

The editor was just going to tell me a little bit about life on a local weekly newspaper. I had no idea why. I turned up in my school uniform. I was shown in to meet a nice lady in an otherwise empty open-plan office, which makes me think now that it was a Thursday afternoon, after that week's paper had been put to bed.[10]

I didn't realise at first that Annie Roycroft was the editor. She was a spinsterish woman, then in her fifties. She was the same age as the Queen. I didn't know she'd been the first female newspaper editor in Ireland, or that there still weren't many others like her in the whole of the UK. Or even that she'd started out as an office girl during the war and gradually turned herself into a reporter.

There were two dogs in the office, two brown Labradors. One was called Caxton, the other Muttley. Miss Roycroft – it was always, until the day she left the paper, Miss Roycroft – casually asked me if I knew why Caxton was called Caxton and I was able to mumble vaguely that it had something to do with printing. I would have been on much safer ground with Muttley.[11] But she seemed pleased with my answer. I was otherwise very quiet. She took out a pen and paper and sat me at a desk and asked me to write 300 words on why I wanted to be a journalist, and my first thought was why the hell would I want to do that? It was also an easy question to answer. I Do Not Want to Be a Journalist. But being an agreeable sort, I wrote 300 words on why I wanted to be a journalist. They might be the finest 300 words of fiction I've ever written.

---

10   Curious term, but still in use. I'd only previously been put to bed because of my drinking.
11   The sniggering dog in the cartoon series *Wacky Races*.

Miss Roycroft must have been easily impressed or fooled, because she offered me a job – or, at least, promised me one if I was prepared to leave school after my upcoming O Levels and go to the Tech for a year to take an A Level in English and learn shorthand and typing. I don't know what she could have seen in me. My responses to her questions had been largely monosyllabic. And the enthusiasm I had shown in my writing – surely she could see through that? My passion for local history? Amateur dramatics? The work of the local council? All bollocks, really.

But there it was. And the idea did gradually begin to grow on me. I was still intent on becoming the Great American Novelist, but wise enough to know that wouldn't happen for at least a few years. What if there was a way to learn to be a better writer – and get paid for it? I had no intention of going to university. Not only had no Bateman ever gone off to college, but I didn't actually know anyone who'd been to one or had plans to go. I'd been reading quite a lot about journalists anyway. About Woodward and Bernstein, who had so recently helped bring down Nixon, via *All the President's Men*. And watching Jon Voight as the investigative reporter bringing down old Nazis in Frederick Forsyth's *The Odessa File*. There weren't exactly going to be a surfeit of presidents or Nazis living in fear of the *County Down Spectator*, but it was definitely a way to get into the business of writing. And I did flick through the paper every week. My favourite bit was David Crossen's Diary. He covered the arts beat. And every week he reviewed new records. That was bound to mean he got them free. And that was rather attractive.

When I went back to school, I excitedly told the careers teacher that I'd been offered a job on the *County Down*

Spectator. He laughed and told me I really didn't want to do that. I should stay and get my A Levels and then go to university. It was the '70s, and jobs were hard to come by, and there I was, not long turned fifteen with a firm job offer and a career path and his contempt was palpable – and so was mine.

I walked out of Bangor Grammar and I was on a mission. I was going to show them that their way, their traditional way, their snooty, stuck-up, rugby-playing, Latin-quoting way wasn't the right way for everyone, and prove that those who can, do; that those who can't, teach; and that those that can't teach, teach PE.[12] I would become the boy with a nose for a good story.

* * *

But not quite yet.

I still had to sit and pass my O Levels. And I still had a lot of cider to drink, girls to be rejected by and the Boxing Day Blarge to look forward to.

The Blarge has entered punk folklore.

It was a day when we did the gig right *here*. But there was a long and winding road to get there.

Punk in England had started as early as 1975, with the formation of the Sex Pistols. It began to grow out of being a cult in 1976, particularly in London, and with the release of that first clutch of singles. It spread out then to the provinces and we were all converts by Christmas, the duffel coats and flares of The Blues changing to drainpipes and leather jackets virtually overnight. But because we were still kids, essentially, it took a while for the creative side of things to grow, it took

---

12 That's Physical Education, not Paedophile Education, though …

time for like-minded individuals to be drawn to each other, to talk about the music, to get parents to sign hire-purchase agreements for guitars and amps and to learn those basic chords; more importantly, to get that first band photo taken, wearing sunglasses, looking cool.

The Trident bar at the bottom of Bangor's High Street became one of the few venues in the country open to punk bands and fans. We were too young to get in. We would stand outside and see punk girls using teapots for handbags. Stiff Little Fingers would immortalise the Trident in their song 'Alternative Ulster'. And that name wasn't just plucked from thin air. Gavin, who'd been the first to bring punk to us in school, wasn't a mere observer. He sprayed 'Bangor's Burning with Boredom' in black paint on The Whites. He launched the first punk fanzine here, *Alternative Ulster*. He initially photocopied it, then had it produced from a print workshop under Terri Hooley's Good Vibrations record shop in Belfast. The fanzine came first, and then the song. Originally it was going to be given out as a free flexi-disc with the mag, but the economics didn't work out. Morrissey wrote for *AU* from Manchester before he decided to form some band. On the odd occasion Gavin would come round to my house to look at my science-fiction fanzines, looking for design ideas. He got to interview all the visiting bands. When The Clash finally managed to play in Belfast, we went up to see them and all snuck into the Europa bar before the gig. We saw them arrive outside through the glass and they looked sensational. Guitarist Mick Jones was clutching multiple bags of Tayto cheese & onion crisps. Their road manager Johnny Green came in and chatted with us while Gavin went upstairs to conduct his interview. He shared a spliff with them. We had no idea what a spliff was. Gavin was the man. He'd also started reviewing gigs for the *New Musical Express*. This was long before I had a single word in print, and he was a proper writer already, and maybe that nudged me towards journalism as well – more jealousy. It was amazing to see, because the *NME* was the Bible; it shaped everything. But we were always slightly behind the curve. Punk was already morphing into something else on the mainland. But no matter. It wasn't a race.

A band even grew out of nice Bangor Grammar. They also drank at The Blues. They wrote songs they could play and occasionally keep a beat to. They wrote about growing up on our tough cul-de-sacs. They were called The Doubt.

Clarkey, Scotty, Chad and Corkey.

For a while Clarkey was my best friend. He was the mouthiest kid I ever met. He could always rescue defeat from the jaws of victory. He didn't play drums for a year because he ripped his Achilles tendon breaking into Caproni's Ballroom, which was just around the corner from The Blues. The ballroom had been a huge attraction for years. I'm sure my parents went there. They might even have met there. People came from all over Northern Ireland to dance there. But it hadn't operated as a ballroom for a long time. It had become a glorified ice-cream parlour when we hung out in The Blues. The polished ballroom floor was still there, but they wouldn't countenance putting a punk band on. Clarkey decided the contents of their cigarette machine needed liberation. He kicked through the glass, and the glass ripped his leg open.

Clarkey was great fun, but you couldn't trust him as far as you could throw him. He would routinely borrow records, then next day in school you'd find him handing out a list of records he had for sale, and damn sure you'd find your own on there.

The Doubt only ever played a handful of gigs, but that didn't matter; they made a racket, they had songs, they were our mates, they did things for themselves. Gavin set up a gig in the church hall in Ballyholme. Our church hall. A punk gig. We could hardly believe it. He invited punk bands from Belfast – Ruefrex, The Androids, The Idiots, and added The Doubt to the bill. There were our *friends* blasting out 'Pills' by the New York Dolls. There weren't many people there – fifty, sixty maybe, and most of them wallflowers, while we were pissed and pogoing madly at the front. I was wearing eyeliner. I had written a big R (for Ruefrex) on my forehead with a felt-tip pen. We were in heaven. When the gig was over, we adjourned to the Steak Out chip shop next door to the church and were on such a high, still pogoing and singing, that the police roared up in their grey meat wagon to quieten us down; but I just could not switch off or understand why they were there when we were just having fun. I let them know my important thoughts, and next thing a policewoman had arrested me and put me in the back of the Land Rover. I demanded to know why and she said because I was chirping like a little bird, which I wasn't entirely sure was an offence. Neither were they, clearly, as they released me not long after arriving at the station and didn't even alert my parents, so I was spared a *Rebel Without A Cause* showdown with them.[13]

The Boxing Day Blarge was an inspired piece of punk performance art. Christmas with your parents, with your perm-

---

13   Or Rebel Without Applause.

129

headed brother and your crocheting auntie, your migraine-suffering mum and your crazy-paving dad was just something to be endured. We needed a diversion, and someone came up with the idea for the Blarge[14] – it was to be our Woodstock, it was our Live Aid years before Live Aid was thought of, and the only people who benefitted from it were ourselves.

One of our shelter's gang was Michael Crowe, also known as Big Bird. His younger brother was known as Little Bird. He had a huge St Bernard called Barney. Big Bird's house was at the very corner of Ballyholme Park, opposite the shelters. Multiple cables were run from his kitchen, across the park to The Blues, where amps were set up. Rudimentary posters advertised the gig, but no one knew if anyone would come.

Come the big day, not many did.

It was Boxing Day, for fuck sake.

But enough did. Park drinkers of an older generation arrived to see who was making all the noise. The Doubt were. And so was a variety bill of talentless wastrels too drunk to turn down the opportunity to blast their profanities out over a PA that could be heard all over Bangor.

Boker gave it a go. Even Barney managed a few barks into the mike. Most of Ballyholme eventually came out to see what that fucking racket upsetting their Boxing Day was, and the Peelers came too and yanked the plugs and we chanted SS/RUC, although very quietly, because deep down we were good boys, we'd had our fun, and for maybe an hour Bangor wasn't burning with boredom.

---

14   Blarge has a dual meaning – to approach a task haphazardly, or to over-indulge in alcohol. Both applied to the Boxing Day Blarge.

6

Woodstock & Wine Barrel

I WOULD GET THE BUS home from work and it would pass by The Blues and The Whites, and I would want to get off and join my friends drinking cider in the sun, but knew that I couldn't because I had work in the morning and my hangovers were lethal while they were all gloriously unemployed, with their drinking being sponsored by the government. I was seventeen and I was madly jealous of their freedoms and a little ashamed of my own conformity in the age of anarchy. But I would have to stick with it if I wanted to be the Great American Novelist.

There is probably a right age at which to become a writer, and that can be a different age for everyone – seventeen or seventy. But I couldn't do it at seventeen, I didn't have anything to really write about.[1] I was also self-aware enough to know that I needed to learn how to write proper.

I was still painfully shy, and the open-plan design of the *Speccy* office did not help. It meant everyone could listen to me making a fool of myself on the phone. And I did, and often. One of the first things Miss Roycroft did was hand me the

---

1   Although obviously I did, see Chapters 1–5.

Belfast Telegraph's page of death notices. She told me to find out if any of the recently dead had lived in Bangor and then to track down their closest relatives, phone them and ask if their dearly departed had done anything interesting in their lives in order for me to write them an obituary. That was an ordeal. I'd barely had a serious conversation with any adults, let alone any grieving ones; and most people *don't* live interesting lives, so extracting usable information was like flogging a dead horse, so to speak. I melted, and I melted, and I melted. It gave me a lifelong phobia of using phones and other electronic devices. I can receive calls, but I've great difficulty making them. I even have difficulty using the drive-thru at McDonald's. My son still has to shout what he wants at the speaker on the way through because I find it hard to engage. He thinks I'm on the spectrum. He can fuck off.

I was the cub reporter. Probation for six months, and then three years of training before you become a senior journalist. You're tipped in at the deep end right at the start. I wasn't driving yet, so that meant my work was pretty much confined to the town centre, or further afield if a photographer was going with me. There were two photographers on the paper, and between them they couldn't hope to cover half the assignments that needed covering. A local newspaper thrives on covering *everything*. This is in part so that it gives the fullest possible picture of what's going on in the town, but also sound business sense – if a photograph appeared on our pages then the reasoning was that everyone in that picture would go out and buy a copy of the paper, and that would drive circulation. The jobs that the photographers couldn't cover were re-assigned to the reporters. On my first day I was handed a camera and a list of events I had to cover, all within walking distance of the office. The photographic training I was given consisted of being shown where the automatic button was on the camera and how to screw on a flashgun, and then I was sent on my way. This didn't allow for any nuance, or, frequently, any kind of focus. There were literally hundreds of photographs I took that were too dark to make out the faces, because the flashguns were never quite strong enough. There was certainly no art to it – the subjects of photographs lined up in neat rows and smiled at the camera. The more you could cram in the better.

On my first day I was sent out to take one photo in the town centre and soon realised that this town that I knew so well, I actually didn't know so well. It was pouring down, really lashing, and my target was a blood-donation session in the Dufferin Hall. Simple task – man or woman smiling at camera while an armful of blood is drained away. Any reasonable person might assume that the Dufferin Hall was to be found on Dufferin Avenue, which was the next street up from the *Speccy*. Well. I tramped that street up and down for forty minutes looking for it, getting drenched to the skin in the process, but refusing to admit defeat or ask directions. I would find it. It was my town. It was here somewhere. I walked every sodden lane, peered behind every dripping bush.

Eventually, on the point of hypothermia, I returned to the office adamant that there was no such thing as a Dufferin Hall and convinced I was the victim of a not-very-elaborate first-day prank, until it was gently pointed out that the Dufferin Hall was actually on Hamilton Road, and so out I went again to take the photo and then directly to hospital. Or, indeed, my desk, to steam away the rest of the day.

Bangor is and was Northern Ireland's third-largest town, and the newspaper it supports then sold around 16,000 copies every week. Maintaining that level of sales was difficult. Every year circulation dropped a little, even as the population grew. But it was still at the heart of everything, still essential reading, even for those who so easily dismissed or disparaged it. It was the paper of record in a way that the so-called papers of record rarely are – because bigger newspapers have to be selective, or reductive, whereas the *Speccy* reported everything, and at length. Every word of a court case or a council meeting, every meeting of every club or society, every football match, every speech festival.

If a tree falls in the woods does it make a sound if nobody hears it? The *Speccy* heard it. It was the arbiter of justice in a way that the local magistrate's court couldn't be. While there would be obvious consequences if you appeared in court – whether for shoplifting or gross indecency or for careless driving – was justice truly being done if nobody knew about it? Often the true punishment wasn't whatever fine or occasional custodial sentence was handed out, but the shame of having your sins described in the local paper.

The paper had a hard-and-fast rule: every case went in and every address was published. It didn't matter if it was one of your relatives or friends, it went in. It was the only fair way to do it. People would always beg us to change an address – their dad was on heart medicine and he'd die if their name appeared, or can you use this address instead, the court made a mistake; or the ultimate bargaining chip: if you publish my name and address, I'll kill myself. They never did. Employees of the paper, or indeed, owners, were no exceptions; if they did something wrong their name and address went in.

At first, I accompanied a senior reporter to the magistrate's court – there were two, one in Bangor on a Wednesday morning, and one in Holywood on a Friday. An hour before court we collected the summonses from an office upstairs. We'd take them into the court itself and sit at the press table and meticulously copy down the charges. Often there'd be over a hundred cases. Of these maybe half would eventually be adjourned to a later date, but you had to have them down in case they weren't. Most of the rest would be traffic offences, dealt with by way of minor fines. Then there would be the criminal cases of drunkenness, disorderly behaviour and assault, where the defendant admitted their guilt. Contests, when those being prosecuted pleaded not guilty and decided to fight their case, were generally pushed back to the end of the list.

If you were lucky, you got a good meaty courtroom fight that you could turn into a cracker story. Mostly you got tedium: two underachieving local solicitors debating the finer points of a minor traffic violation. You still had to sit through it. You still had to record every word. Then you had to keep your notebook for at least six months in case there was a dispute over your report so you could show your verbatim notes to prove that what you'd written was accurate. That was the theory. I'm not sure if any reporter in the local court system has ever been asked to prove the veracity of their stories. No other account of what is actually said in a courtroom is taken,[2] so we were, literally, the paper of record.

---

2   That's reserved for Crown Courts.

After a couple of weeks, I was on my own. The thing about a magistrate's court is that the odds are always stacked against the defendant. You are expected to plead guilty. If you plead not guilty, in nine cases out of ten you will be found guilty anyway. It is understood that the magistrate will believe the prosecution case and that he will attach more credence to accounts given by the police than the defendant. In many cases witnesses will stumble in their evidence and be confused by cross-examination, because it is not their natural environment. Solicitors are used to picking evidence apart; police are expected to deliver their evidence in an authoritative manner. Wearing a uniform means you've already won half the battle. The magistrate will find you guilty as charged. That's what he's there for, to uphold and reinforce the rule of law. If you really, really feel that you're not guilty, then you have to appeal against your conviction at the next court up, the Crown Court. That's where justice is actually handed out, and the odds are still stacked against you. The damage has already been done anyway, because a young journalist with inadequate shorthand has already published his version of your case and the good people of the town already know about your shameful perversion, shoplifting or speeding, and occasionally all three, and no amount of appeals are going to overturn the court of public opinion.

Once the court was over it was then a race back to the office to type up my reports. Reporting generally was quite leisurely because we had a week to put the paper together, but as that week progresses the pressure ramps up. The *Speccy* hit the shops generally about 3 p.m. on a Thursday, with the finishing touches being added right up until about 1 p.m. Then the finished pages would be rushed up to the printing presses at the Balloo Industrial Estate on the town's ring road. Getting the court reports written in time, often with up to fifty cases of varying lengths, was always stressful – particularly as I was often staring at pages of barely decipherable shorthand, because, despite my year studying it at the Tech, I never quite grasped it. Frequently it was guesswork. Often puzzled defendants would appear in the office and complain that *that* just didn't happen. But as long as I got the name and address, the charges and the general gist of things and the verdict and the punishment right, I got away with it.

Miss Roycroft sat at her own large desk facing half a dozen smaller ones, each manned by a reporter with his own typewriter and ashtray. Every morning it was the job of the cub reporter to open the mail, which would be a mixture of handwritten or typed reports from the weekly meetings of a bewildering variety of clubs and societies – the Trefoil Guild, anyone? The Soroptimists Society? – and articles sent in by public-relations agencies. Often these would be in the form of competitions we could run, offering prizes to those readers who could be arsed entering them. The prizes erred towards the valueless. It seemed unthinkable that anyone could be bothered going to any effort at all to win a month's supply of cheese strings, but people did – often in their hundreds.

Everyone was a reporter, everyone was a photographer and everyone also had their own speciality or column. By the time I joined, David Crossen of *Crossen's Diary* and the free records had just left; part of me expected that they would just hand the reins over to me because I was young and cool and punky, and I was somewhat put out when someone who actually knew what they were doing, someone who had actually written a story with their by-line on it, took over. That was young and vivacious Maxine, whose husband played bass guitar in a local showband. Then there was Barry, about whom the whisper was that he might be, you know, GAY, based purely on the evidence that he ran the Fashion Page, and also that his hair was tinted burgundy and he had a campy manner about him. But just to confuse matters he also wrote the Motoring Page, which was clearly a heterosexual endeavour because actual gay men would surely be prancing through meadows, not showing an unlikely interest in camshafts. Peter, living in Holywood, ran the Holywood Maypole Page.[3] He was always up to something. He'd been a printer initially, and so was at one with the lads, but had stepped sideways to become a reporter and always had what today we'd call a side hustle going on. Peter and I frequently went for lunch together, usually a three-course meal in a Chinese restaurant at the end of Queen's Parade. It was really cheap. Also, we never ate Chinese food. It was always traditional British food but cooked by Chinese people.

We all worked late on a Wednesday night. There was a smaller Newtownards edition of the paper, which hit the shops first thing on Thursday morning, so that had to be finished. Then the main paper would be completed on Thursday morning.

Joy was our deputy editor. We never hit it off. She was our 'Star Writer', having won awards for her journalism; she was English; she was a big woman; she loved and rode horses; within a few months of me arriving it was announced she'd

---

3   Yes, Holywood has a maypole. On May Day, street urchins dance around it.

been given a publishing deal for her first novel; a science-fiction novel, *The Matrix*.[4] Of *course* I disliked her intensely.

I never once mentioned that I was hugely into science fiction. I kept it well hidden, preferring to promote the fact that I was a punk rocker. I did this by exclusively wearing black, sporting a lapel badge promoting The Clash and by not speaking to anyone unless cornered, which was clearly because I had *attitude*, not shyness. Joy was thirty in 1981 when her first book came out. I was not going to wait until I was thirty. That was ancient. I'd already started my first novel. It focused on drinking and punk in our beloved Blues. But I only ever got a few pages into it. It was largely incoherent gibberish, or exactly like a night at The Blues. I would tinker with a version of it for years, and even hijacked the title of The Mighty Wah!'s hit single 'The Story of The Blues' for it in 1982, but I never got much further with it than that. I still haven't. As a writer, there are things you *want* to write about, and things you *can* write about. I've never quite been able to crack The Blues. At seventeen I was already beginning to think that maybe I wasn't a writer at all, that in fact I was just in love with the idea of being a writer. Perhaps I should just concentrate on being the next best thing, a journalist, and tracking down Nazis.

The *Speccy* was as chaotic and disorganised and idiosyncratic as only a family-run business can be. It hadn't missed a week since it was founded in 1904. It survived two world wars, loyalist power strikes during the Troubles when the presses had to be hooked up to farmers' tractors, and it was only briefly silenced during the worst of the Covid-19 pandemic.

---

4   Unfortunately, not *the* Matrix, of Keanu Reeves fame.

The open-plan office also housed the advertising and clerical staff and was divided by large windows from the make-up area, where the newspaper pages were put together, and 'the bungalow', a smallish room where the typesetters worked. There was also a large area where the 'jobbing' work took place – the printing of business cards and flyers and church magazines, usually on machines that had barely changed since the war. All of the printing staff and typesetters were male; all of the clerical staff were female, with the exception of the advertising manager. The managing director was David Alexander, or sometimes 'young Mr David', as opposed to his father, who was always 'Mr David'. Mr David was long retired when I joined, but he was still in and out of the office two or three days a week. He was one of life's eccentrics, an obsessive ornithologist famous for leaping out of his car and pursing birds through strangers' gardens. Young Mr David's wife, Pat, was a glamourous and somewhat aloof[5] ex-model who had been *married before*, and was therefore somewhat suspect. Her husband drove a Porsche. His cousin Ian mainly ran the *Speccy*'s sister paper, *The Newtownards Chronicle*,[6] with whom we maintained a friendly rivalry. Young Mr David was friendly and approachable, Ian was regarded as the hatchet man: when there was someone to be fired or pay negotiations to be abruptly terminated, Ian was your man.

I was photographer, letter-opener, court reporter and I was in charge of The Morgue. That's where the bodies were kept. Metaphorically. My task was to strip stories and photos out of each week's paper and paste them onto cards and then slot

5   i.e. out of my league.
6   Routinely referred to as *The Newtownards Crocodile*.

them into alphabetical files, so that if their names cropped up again and you couldn't quite remember who they were, you could 'check The Morgue'.

All of this was designed to get me familiar with the inner workings of a newspaper, but of course that wasn't enough for me. I wanted my name out there. I wanted my friends to see what I was doing, so they could understand why I wasn't in The Blues as much. I wanted the fame, the identity, the glory. And I had an idea, based around indignation and punk.

The Sex Pistols' first album, *Never Mind the Bollocks*, had come out eighteen months earlier, and many of the 'proper' shops had banned it – as much for its title as its content.[7] But now that the controversy had died down the shops that had banned it had quietly slipped it onto their shelves, because they were a business and there was money to be made and also because they were HYPOCRITES.

Where you're a teenager you can get exercised about whales and political prisoners and HYPOCRITES. I wrote a short article about this HYPOCRISY, which was really more of a polemic than a news report, and sheepishly handed it in to Miss Roycroft. She read it and then called me up to her desk. She pointed at it and said, 'What's this word here?' I got very red faced and said quietly, 'Bollocks'. I had asterisked most of it out. Miss Roycroft's reply rather stunned me. 'If it's called Bollocks, then Bollocks it is.' And so Bollocks went into the paper.

It might seem insignificant now, when we routinely bandy about words like fuck, cunt, wanker, twat, shite face, cum-

---

7   Their single, 'God Save the Queen' had been banned from the airwaves and even censored from the official charts in what was the actual Queen's Silver Jubilee year. It still went to number one.

trumpet, ballbag, shitmagnet, arsehole and Manchester United, but it was little short of revolutionary then. I don't think any other weekly or even daily paper in the UK would have allowed it – and most still wouldn't – but Miss Roycroft, our prim Sunday School teacher editor, was all for calling a spade a spade, and so my first ever by-lined article appeared in print and it was literally a lot of bollocks. But I was officially launched as a journalist – a music journalist, even. If it wasn't quite the *NME*, then it was at least something, and to my eyes, almost as important.

About a year later, perusing my Thursday-morning copy of the *UK Press Gazette* during my Coke break in work, I spotted a job advert for a sub-editor on the *NME*.

By this time Gavin had decamped to London to work for them full-time and, being at the heart of everything and meeting and interviewing punk and rock stars every day, had slipped out of our orbit. But when I saw the advert my brain went into overdrive. Half my job was turning contributed notes into something printable, cutting them down to size and adding headlines, so sub-editing was already a big part of my job. Could I actually do that for the *NME*? It would be like going from the Isthmian League to playing for Liverpool, but sometimes those things happen. Could I go from Bangor to live in London? I got dizzy any time I had to get the train to Belfast, and the only time I'd spent away from home without my parents was at the Christian-and-Paedo Camp on the north coast, so how could I possibly survive in London – unless, of course, I was able to call on the support of what were bound to be my new friends in The Clash and the Pistols. I'd be in some grotty squat having crazy sex with that sub-section of groupies who only slept with sub-editors on music papers. Gavin was already a hip young gunslinger, and I could be his sidekick: he could provide the dazzling words and I would provide the puntastic headlines. I loved Bangor, but I would soon forget it. Sub-editing would only be a temporary thing anyway; soon they would realise what a great writer I was and send me around the world to hang out for extended periods with the Stones or Marvin Gaye. I would be the *NME*'s answer to gonzo journalist Hunter S. Thompson. I wouldn't just report stories, I would become part of them, and often the most interesting part. I was a child of the Troubles with a unique perspective that would blow the readers of Britain's top music paper away. Sooner or later I'd get a call from someone in publishing who liked my style and who was wondering if I'd ever thought of writing a novel and I would say actually, I have one, *The Story of the Blues*, and I would describe it to him and he would be desperate to read it and I would say I just have to tidy it up before I sent it to him and then I'd spend the next seventy-two hours high on speed whilst the words spewed out of my typewriter at an incredible rate, I would not eat or sleep, stopping only to have wild sex with Debbie Harry who had heard about my sub-editing skills and tracked me down.

There wasn't an application form, that was for the straights, the greys, the squares. All you had to do was write a letter. I wrote a letter. I told them about my love of music. I sent some of my articles from the paper. I presumed there'd be thousands of applicants. It was the leading music paper in the UK, and probably the world. Even if I got some kind of acknowledgement from them, that would be wild. A few days later I got an actual phone call from the *NME*. The *NME*! They not only wanted me to come to London for an interview – they would pay for my flight as well. I couldn't quite believe it.

Then the nerves kicked in. And the Northern Irishness kicked in. That meant negativity. That meant poor self-esteem. That meant we're not worthy, that meant we're not good enough. We were a country that said No. Part of me was thinking that I shouldn't risk killing the dream by actually going for the interview. Imagining working for them would be much better than actually having to do it. I was *Billy Liar* in drainpipes and a Clash badge. I was happy at the *Speccy*; why risk that for an exciting life full of sex and drugs and rock'n'roll? As long as I wasn't actually rejected by them, I could still dine out on telling everyone I met that I'd been invited over to the *NME* but chose not to go, because my loyalties were here – and they would respect me for it, or call me a dick.

On the morning I was due to go to London I woke up with a head cold. Reason enough to cancel. But I felt obliged to go, what with having bragged about it far and wide. My dad gave me a lift to Aldergrove Airport. During the flight the air pressure began to work on my ears, which grew painful. By the time I got off the plane I couldn't hear out of one of them. My balance was affected. And the cold had turned into a flu. I felt miserable. I somehow made it into the centre of London. The *NME*'s offices then were on Carnaby Street, which was just off Oxford Street. I had a street map. But for the love of God, I still just could not find Carnaby Street. Partly it was how sick I was feeling, some of it was being unable to read a basic map, much of it was stupidity – but whatever it was, I just couldn't find Carnaby Street. I was up and down, up and down Oxford Street, squinting at my map, going down blind alley after blind alley, in much the same way that I wasted so much time looking for the Dufferin Hall on Dufferin Avenue, and all the time the clock was ticking closer to the time of my interview, 3 p.m., but I just couldn't find fricking Carnaby Street.

As the panic and nausea continued to build, I decided to do what no man should ever do, and that was to reduce himself to asking directions from a policeman. From a London bobby.

I went up to the first one I saw and said, 'Excuse me, could you tell me the way to Carnaby Street?'

And he said, 'Yes, Bacon, it's down there on the left.'

For a moment I thought my duff ear was playing tricks, or that I had slipped into psychosis, but then I saw the copper was smiling at me and that there was something familiar about his face, and in a moment I realised it was Derek Larmour, the speedy winger from my primary-school football team, Derek Larmour who had lived just a few streets away from me in Ballyholme, Derek Larmour who had clearly now left home and joined the Met and was a copper on patrol in central London – but still, the chances of randomly approaching him of all people to ask directions in a city of nearly seven million people were so incredible that to this day scientists remain baffled as to how it actually occurred. I hardly even had time to thank him or explore the peculiarity of our meeting because it was almost three o'clock, I had to *run*.

I arrived breathless and sweaty and just about on time. Far from the Bacchanalian free-for-all I had expected, I found a cramped newspaper office with desks crammed into every possible space. There wasn't a Pistol to be seen; not even a Ramone; just a nice, prematurely balding man called Neil Spencer, the editor, who took me into his office and said something and I said what, because I was still half deaf, and he repeated it, louder. He thought my application letter was really well written, and I thanked him and began to tell him how much I was into music and what a thrill it was to be there, and he said what, because my accent was so thick, and so it went on, with him shouting and me declaiming every word like the worst kind of Shakespearean actor. He asked me who my favourite band was and I said The Clash, which was the rock'n'roll equivalent of saying blackbird to prove my ornithological knowledge. There was so much I could have said, so much back-home music I could have enthused about, but nothing would come. He ended up showing me what a sub-editor was expected to do, explaining it as if I was the village idiot, and I was; I sub-edited every day at my paper, but he couldn't have told it from our chat; I was the nodding dog in the back of the car. Gavin wasn't even there to smooth my way or explain my words or lack of them; I hadn't thought to let him know; I had thought of the *NME* in terms of the *Speccy* and presumed that he would just be there, sitting at a desk, eating Midget Gems, waiting for me. But he wasn't. And I didn't really care because I felt so crap. I stumbled back out onto Carnaby Street, knowing already that I had failed the first proper job interview of my life, and what might turn out to be the most important one. And in a way it was, because even though I was feeling miserable, I was also feeling homesick. I'd only been gone a few hours, but I missed it, I missed Bangor. It was an interview that ultimately showed me exactly what I didn't want.

I wasn't even staying the night. My first time in London, and I was determined to get home. I got on the Underground, and after travelling for half an hour towards Heathrow I began to realise that actually I might not be doing that at all but going in the opposite direction. I couldn't make head nor tail of the Underground map, and with a growing sense of panic I decided to throw caution to the wind and asked a ticket inspector if I was going the right way and he said, 'No, Bacon, you're on the wrong train,' and it turned out to be Smelly McDade, and he was still wearing armbands on his feet, and not only was I lost but I was growing delirious.[8]

Of course, I made it home. I recovered. I didn't get the job, and I wasn't disappointed, or surprised, and the biggest thing I took away from it was that I didn't want to live or work in London; in fact, I didn't even want to live or work in Belfast and that was only ten miles away. I liked where I was. I didn't like it all the time, and I didn't like all of the people all of the time, but at least I knew them.

* * *

The Red Harringtons were amongst the people I didn't like. They were a gang from the wrong side of town. Or, at least, the other side of town. They were so called because they wore duffel coats. No, because they wore red Harrington jackets.[9]

---

8   I haven't seen Derek Larmour from that day to this. But I'm still stunned by bumping into him like that.

9   The first Harrington-style jacket was made by the British company Baracuta in the 1930s but was popularised in the 1958 Elvis Presley movie *King Creole*. The jacket got the nickname 'Harrington' from a character in the 1960s prime-time US soap opera *Peyton Place*, Rodney Harrington, who was often depicted in the Baracuta-style jacket. Rodney Harrington was played by Ryan O'Neal, who became internationally famous in *Love Story* but also starred in *A Bridge Too Far*, about the Battle of Arnhem, where my uncle fought and also became a film star. Small world.

American-style zip-up jackets. There was maybe a dozen in their gang, possibly thirty, maybe even a hundred and fifty. The size of their gang grew in the telling.

We virtually never ran into the Red Harringtons and I don't quite know why we were mortal enemies. At least one of them had been in my class at the Grammar and he had seemed all right. We had grown up scared of the Churchill Tartan, but we weren't scared of the Red Harringtons. We just didn't like them. Besides, we were our own fearsome gang. We were into anarchy, so didn't have a dress code. Having a dress code made you seem organised. A uniform suggested tactics and a command structure and possibly a bugler. We were spontaneous. We laughed at tactics and grotted on command structure. We didn't know any buglers, only players of imaginary flutes.

Clarkey might have been one of the reasons for the animosity. Possibly he borrowed their records and then sold them. More likely he was just gobby with them and it festered. It's a peculiarly teenage thing to walk down a street and be fearful that you're going to be jumped by a gang and beaten up. That fear just seems to go away when you reach a certain age. Being a teenager and in a gang gives a kind of security. Having a uniform shores you up, unites you. We not only didn't have a uniform, we didn't even have a name. We could say, here come the Red Harringtons. I've no idea what they said about us. Here come ... that lot. They could also take off their red Harringtons and become anonymous. We were anonymous to start with.

They might have been inspired by *The Wanderers*, the 1979 film about an Italian-American gang vying for respect on the tough streets of the Bronx in 1963. They fought with the Ducky Boys and the Fordham Baldies and learned some difficult lessons about life and love. Everyone went to see that at the Tonic. We loved it.[10]

We always went on a Sunday night – the council had only recently relented and allowed screenings on the Lord's Day. After two nights of drinking, we were all shattered on a Sunday, and went to see whatever was on. We sat transfixed during *Taxi Driver*, not so much by the directing skills of Martin Scorsese or the bravura acting performance of Robert De Niro, but by our first ever glimpse of pubic hair on a big screen.[11]

You were taking your life in your hands even entering the cinema. We'd sit in the cheap seats near the front, but that always came with the risk of being hit in the head by an Opal Fruit flying at thirty miles an hour fired from the balcony above. There were more people injured by Toffets during the showing of *Apocalypse Now* than there were during its infamous 'Ride of the Valkyries' helicopter attack. You also risked a beating if you tried to leave the cinema before the national anthem was played. They played it after every screening. And a beating was also on the cards if you didn't stand for it. We were conflicted – we were punks whose own national anthem was 'God Save The Queen' by the Sex Pistols, and we were supposed

---

10 The movie was based on a novel by Richard Price. I loved it too, even though he wrote it when he was twenty-four and was therefore an over-achiever.

11 I don't mean just a piece of pubic hair stuck to a big screen. That's just gross. Jenny Agutter had also displayed pubic hair in 1971's *Walkabout*, but we'd had to wait a few years to see that on the small screen. And it had just confused us. There was something *beyond* boobs?

to despise everything about the royal family, but we were also good Prods whose identity was all about celebrating the Queen and waving the Union Jack; usually we tried to cover both bases, standing at half-mast while the dirge played out.

There was never a showdown between the Red Harringtons and our lot.

There was no *West Side Story*-style ballet-rumble in Ballyholme Park. There wasn't even a fight over a girl and her choices; our girls had made their choices, which was not to be with us. None of us had girlfriends. Occasionally there were girls there, but they never lasted long. We lacked charm. And attractiveness. Not even very drunk girls with neither of those attributes themselves were lining up to be fingered in the toilets behind The Blues. They wanted to be fingered by a better class of teenage hoodlum: hoodlums who were at least colour co-ordinated.

No showdown, but there was a reckoning – at least for me.

My public profile was growing week by week. After that first by-line, there was no stopping me. I followed it up with a review of a gig in a Nissen hut attached to Ballyholme Methodist Church. It was headlined: '70% Proof, or Two Punk Bands in a Tin Hut'. It was a first gig for both the aforementioned 70% Proof and also The Co-ordinates, the latter formed by Clarkey and Chad, who had by now left The Doubt, and formed their own band with singer Mouse, guitarist Colin and bass player Robin. The Blues crew got drunk and turned up at the gig, not expecting much, but I was blown away by The Co-ordinates, though both bands mainly played cover versions, The Co-ordinates had this one self-penned song called 'Government Warning', a not-veiled-at-all attack on Maggie Thatcher, which was both raucous and catchy, and I was immediately smitten. They became my new favourite band.

Within a few weeks I was their manager.

I had no qualifications for being a manager, and I proceeded to show them why. Although the role was ill-defined, it mostly involved telling them how good they were and arranging to have their photographs regularly placed in the *Speccy*, the only place in the known universe where I had real clout. While in my head my managerial nous had me somewhere between Brian Epstein and Svengali, in reality I still had trouble making phone calls, and in the era before emails that was going to be a problem if I was to guide them to global superstardom.

To be fair, they didn't expect much.

The Undertones were famously homesick every time they left Derry for London or to tour the USA with The Clash; The Co-ordinates never even left Bangor. They practised every Saturday morning in Project Bangor, a community centre specifically provided for young people at the foot of Dufferin Avenue. Every week they got better, and their own songs began to dominate their set. One, the superbly poppy 'We're Only Monsters', even managed to get antidisestablishmentarianism into the chorus, which should be in the *Guinness Book of Records*. Mostly they rehearsed; occasionally there was a local gig. Their biggest was playing at Youth Expo, an otherwise tedious day-long annual event put on by the council featuring various worthy organisations strutting their stuff, but on this occasion, probably by mistake, they invited local bands to play on a small stage in Castle Park. The Co-ordinates really rocked it in front of hundreds of local kids. Their most audacious gig took place in the Sunken Gardens, just beside Bangor's McKee Clock, which is like Big Ben but smaller.[12]

Clarkey and I were passing through on a Monday afternoon when we noticed a stage being built for some brass-band performance the following day. More importantly, I noticed an electrical socket beside the stage. Being the visionary manager I was, I suggested the band just turn up that night with their equipment, plug in and play. Which is what they did. And there was no one to stop them. It was punk. It was anarchy. It was the Sex Pistols barge along the Thames at the height of the Silver Jubilee, except the cops couldn't stop us.

The band were by now good enough to go into the recording studio, or at least a kind of semi-pro studio run by local heavy-metal combo Krawler in King Street. The resulting six-track tape was then duplicated a hundred times using machines at Seacourt Teachers' Centre, a cover 'designed' and then the finished package was released to overwhelming silence.

I sent off copies to record labels all over the UK but heard back from only a couple, and those were hard noes. However, there was one person we were pretty sure could set us on the road to global domination and he was right on our own doorstep.

Terri Hooley was the biggest non-rock-star rock star we had. He ran a second-hand record shop in Belfast, Good Vibrations, but made an international name for himself by setting up a record label with the same name. His first release

12 The McKee Clock was named after a former borough rate collector who, amazingly, worked on a commission basis. He was thought to be the richest man in town. It was unveiled in 1915. A member of the McKee family still goes down every night to wind it up.

was 'Big Time', an instant classic by Rudi and still one of my favourite records. Then came Victim, 'Strange Thing by Night', which was almost as good, and The Outcasts, Rudi's fierce rivals, with 'Just Another Teenage Rebel' and a reputation, mostly deserved, for violence. None of these made any money, and probably lost it. Terri's big break could and should have been with The Undertones' 'Teenage Kicks', but he just wasn't a businessman and allowed the band to sign for a major label for a tiny amount of money and a promise of a record signed by '60s girl group The Shangri-Las, which he never even got.

We had no idea that the Good Vibrations label was losing a fortune, but soon found out first-hand how careless Terri was with money. I'd spoken to him a few times on the phone as a reporter, while subtly trying to foist The Co-ordinates and their tape on him. He had retreated from the dangers of living in Belfast to the rather more peaceful Helen's Bay, just a couple of train stops from Bangor. He invited me up to the house to give it a listen and, seeing as that was just about within my comfort zone, I agreed. Clarkey went with me for moral support. For alcoholic support we invested in several bottles of cider and were very drunk by the time we fell off the train.

As we stumbled up Terri's driveway we noticed a large bundle of cash tied up with an elastic band just lying on the ground near his front door. We stopped and stared at it and wondered if this was some sort of a moral test or his understated way of offering to finance our first single, or at least plenty more alcohol.

We debated it. Clarkey, with his history of petty larceny, must have been tempted. It would have been the rock'n'roll outlaw thing to do. But we were basically nice boys from Bangor, so we rang the doorbell and handed it over, and Terri didn't seem overly surprised that we should find what was for us – and given what we now know about his chaotic approach to finance – a huge amount of cash lying unmissed outside his house.

The rest is history – impressed by our values *and* our music, we signed a huge record deal, had a number-one record, toured the world and I got 10 per cent of it all; and then we woke up with a Strongbow hangover and a vague memory of it being a brief chat and 'I'll give it a listen.'

Most rock'n'roll stories usually end with 'and then the drummer quit'. That's what happened to The Co-ordinates. My negotiating skills – smiling, but saying nothing, and so appearing both savvy and inscrutable at the same time – did not result in an instant record contract with Good Vibrations. But we were inspired to record our own single. This took place at Downtown Radio's studios in nearby Newtownards. We should have known better, for no good things come out of Newtownards apart from the road, and me.[13] There had been some tensions in the band prior to the recording, but they came to a head in the studio, exacerbated by an uninterested producer-for-hire who didn't even turn up for the first session, and then further by the drummer's consumption of magic mushrooms.

There was one last hurrah.

A final gig at BJs.

---

13 Confession – I was actually born in Newtownards Hospital but escaped to Bangor very quickly. It's a source of eternal shame, and why this is a footnote.

BJs being the old Milano's Ballroom on Seacliff Road, which had recently been turned into a vast teenage disco. This is how naive, how cosseted we were – none of us ever twigged to what BJs stood for. We thought it was somehow cool and American. 'Hey, let's all go down to Eddie's Diner!' 'Let's all go to BJs!' Even our parents, who should have known better, should have guessed about BJs. It wouldn't have taken much – just spelling it out. 'Hey – let's go down to Blow Jobs!' Perhaps it was chosen ironically, because there weren't many BJs going down at BJs for The Blues crew.

The Co-ordinates were to be the support act to Rudi. A final farewell for my band, and ultimate punk rock from my first local heroes. I set up the gig, I promoted it through the paper and I was there on the night with a camera slung round my neck to record it, striding around cool as begot.

It should have been fantastic. And it was fantastic. But by then I also had a price on my head. Kind of. A very small price, because I was being widely accused of trying to ruin everyone's lives, and by lives, I mean their drinking.

Teenage entertainment then revolved around drinking in public parks. There was nothing else to do. We were too young to be truly comfortable in pubs, or just too young. We were certainly too old for youth clubs, and much too sensible for the other God-related alternatives. Come rain or shine, each Friday and Saturday night hundreds if not thousands of young drinkers thronged Ballyholme Park, Ward Park, Castle Park and all pieces of waste ground in between. In autumn there were more Wine Mark bags floating in the breeze than leaves. There was no law against it. Yet. We would roam the parks like vast herds of apple-infused wildebeests while the Peelers waited in the long grass to pick off the young, the infirm and the inebriated. They could get you on age, they could get you on being disorderly, they could get you for pissing in bushes, but they couldn't get you on just sitting there drinking.

In the autumn and winter, with the early dark, it was generally fine, but once the spring and summer months came round we were a nightmare: old folks out for a stroll, families out for a pleasant walk or cycle were confronted with us hordes of drunks – punk blasting, boke flying, bottle smashing, duck molesting – and were rightly horrified. We were mostly harmless but undoubtedly intimidating. They all wanted something done about it, and if the police were powerless and the council slow to enact a by-law, they wanted it exposed in their local paper so that the authorities could be shamed into doing the right thing. And the local paper agreed. They would put their finest reporter on the case. One young enough and brave enough to go in undercover and report on the weekly mayhem, who could befriend them and learn their degrading secrets and then expose them in the paper. The oxygen of publicity would force the council to take action to finally end the scourge of park drinking. Unfortunately, their finest reporter wasn't available.

I didn't go into it to betray my friends, exactly. I went into it to report on a genuine phenomenon. I wasn't sanctimonious. But the very drawing attention to it was what caused the problem. It was the pointing to the huge and obvious boil on the side of someone's face, a boil that clearly demanded lancing.

I went to the police to interview the station sergeant about the 'problem' drinking and with a knowing glint in his eye he said let me just show you what we're up against, and he took out a file bursting with reports and put it on the desk before me. He tapped the cover and said these were just reports of arrests and incidents of public disorder in Ballyholme Park, and he knew, he fucking knew, that my name was laced all the way through them. I said nothing, he said nothing, but a lot was said.

My report was *long*, broadsheet long. It highlighted the lack of amenities for kids and their boredom. There was a photograph of The Whites with Gavin's 'Bangor's Burning with Boredom' spray-painted across them. And the truth is, we weren't really that bored at all. We were having a great time. The Troubles hardly affected us, we had youth clubs and cinemas and pubs and yes, park drinking, but we didn't drink there as an expression of some underlying malaise or societal dissatisfaction – we drank there because it was good crack.[14] We weren't lacking for something to do; we were doing it. We were teenagers and it was our job to be pissed off, and to piss other people off. We were happy to be bored. Because then we could complain about it. We were happy with The Blues and BJs. We did not expect the Hanging Gardens of Ballyholme.[15]

The article was not a polemic, it was balanced; it gave as much space to the police and the councillors and the community workers as it did to the kids with the flagons of cider raised to their lips. But when you're young you don't really see that balance, you see your gang being picked on, you

---

14 I use here the unionist 'crack' as opposed to the republican 'craic', which is the same but different.
15 No one expects the Hanging Gardens of Ballyholme.

see your mates being turned into something you knew they weren't – antisocial delinquents. And you also knew who was responsible for writing it: yon big-nosed skinny wanker with the camera round his neck thinking he can dance to Rudi.

That's where I was, having the time of my life after my band had bowed out, pogoing along to 'Big Time' and thinking life can't get any better – gloriously unaware that the forces of retribution were gathering around me, or that they were all wearing matching red jackets.

It started with a shove, but everyone was shoving; that was the nature of the dancing. Then a punch and a shove and a kick and a sudden realisation that the space around me was growing as people made room for what was surely coming. I pretended not to notice, and made my dancing even more vigorous, which allowed me to pirouette to the edge of the dance floor. I looked about desperately for some sign of my friends, but no joy. Deciding that discretion was the better part of being a chicken, I fled through the crowd, out of the dancehall and into the car park across the road.

I stood there, breathing hard, waiting for my mates to arrive, waiting to tell them about the lucky escape I'd just had. We would surely talk about the counter-attack we were going to mount, while at the same time walking back to The Blues to avoid any real chance of conflict. 'Big Time' was Rudi's most popular song and surely their last of the night, so my friends would be there in a minute. Except it wasn't their last, they had an encore to do, and as the music started up again, achingly muffled, I came to the conclusion that the Red Harringtons weren't that fussed on the encores either, because they were there, all of them, and they waded in.

It wasn't a question of me going down with all guns blazing like Custer of the West. If it was Belfast there might have been a knife or a breeze block. In Bangor it was wannabe hoods in Clarks Commandos. But a well-aimed foot can do a lot of damage. I was on the ground, curled into a ball, protecting my head as best I could, and took my kicking while praying for the cavalry to arrive. The only problem was that the cavalry was still dancing.

After what seemed like an eternity someone said, 'He's had enough,' and it stopped.

I breathed a sigh of relief, which was a mistake, because it showed I was still alive.

Another voice said, 'No he hasn't,' and the kicking started again.

They left me lying there in a very small pool of blood. My friends finally showed up. They helped me up off my gravelled knees and cleaned me off, and I staggered back to The Blues, minus my camera and dignity. My heart wasn't in any further drinking and I soon slipped away home, my head throbbing and my bones aching, trying desperately to think wise, philosophical thoughts that might allow me to put this experience into proper perspective, but nothing would come because I was drunk and I wanted the comfort of my mum and my dad and my dog, though I told only my dog. I was not noticeably a different, wiser person when I woke the next morning, although I could now speak Japanese and do needlepoint.

It wasn't a life-changing experience, though it gave me a lifelong aversion to getting a kicking. The Red Harringtons had either tried to stifle the freedom of the press, in which case I was both victim and hero, or they'd given me a hiding because I was an obnoxious wanker, in which case they may have had a point. I would never know. If they compiled a report afterwards, nailing down exactly why I was jumped, it now languishes somewhere in their long-lost files.

Now that I think about it again, with the benefit of hindsight and the best part of forty years of life behind me, I wonder to myself, who really won the fight outside BJs that night, in a damp car park with the dull thud of punk rock in the background and with nary a BJ in prospect? For I am still writing, while the Red Harringtons are long gone, destined to be nothing more than a tiny footnote in an obscure social history.[16]

---

16   Right here.

7

Half Man Half Biscuit

MY AUNTIE LILY HAD LIVED with us my whole life. From the house on the High Donaghadee Road, to Wellington Park, to Ballymacormick Avenue. She was part of the furniture, without actually being a chair.

She never drove, so I walked with her everywhere. I don't remember ever walking anywhere with my parents. We spent hours in Castle Park with my binoculars and guidebook at the height of my birdwatching phase. We walked on the beach at Ballyholme. She bought me a Mars bar and I took it out of its wrapper and threw the bar in the sea, instead of the wrapper and we laughed for a long time about that. Those were the days when you just threw litter away. There weren't as many people, so there wasn't as much litter, so it was okay.

She took me into Bangor on a Saturday morning. She was surprised I had enough money to buy two boxes of Wee Soldiers. Then we got home to my furious dad – furious because he couldn't find the cigarette money he had squirrelled away in his jacket, and then he saw me with the two boxes and knew I'd stolen it, and that was me away upstairs to get my arse smacked. I cried my eyes out, although part of me was thinking, how long before he caves in and gives me the Wee Soldiers back? But I learned my lesson; I've never stolen anything since, apart from hearts.[1]

I don't know if Auntie Lily ever enjoyed a racy single life, but there were certainly nights out with her workmates, and friends like Billy and Nan, and Lena. But then she had a stroke. She had to retire. She was never quite the same busybody again. She had lost the use of one arm and could only walk with the aid of a metal brace on one leg. The caliper. At first, she couldn't talk very well either, her face being all lopsided and her mouth droopy. But her arm improved and, after a determined effort, her mouth firmed up again, mostly so that she could properly smoke. You can achieve anything if your nicotine addiction is bad enough.

During this time she had huge fights with Boker. He was subsisting on a small civil-service wage while living the high life of a disco-dancing, booze-guzzling, perm-headed, platform-heeled Lothario, and the only way to finance that was to borrow money from Auntie Lily. The borrowing was fine, the returning less so – so they would rage at each other, Boker swearing he'd pay it back and Auntie Lily, an inefficient Shylock with an orange nicotine tinge, knowing he never would while simultaneously lending him more.

The only thing that stopped their fighting was my brother getting married and leaving home, which was something of a surprise to me as I hadn't realised he was going out with someone. But there he was, twenty-four years old and marrying Diane, despite the fact that she came from Newtownards, and

---

1   Yeah, right.

who would henceforth always be referred to as the Duchess. I had no idea why she was called that, and didn't dare ask, because by then David and I weren't getting on.

Much of it stemmed from the fact that up until he got married we still shared a bedroom and he'd come home in the early hours and put on Downtown Radio when I was trying to sleep, and it always seemed to be playing 'Bat Out of Hell', and then he'd fall asleep with it still blasting out and I would get in a rage about having to get out of bed to turn it off. Once, he was too drunk to make it to the toilet, and instead pissed in my upturned typewriter case. You can see how we might have fallen out.

By the time he was getting married I was lucky to score an invitation to the wedding.

On the morning of the wedding, he chased me up Ballymacormick Avenue with a knife.

I can be *really* annoying.

I never borrowed money from Auntie Lily, but I was bad in other ways. She was nosy, smoked like a train and smelled of pee, and I didn't mind telling her. She was slow and would block doorways, and she would want to know everyone's business, and all those lovely walks were conveniently forgotten. Neither of us had any sympathy or understanding for her. We were just too young or too self-absorbed, but it's a fact that you can be awful to family in a way you would never dream of being awful to a complete stranger.

With her illness, contact gradually lessened with her old friends. She became quite cut-off. She stared out the window a lot. She could have bought a Sherman tank with all the cigarette coupons she had. But she didn't.

Richard returned briefly from America for a visit, bringing with him an American accent. He was in our house the afternoon Auntie Lily collapsed in the kitchen. We were more interested in the fact that we'd just acquired the new single by The Jam. We thought she'd just fallen over. But they took her to hospital and she died there. I saw her body in the hospital, and I swore I would never look at one again and I haven't.

It wasn't all bad. I lost an auntie and gained a study. I'd like to say it's what she would have wanted, but I doubt it. She'd have preferred to still be smoking. She had lived nearly her whole adult life with Mum and Dad. With her little sister. She was just always there. The three of them sitting around the kitchen table at night, or all five of us watching telly. I don't know if she paid rent. Maybe she was the difference, maybe she was the perks, maybe she was the fridge and the rented colour TV, the crazy paving that wasn't stolen. We only had a few holidays – to Ballycastle, to Portrush, to the Isle of Man – but she never came with us. Maybe she had mad, drug-fuelled orgies when we were away. Perhaps not.

In the early days, actually, there were six of us. My granny lived with us too. I don't remember her. My brother does. She was old and infirm and there were stories of my mum, eight months pregnant, trying to carry her up the stairs. There was another, younger sister, Hetty. The handed-down story is that she wasn't much help with their mother, too busy out having a good time, and there was a falling-out because of that. She was young though, and you do that.

Auntie Lily's room was quickly cleared out, my dad and I bought a desk and swivel chair from the classified ads in the paper, and I sat in there for hours – not writing a novel but imagining that her ghost was watching over me. Because although I couldn't see her, I could certainly smell her – that or the cat next door. Either way, the novel wasn't written, because although I now had my own space in which to begin it, I didn't have any ideas, and I had a full-time job, and I had a girlfriend.

Yes, indeed.

Marie-Louise introduced herself to me at a gig by The Outcasts. It was held in the Market Hall, a smallish, underused venue owned by the local council and situated directly behind the *Spectator* offices, which backed on to Market Square. It hadn't been used for gigs since the '60s, but one day I thought, why not, and ended up hiring it out. I put on a gig by The Co-ordinates, and it went well – so I booked The Outcasts, and it didn't. They were then one of the biggest draws on the punk scene. I promoted it through my own entertainment page in the *Speccy*, Maxine having given it up in favour of grown-up journalism. I was now pulling the strings of the music biz, albeit only in Bangor. It was deeply unethical, but cracking fun.

The Outcasts came with a reputation for trouble, and they didn't let us down. It wasn't so much the band themselves as their followers. They were hardcore punks in studded leather jackets and peroxide Mohicans. They were all mates of the band, so they blustered in without paying and were welcomed into the large dressing room upstairs, together with their carry-outs. Because the toilets were deemed too far away, they pissed down the stairs when the need arose. They clashed repeatedly with our local punks once the gig started. The atmosphere was poisonous and faces were smashed, and

I would have been very annoyed except a girl came up to me and asked if I was that fella from the paper and said she read my stuff and can I look at your camera and a few moments later she was snogging the face off me, which was A Good Thing. Before I knew it I was out of there and fumbling for the key to the *Spectator* office and I was jabbing in the security code[2] and then we were stumbling through the print works to the editorial office and I was showing her where I worked and then we were lying on the desks and fumbling some more and I'd no idea what I was doing, but my hands were everywhere and I was in seventh heaven and also I was nineteen and this was LONG OVERDUE. Typewriters, ashtrays, towering columns of newspapers hit the deck as Marie-Louise, clearly lacking prescription glasses, showed me what was what, and if we didn't quite go the whole way, we very nearly did, and I did not give one damn about all the punk mayhem happening a few yards away. The hall could have burned down with everyone in it for all I cared: I was with a girl, a good-looking girl, who wanted to be with me, a good-looking girl blinded by my local celebrity and with jeans that unbuttoned and a bra … well, just a bra, a bra – what a few years ago I would have called an Over-Shoulder Boulder Holder, but which I now called Heaven.

Marie-Louise was seventeen. She went to Sacred Heart of Mary Grammar School. She could not have been more Catholic if she'd been called Virginia O'Mary. She lived in the Bloomfield Estate, just on the other side of the ring road. Or, as it was frequently called on the news, the loyalist Bloomfield

---

2   3861. I'm sure they've changed it.

Estate. Being a Catholic in Bloomfield was rare; not being firebombed out of there was rarer still.

She was smart and funny and we hit it off. I went on my first ever proper date with her, a meal in the Cartwheel Restaurant in High Street. You would know the Cartwheel because there was a large cartwheel stuck to the side of the building. I don't know which came first, the restaurant or the cartwheel, or how it got there. Perhaps there had been a crash and the rest of the cart still lay in a ruined heap in the attic, possibly with a mangled corpse within.

I was nervous, that first date – not so much with Marie-Louise, but with being in a proper restaurant. I didn't recognise half the dishes on the menu. The waiters were over-attentive with their offers of bread. I hadn't realised there were so many different types of bread. I thought there was only white, Nimble and Veda.[3] They kept coming back with more, and I found them intimidating and felt under pressure to eat more and more bread so that I began to puff up like the overfed ducks in Ward Park.

When they finally came to take our order, I thought I would play safe and order roast turkey, except when it came to saying the words out loud I panicked and asked for 'raw stork'. They then looked at me like I was a fruitcake, which, incidentally, was also available in the breadbasket.

Otherwise, all was going swimmingly. So swimmingly, in fact, that a few dates later, on a warm summer's evening, on

---

3   Veda is a popular malt bread invented in 1904. Not to be confused with VD, which is a popular sexually transmitted disease. Veda bread is traditionally sold unsliced. Many fingers have been lost in the slicing of it, but it's generally worth it.

the way home from the pub, I lay my jacket down in the grass behind some bushes in Castle Park like the gentleman I was and, watched only by badgers and bats and red-eyed rabbits, the virginity was lost and heavenly choirs sang and I was finally A MAN. It was the best thirty seconds she ever had, she assured me.

But we were off and running.

I had passed my driving test at the third attempt, thanks to the patience of a flatulent instructor, and so we had access to one of the paper's delivery vans, which the journalists routinely used to cover stories at night and then held on to until the next morning. We found it wasn't only good for delivering papers, but also for having undisturbed sex in. Thus, we would find secluded car parks, clamber into the back, zip two sleeping bags together for comfort, and enjoy ourselves in the only way two fit, healthy and curious teenagers can where it doesn't involve a trampoline.

Marie-Louise was not initially welcomed with open arms at home. My dad said, 'So you're going out with a Fenian,' though I think he was just trying to be funny. But still. It registered. My brother marched with the Royal Black Preceptory and had obvious reservations. But I was never told not to see her, and gradually they got used to having her around. After a few months it wasn't an issue.

Months! I was going steady. *We* were going steady.

We started out hogging the living room, exiling my parents to the kitchen. Then we slipped into my bedroom, ostensibly to watch TV on a portable black-and-white set so that my parents could reclaim the front room, but always with the door half open so it could be seen that we weren't getting up to no good, but that soon progressed to the door being closed and then the door being locked and then we couldn't keep our hands off each other.

I was doing exactly what I'd laughed at others for doing – I'd met a girl and was now slowly withdrawing from The Blues. It wasn't the sort of place a girl wanted to hang out, and increasingly, given the alternative attraction, neither did I. A winter's night in a force-ten gale with Wine Mark bags on your feet to keep you warm, or curled up in bed with a beautiful woman? There wasn't much of a choice. My friends were changing anyway – being involved with the band and the whole local music scene had introduced me to loads of different people, few of them from Ballyholme. Some were from as far away as the other side of town.

Music was changing too. Punk wasn't dead, but it had splintered. The second wave of bands was more hardcore, lacking in melody and smothered in glue, but the punk spirit had also fed into an explosion of ska, mainly through the 2 Tone label, with The Specials and The Selecter and Madness. Then there were the New Romantics with toned-down glam and lovely hair. There was also a huge Jam-inspired mod revival. It was hard to know quite what you should be.

Easter Bank Holiday Monday was one of the biggest days of the year for the town and for the paper. Hordes of visitors came down from Belfast. Orangemen marched. It had also become a tradition for punks and rockers to fight each other. There'd be running battles all over town. It was like the Wild West. Punks and rockers, and then intemperate Orangemen would chip in.

The Wednesday magistrate's court immediately after the bank holiday was the biggest petty sessions of the year.

Hundreds of kids would be brought up on charges of disorderly behaviour, assaulting the police, drunkenness and generally being a pain in the arse.

The resident magistrate was J.D. Wishart Mills, a grumpy bugger who would have been known as the Hanging Judge if he'd been allowed to be. He did not suffer fools, at all. My job was to sit at the press table desperately trying to note down the evidence with my dodgy shorthand, while at the same time trying to hide my face from the accused, because I knew half of them. But for chance and circumstance I *was* one of them. It rarely worked, and I'd be routinely besieged after court by teens anxious for their names to be kept out of the paper. I would patiently explain that everyone's name went in and that there was nothing I could do about it, that it was the only fair and democratic thing to do, and in response they would patiently explain how they were going to kick the living shit out of me. It went with the territory. I never did get another kicking, though the odd time I had to scarper quickly out of parties when someone I recognised from the dock came in.

As the trends and tribes changed, punks v. rockers gradually gave way to mods v. rockers. The main difference was that there just seemed to be so many more mods than there ever were punks. There were, literally, thousands of them. On a Bank Holiday Monday the town was abuzz with the sound of Vespas, the flap of fish-tailed Union Jack parkas and the music of The Who and The Jam.

And that got me thinking.

Having tried and failed to play in a band, and having made a dog's dinner out of managing one, the obvious next step in my road to the bottom was to build on my success in promoting

The Outcasts by finding a band that the mods might flock to. Surely there was a fortune to be made there. The Who and The Jam were slightly out of my league, but might there be another band I could ruthlessly exploit? No, as it turned out – at least, not in Northern Ireland. But I was still buying the *NME* every week, despite their callous rejection, and in one issue I found exactly what I was looking for – a band called Squire, who'd recently released a single, 'Walking Down the Kings Road', which the mods were loving but which hadn't sold much outside of their niche market. They'd played some small club gigs in the capital, but not much beyond. Surely local mods would eat them up?

I shared my idea with Robert, another newish friend who was interested in getting involved in promoting gigs – maybe we could do it together? He could do the practical stuff, like booking the venue, and I'd talk to the band and do the promoting through the paper.

We decided to go big – most of the mods were still in their mid-teens, so a bar wasn't going to work. Although Mod Central was Belfast, we were determined to keep it local. The Market Hall was much too small – but the Queen's Hall in Newtownards might work.

Robert looked after that, and I booked the band through their manager, Dave Fagence, and they agreed to fly over for their Irish debut. The tickets went on sale on a Saturday morning through Caroline Music in Belfast. We were hoping at best to sell a couple of hundred. By the following Monday we had sold 800. A complete sell-out. We were stunned and a little shocked, and then very full of ourselves. We were the bee's knees. We had our fingers on the pulse. All of those big promoters didn't have a clue. We had sold out a huge venue. Money in the bank.

The band flew in for the gig. We picked them up at the airport and drove them to Caroline Music, where they signed autographs. Then we took them to the venue. As it was too expensive to bring their own gear, apart from guitars, we were providing everything else, including the drum kit. The drummer burst out laughing when he saw what he was supposed to play. It was, basically, a child's kit, the drumming equivalent of my Chad Valley typewriter. As the mods began to arrive, we were still racing around in a blind panic trying to get a replacement kit.

Eight hundred had tickets; many more came along for the ride. We hadn't thought to alert anyone in the town to the coming invasion. That's what it was. And we had no idea that Belfast mods divided along sectarian lines. Half of them turning up that day didn't sport Union Jacks on their parkas; they displayed Irish Tricolours, which did not go down well in loyalist Newtownards, or with other mods.

They came by scooter, they came by car and bus, and they besieged the local off-licences as soon as they opened. Then they were getting pissed out on the streets and smashing bottles and pissing in corners and generally overwhelming the local police, who'd been expecting a rather quieter Saturday afternoon. Most of the mods were legless by the time they started queueing up. We'd decided to make it an afternoon gig but had somewhat naively imagined that this might mean they would all assemble quietly, stand appreciatively to watch the band and then quietly disperse afterwards.

Ahm, no.

We began to panic as the first windows were kicked in. And then the doors. At this point at any other rock gig a crack security team would leap into action, root out the troublemakers and restore order. That would have worked for us if we'd had a crack security team. If, in fact, we'd had any security team. We had neglected to employ security. That's how naive we were. We had corralled a couple of mates into acting as stewards, but with the understanding that all they were expected to do was check tickets and direct people into the hall, not wade into gangs of drunken youths who were only interested in smashing the hall and each other to pieces.

I stood at the back as the crowd surged forward in anticipation of the band's imminent arrival, thinking what a lot of little shits they were and feeling desperately sorry for our bouncers – friends of friends had been rushed in to try and help, but it was really a losing battle – them all looking battered and bloody, and decided that it was the worst day of my life and that I never wanted to see a mod again, or promote a gig, and the only relief was that at least it couldn't get any worse and would soon be over. At that point the lovely red velvet curtains that were closed across the stage, curtains that were massive and worth thousands, were ripped from their moorings and came floating down over the crowd, and as the full horror of that began to sink in, Robert came up and whispered in my ear that we'd neglected to take out any insurance and that we were, in fact, fucking idiots.

Without realising it I had done the most punk thing of my life. I was like a miniature Malcolm McLaren, accidentally creating anarchy with the Sex Pistols. The only difference was that he had ruthlessly exploited it and forged a career based upon it, whereas I went home and hid my head under a blankie.

I had a terrible headache that night. A migraine. I'd never had one before. Marie-Louise tried to soothe me, but nothing would work because I was dreading the following day, when I was going to have to do it all over again.

Not only was I crap promoter, I was also a greedy crap promoter.

I'd arranged a second gig. This time in a smaller venue. This time in Bangor. In Rollerama, which had recently been converted from an abandoned ballroom on the seafront into a roller disco. Roller-skating was enjoying a comeback destined to last as long the mod revival, which is to say, not long at all – only long enough for businessmen to invest in expensive premises to exploit the craze and then lose their money.

I decided, as the band were already here and clearly very popular, to put on this extra gig just four miles away, not thinking once that we might already have exhausted the market. Robert, being slightly more sensible, decided not to partner with me on this one.

I had such a sense of dread on the morning of the gig – not only because of the riot the day before, but also because I had sold precisely forty tickets for it. Mods were not only little shits, but they weren't even prepared to shell out for two gigs in two days. I was facing a colossal loss on this second gig, unless hordes of fans suddenly turned up at the last minute. And I didn't even want them to turn up in case it turned into the kind of anarchy we'd just about lived through. I would be screwed whatever happened.

As it turned out the band was great, the sound was perfect; this time they loved the drums. All they lacked was an audience. I had to drive home after the gig to get my dad to write me a cheque to cover what I still owed the band, having lost all of the profit I'd made the previous day. Home to Daddy. It wasn't like he was a millionaire indulging his spoilt son. He was merely trying to keep me out of debtor's prison or getting another hiding. Meanwhile, Robert was laughing all the way to the bank, or at least quietly giggling, because by then he knew that the council, owners of the Queen's Hall, were going to cover the damages.

A few days later the first Squire gig was the front-page lead story in the *Newtownards Chronicle*, with multiple witnesses attesting to the scenes of mayhem which had so disturbed a normally peaceful Saturday afternoon. Unusually, there was no comment from the concert's promoters. Inexplicably the reporter had been unable to track them down. I don't know if he knew at least one of them was hiding in plain sight, but somehow I got away without being exposed.

The gigs were a harsh lesson. I was not cut out for concert promotion. I had good, original ideas, but I wasn't equipped to properly see them through. I couldn't handle the stress. I also didn't have the skills to manage a band to superstardom even in their own home town. And my one attempt at joining a band by playing a synthesiser/car alarm had been an embarrassing failure. I was not supposed to be an entrepreneur or a performer or a manager. I was supposed to be a writer. I was supposed to write that Great American Novel. And the only thing stopping me was that I still couldn't think of a single thing to write a novel about. I had a typewriter, I had a desk, I had my dead auntie's bedroom, I *had* to make a more determined effort.

* * *

Nope.

Nothing would come.

My only excuses or distractions were a full-time job at the cutting edge of nothing and a girlfriend who had lately begun studying at Queen's University and was beginning to show a distressing amount of interest in hanging around with other students up in Belfast.

There was only one way to deal with that.

We got engaged.

I don't think either of us had any intention of getting married. It could have been prompted by her getting pregnant, because we were utterly naive on that front, or reckless. The only kind of protection I was familiar with involved a balaclava and a baseball bat. Pregnancy would have been the natural and traditional progression. But she wasn't pregnant. I think it was mainly so that we could say we were engaged and become the first of our friend group to make that claim, to make that stride towards being adults, when we were clearly very far short of that.

We went up to Belfast to look at rings. We got one with a tiny diamond for £300. We paid for it with hire purchase. £10 a month. And when I say we paid for it, I mean I paid for it. I was then earning about £30 a week. £30 a week seemed like a lot, although you'd get £40 in the Royal Marine Commandos. I had no other real expenses – £5 was paid into the house. The rest went on records and cider. That was the way to live.

Music, cider, girlfriend, sex, use of van, top journalist and former rock'n'roll entrepreneur now focused on writing. Life was good.

When I wasn't snuggled up with Marie-Louise, the park drinking continued, but no longer at The Blues – mostly now in Ward Park, a different group of friends, more united by music and bands and not so much based on where we lived. It was also closer to the pub. We were making that shift from largely drinking in the wild to treating it as an aperitif.

Our pub of choice was Hunter's, at the corner of Queen's Parade and Main Street. It was over three floors, the bottom bar being a regular spit-and-sawdust kind of a working-man's bar, the middle made up of comfortable booths with a well-stocked jukebox and the top bar boasting pool tables. We would often start off in the bottom bar, but the middle was our natural home. We rarely ventured up top – that was where the 'hard men' hung out. There was a vaguely paramilitary air to it. Perhaps for that reason Marie-Louise wasn't really into hanging out there. She was either up at university or I'd spend the early evenings with her at her home in Bloomfield before slipping down for a few pints with my mates.

The owner's son, Colin Hunter, was a permanent fixture, always keeping an eye on the middle and top bars. He was around our age and an affable sort. He later opened his own nightclub but had a falling-out with his business partner. The partner stabbed him to death on the premises after hours, then panicked and hid the body in the bins behind the club, meaning to remove it for secret burial later. Except he forgot the bins were collected early the next morning, and so Colin's body was emptied into the bin lorry and mangled in there before being removed to the local dump. It was eventually retrieved, here, there and everywhere. His ex-business partner, even though he was quickly the chief suspect, audaciously attended the funeral and the reception afterwards, where we saw him sympathising and commiserating with family and friends.

Colin Hunter's murder was one of those shocks you occasionally get in a small town – the sudden death of someone everyone knows. It didn't happen like that in Belfast, not in the '70s and '80s, when death was every day, death was mundane, violent death was almost passé. In Bangor it was out of the ordinary, and that's how it should be. Sudden, violent death shouldn't be routine, it shouldn't be greeted with a resigned nod or a sigh, it should shake the foundations.

A young Bangor policeman, Gary Martin, married with two young sons, attended a hijacked delivery van in Andersonstown in Belfast. The van had been blocking the road. He volunteered to move it out of the way so that the traffic could flow again, but as soon as he moved into the front seat, he set off a mercury tilt switch and a bomb exploded. His funeral service was held at Ballyholme Presbyterian Church, where I'd marched up and down with the BB. His widow asked for no retaliation.

In August 1981 the IRA set off a 150lb car bomb at the bottom of Main Street. It caused substantial damage to the Co-Op and many other shops. Part of the car was later found on the roof of Boots, right at the top of Main Street. Two policemen and a woman were injured by flying glass.

Then we continued with the Groomsport Gleanings and the Bangor Camera Club, and Lolita Alexander wrote her columns about Spanish art.

It was normal, normal, normal, bang, normal, normal, normal, bang, normal.

In September RUC Constable Alexander Beck, who lived on the Clandeboye Road, was killed when his Land Rover was struck by a Russian-made RPG-7 missile. The IRA did it. He had two young children. The other officer in the Land Rover lost both his arms and a leg.

I ran reviews of punk gigs and the latest video releases. Normal, normal, normal, bang.

In November 300 cars took part in a cavalcade around the town to protest against the upsurge in violence, and then they all went off to Newtownards for a rally by the Third Force, the latest in a long line of loyalist paramilitary outfits, this one inspired by and later disowned by the Rev. Ian Paisley. He declared his intention to exterminate the IRA, egging on the crowd packed into Conway Square.

It was a dark, miserable winter's night, a sea of green parkas and balaclavas, with febrile roars and salutes and promises, and it was Paisley doing his Grand Old Duke of York routine, leading them up to the top of the hill, but never quite into battle.

Normal, normal, normal, bang.

Ninety-nine per cent of the journalism was councils and court cases, speech festivals and blurry photographs of winning darts teams, it was endless afternoons fighting off hangovers in the garden shed that passed for the press box at Clandeboye Park as The Seasiders hacked their way through another muddy ninety minutes before a paltry few hundred supporters.

The only time there was any real excitement at Clandeboye Park was when perennial champions Linfield visited from Belfast – and that wasn't because of the football, that was because of the thousands of unruly supporters they brought with them. It was the footballing equivalent of The Outcasts coming to town. Afternoons when the ground rocked to sectarian chanting, when even the cows being herded into Bangor Abattoir immediately behind the ground were uncharacteristically skittish.[4]

Once it was discovered that I liked football, I was rapidly promoted to being the *Speccy*'s football correspondent. This meant attending all of their home matches and none of their away matches. If I'd had any sort of real interest in them, I would have travelled; but I liked football, not Irish League Football, and fortunately Miss Roycroft didn't insist on it.

Other papers might have employed freelance correspondents to cover the away games, but not us. What we did, what we had always done, was we picked up our reserved copy of the *Saturday Night* sports paper every Monday morning, we clipped out the report of our away fixture, and then we rewrote it as if we had actually been there.

This became my job. It was tedious watching the home games, but twice as bad rewriting someone else's report of a tedious away game. Occasionally I would liven things up by throwing in odd details which couldn't have occurred, just to see if anyone would notice. Chickens that ran onto pitches, bomb alerts that no one could recall, players who had never existed. Nobody ever did, or if they did, they never

---

4   One game was delayed by an escaped cow. That doesn't happen at Anfield.

180

complained, or perhaps doubted their own recollections, because the reports were clearly put together by professional journalists. One particularly inattentive week I got the score completely wrong and turned a defeat into a victory. Someone did notice that, and I was hauled in for questioning. I couldn't even claim it was a typo, because I had lifted completely the wrong game from the paper. But I got away with it. I always got away with it. I either had chutzpah or looked on the verge of tears.

The home games were rarely entertaining, but the press box usually was, because there were reporters there from the *Saturday Night* (blissfully unaware that I was ripping off their stories every other week) and the daily Belfast *News Letter*. They were usually old-school sports journalists, some of whom had been covering the Irish League and other local sports since before the war. One wrote a column for the *News Letter* under the nom de plume of 'Omar's Moving Finger' and spent most of the games recounting stories about the good old days when boxer Rinty Monaghan had packed out the King's Hall, or when referee Norman Boal had been in charge of an infamous match between Linfield and Belfast Celtic that erupted into a riot. Norman had his leg broken in the melee. Belfast Celtic never played again, and Norman moved to Newtownards to become editor of the *Chronicle*, which was arguably a worse punishment.

One week there was an unfamiliar freelance reporter in the press box, and we got chatting. His name was Keith Seddon and there was something familiar about it. I told him mine and he went kind of quiet, and then it gradually dawned on me that he shared a name with the editor of *Vortex*, the glossy, richly illustrated science-fiction magazine I'd submitted my story to. I said to my new friend Keith, funny, you share a name with another Keith Seddon, another Keith Seddon who edits a science-fiction magazine, and he said yes, that's me, and I said that's impossible because you're here in the Clandeboye Road press box, right next to the Abattoir End, reporting on Bangor v. Carrick Rangers, when you should be editing tales of intergalactic warfare. He said, well, *Vortex* went bust and I said, oh, and he said, I remember your story, and I looked at him hopefully, because at least a kind word would have helped my fledgling writer's ego, and he said, 'It was too long,' and then we watched the rest of the match in complete silence and we never spoke again.

Whenever Linfield played, the press box would also take on an entirely different atmosphere because it meant the most famous journalist in Northern Ireland was in the building.[5] Malcolm Brodie was a Scot evacuated to Portadown during the Second World War who went from local journalism to setting up the first ever sports department at the *Belfast Telegraph*. He was their sports editor for forty-one years, and when he arrived in town he carried with him the weight of history. He got the best seat, with the best view, and first choice of the biscuits. He had his own phone. In fact, every paper there had their own phone – every paper except for the *Speccy*. They all had their own phones because they needed to get their reports in before their deadlines. I had the best part of a week to get mine in. I had the time to compose my report in iambic pentameter, but not the skill.

---

5   Shed.

Actually, there was a certain pressure – one of the debatable perks of the job was that I had not only to write my own story, but also provide a report for the BBC TV's teatime sports report. It was usually only a couple of paragraphs, but because the programme went out only half an hour after the end of the match, you had to call it in as soon as the final whistle blew. With all the phones in the press box tied up, it meant dashing out of the ground, around the perimeter and straight into Texas Homecare, the big DIY wholesaler next door. They had a public phone box. You had to have the right change, but first you had to actually get at it because invariably there was someone already using it: some old Aggy trying to persuade her husband to come and pick her up. I got lucky most times and would call in my story then drive home in time to hear it being read out, which was satisfying, plus the knowledge that a cheque for a few pounds would shortly arrive for my trouble.

The Seasiders rarely won and being weighed down by decades of mediocrity didn't help. They were formed in a rowing boat in Bangor Bay in 1914. Until then the leading teams in the town were Bangor Rangers and Clifton Amateurs, but when the Great War was declared most of the young men rushed off to fight and the teams folded. Two players who got left behind couldn't face a winter without football, so, while out rowing in the bay, they hatched a plan to form a new club. Bangor FC was launched – but lasted just a few years because some members felt it was wrong to be playing sport when so many young men were being slaughtered in Flanders. Out of the ashes of that club grew the current one. They played their games at Ballyholme Showgrounds, which were situated just behind the Esplanade and, being sand-based, had one of the best surfaces in the Irish League.[6] But surfaces don't make for a good team, so they moved to Clandeboye Park and laboured through the '40s, '50s and '60s, then on into the '70s and '80s – essentially making up the numbers in their league while constantly narrowly avoiding relegation.

It was therefore difficult to give their long, disappointing history and current miserable form a positive spin. Season in, season out, my reports were relentlessly gloomy. Managers came, managers went; it never made any difference. The social club thrived, the team did not. Rumour had it that the social was run by paramilitaries, but then everything was supposedly run by paramilitaries. Taxi firms were run by paramilitaries. Every bouncer in every pub in the town was supplied by paramilitaries. Even the paramilitaries were run by paramilitaries. Paramilitaries were ubiquitous and, just like the Churchill Tartan, no one was quite sure if they actually existed – or, if they did, how many of them there were or how dangerous they might be. There might only have been one solitary paramilitary in the whole town, a drunk with a home-knit balaclava and a water pistol, but the very idea of him was enough to spread fear. But no amount of threatening or protection money could ensure a good performance on the pitch. You couldn't pay the players to throw a match when they did that every week by accident. You couldn't pay them to win one, because you couldn't pay them to win one. You could

---

6   The Ballyholme Showgrounds were built over with houses, forming the current Sandringham Drive. That's where I live now. Sometimes I can't sleep at night for the sound of ghostly studs on vanished changing-room floors and the loud sighs of spectral strikers as they miss another sitter.

pay the opposing team to throw a match, but that would mean dealing with a different paramilitary from his own town and with his own agenda and home-knit balaclava.

Eventually Bangor's managing director, Victor Haslett, had enough of the negativity and asked for a meeting. I thought he might want some advice on where they were going wrong on the field, as I fancied I knew a thing or two about football because I'd watched a lot of it, and also I played most weeks for Dukla Park.

Dukla Park was our team. Our name was a bastardised version of a song by Half Man Half Biscuit, 'All I Want for Christmas Is a Dukla Prague Away Kit'. We played every few weeks. We did not own a kit. Or sometimes, a ball. We turned up with our disparate shirts in Wine Mark bags on a Sunday morning, often unwashed from the previous week.[7] We played other teams made up of similar hangover-suffering reprobates. Teams with names like Lokomotive Holstein, Carnalea Wine and Cheese, and even a team with rumoured paramilitary connections, Slowvan Balaclava. We played a version of the game that we called Irish No Rules Football. Of course, there were rules, but just not very many. We didn't play offside, because there was no referee to enforce it. You couldn't play offside and judge it by popular vote, because it would always end in a draw. Attacks were known to break down because of severe outbursts of laughter. One opposing player had to go off suffering from a severe cigarette burn.

I always played up front, and was generally our top scorer, but that wasn't saying much. But when I did score,

---

7   The shirts, not the players; though sometimes …

and I got that glorious feeling, I could convince myself that I was actually quite good, and that I might have made it as a professional if I hadn't chosen the career of a crusading, if corruptible, journalist. That was why I thought I was ideally placed to offer advice to Victor Haslett, that perhaps Bangor's road to improvement was to not play offside, or to introduce more humour into their style of play, or to dot ashtrays along the side of the pitch, or even to score more goals, the way I did, and perhaps they would sign me to show them how it was done. But no; it turned out when he sat me down with a drink and the club manager, Eric Halliday, that they wanted me to stop writing negatively about their club because it was demoralising the team.

I pointed out that the team kept losing.

Victor pointed out that I'd only recently printed a completely fabricated match report.

I pointed out that at least they won that one.

They didn't even crack a smile.

Victor was big in insurance with a company called Harris Marion, who were club sponsors. Sponsors don't like negative publicity and didn't take kindly to that publicity being spearheaded by a teenage punk rocker who knew next to nothing about football. I could have countered that if they were sponsoring Bangor, they didn't know much about it either, but I held my whisht.

8

Strolling Along Minding My Own Business

THERE WERE SEVERAL DANGEROUS ORGANISATIONS at large in Bangor's sprawling Kilcooley Estate, including the UDA, the UVF and the Red Hand Commando. Any one of them would shoot you in the knees as soon as look at you.

They all ran protection rackets, dealt in drugs, laundered money and basically espoused gangsterism under the guise of loyalism. Much of it was indirectly sponsored through dubious government schemes, which handed out grants designed to keep the peace, but which actually perpetuated and fomented trouble.

The estate was mainly built between 1967 and 1976 to house those forced to flee the strife of inner-city Belfast, and they brought some of it with them. We had feared the Churchill Tartan, but this was on a different level. This was real danger.

If you were streetwise enough, and knew how to keep your nose clean, you could survive on the estate. If you answered a knock on the door and some little shit in an anorak said he was collecting money for new band uniforms, you handed

187

over what you had. When the Eleventh Night bonfire, which was visible from outer space, began to melt your house, you didn't complain, you threw another tyre on the inferno and told the Pope where to go. If they turned up to your gable-end house and offered to paint a thirty-foot-tall mural celebrating a gunman in a balaclava clutching an Armalite rifle, you asked them to add a foot or two.

But there was one organisation that was more feared than the UVF, had more members than the UDA and a better command structure than the Red Hand Commando – an organisation that literally marched to the beat of a different drum: a well-drilled group of fanatics known as the Kilcooley Strollers.

The Strollers were somewhere between a marching band and a dance troupe, and they were made up of children between the ages of six and sixteen. They marched up and down, they danced, they created music of a sort on kazoos. When I say they were a well-drilled group of fanatics, it is actually bollocks about them being well-drilled. They were all over the place. They were a shambles. They were like spiders who'd sucked all the E-numbers out of a truckload of Smarties and then been let loose on a stage. They were more *Pan's Labyrinth* than Pan's People.

The reason you didn't go up against the Strollers wasn't that they were scary or violent, though they were, it was because of their parents. The paramilitaries in Kilcooley were constantly feuding with each other over territory, protection money and how best to interpret the philosophical teachings to be found in Sun Tzu's *The Art of War*.

Often you would find a drunk Womble addressing a group of spotty teenagers in scratchy balaclavas preparing to rob a lost Avon lady with the advice, 'Move swift as the Wind and closely formed as the Wood. Attack like the Fire and be still as the Mountain,' only to be further confused by a passing Red Hand Commando with, 'Knowing the enemy enables you to take the offensive, knowing yourself enables you to stand on the defensive.' They would still be arguing the finer points while the Avon lady slipped away.

They were undoubted and occasionally violent rivals, but the paramilitary parents presented a united front when it came to their children's participation in the Strollers. Nobody criticised their children. Nobody disparaged the Strollers. *That* was an act of war.

Of course, I had to find this out for myself.

The problem was that I was young enough and misguided enough to treat every show I attended in my capacity as the *Speccy*'s entertainment correspondent as if I was reviewing an opening night on Broadway for *The New York Times*. That is, I went in with knives sharpened. I thought I could make or break a show with my unique insights, which were the insights of a teenage punk rocker still flirting with science fiction. I did not have the wit to differentiate between a professional performer and a bunch of enthusiastic amateurs. If I didn't think they were any good, then I had to say that, whether they were earning thirty grand a night or were being rewarded with gobstoppers.

Opportunity Knocks-winning singing star Lena Zavaroni played the Tonic, and I savaged her so badly I was banned from attending future shows. Frankie Vaughan, Dick Emery, Glen Campbell and other slightly past-it '70s stars had already come in for similar treatment.

189

But the Kilcooley Strollers fared worst of all.

I took them apart.

I knew we were a community newspaper – there to offer support rather than criticism, to offer publicity rather than damn them with no praise at all – but I just couldn't help myself. And Miss Roycroft didn't stand in my way. She printed every word. Perhaps she thought it would teach me something. She must have suspected what the reaction would be, that the Strollers would not be of a mind to take fair criticism on board and learn from it, but rather that they would issue the Free Presbyterian version of a fatwa against me, and henceforth I would become not so much persona non grata in Kilcooley but rather persona kick-his-fucking-head-in-if-you-see-him grata. The dancing wing of Ulster loyalism was out for my blood.

Parents arrived en masse in the office, shouting and waving their fists, and I responded with defiance – mainly by hiding in the kitchen, and when I went out, I wore a big hat. I took a circuitous route home and I spent many hours in a darkened house peeking out through my venetian blinds, jumping at shadows and cats.

I seriously considered entering a Witless Protection Programme and relocating to a safe caravan in Ballywalter, and the only thing that saved me was time being a great healer – particularly on a local newspaper. After a while things began to settle down, the Strollers rolled on and I emerged from hiding none the wiser, because very shortly afterwards I was embroiled in another story that literally brought protestors with placards out on the streets. This time, though, it was different: it wasn't entirely my fault, it was Monty Python's.

Their Biblical satire *Life of Brian* was controversial enough on the mainland, but the prospect of it being shown here was bringing Presbyterians out in hives. It was an AA-rated film, meaning that you had to be over fourteen to see it – but in Belfast the council changed that to an X, restricting it to over-eighteens. As a result, faced with losing much of their intended audience, the distributors refused to show it.

It looked likely that North Down Borough Council would go the same way, but the *Speccy* was determined not to let that happen. We'd never been what you'd call a campaigning newspaper; small weekly papers aren't generally like that. But we set up 'Let Brian Live' to try and ensure the film was shown. God knows there was enough crap going on in the country already; we needed a laugh, and if it was at the expense of the religious maniacs who were responsible for half of it in the first place, then all the better.

Most people here aren't religious, it just seems like we are. We're forced to be. Religious fundamentalism is inextricably tied up with politics. If you feel passionately that you are part of the UK, that you are British, then you vote for the party that you think might best defend the Union; but if that party also has lunatic religious beliefs, then you're forced to accept those as a necessary evil. We could wearily accept that Creationists dictated our lifestyles, but there was a breaking point – and that was when they tried to rob us of the opportunity to laugh.

The Scott brothers, who ran the Tonic cinema, were old-style theatrical entrepreneurs who could see there was a profit to be made in putting on *Life of Brian*, but equally they didn't want to run afoul of the council. They quietly encouraged us in our campaign. As entertainment reporter I was heavily involved, but it was mostly Peter, and Campbell from the typesetting bungalow. We wouldn't have gotten anywhere without cheerleading support from Miss Roycroft. She surprised us all. She was so prim and proper on the outside, but she had a mischievous streak. In her reporting days, covering a Bible-thumping local gospel meeting, she took a photo of Paisley sitting with his big size twelves facing the audience and very clearly showing a large hole in the sole of his shoe. She later quipped in the paper about the state of Paisley's 'soul' and took dog's abuse for it, but it was water off a duck's back. She absolutely encouraged our campaign, which ran for several weeks and attracted thousands of signatures to a petition, which we then presented to the council. As a result they refused to take any action against the film and it was duly shown that July, with protestors from the Lord's Day Observance Society marching up and down outside with placards while generally being laughed at by the huge queues of people waiting to go in. It was sold out for two straight weeks. People came from all over the country to see it.[1] On the opening night we marched up as a group; we had VIP seats waiting for us on the balcony. It was a glorious feeling. After that the film could easily have been an anticlimax, and it wouldn't have mattered. But, of course, it was fabulously funny, and I've never heard such laughter in a cinema, before or since. And laughing longest and loudest? Miss Roycroft.

* * *

---

1   It remained banned from exhibition in the South of Ireland for the next *eight years*.

Life of Brian was the last great hurrah for the cinema, because just a couple of years later the Tonic would close down, falling victim to the times – home video was taking over.

Video shops sprang up everywhere, cashing in on the explosion of interest, the way vape shops are suddenly flourishing everywhere today. In Bangor, Richard Morrow had the first. He was a smooth-talking, charismatic ex-rock'n'roller who had nearly made the big time with his band The Carpetbaggers in the '60s, but eventually signed up to the family estate-agency business. However, selling houses proved too quiet and respectable for him, and when video recorders began to arrive in the early '80s, he saw an opportunity. Until then you could only ever see films in the cinema or wait years for them to turn up on TV, but now you could watch them in your own home. Richard began renting video tapes out of a back room of his Ward Avenue home. The business took off, initially by word of mouth. Soon competitors began to spring up in different parts of the town, until it seemed like every mom-and-pop operation was offering tapes for hire. Richard's old music-biz showmanship, combined with his estate-agent canniness, soon came into play. He moved to larger premises and began an aggressive marketing campaign, spending his way to success. He took out half-page adverts in the *Speccy*, spending thousands. It was a broadsheet, so they were huge, and he took them out *every week*. He sponsored sports clubs and charity events, handing over those big mocked-up cheques and posing for publicity shots which ended up in the paper, often two or three times in every issue. He blew every other upstart video club out of the water. Yet there was always something not quite right about it. His advertising debt at the *Speccy* rocketed up into the tens of thousands, and just seemed to grow and grow. Occasionally he would make a token payment just to prevent his adverts being removed, but the debt never seemed to shrink.

Rumours spread that he wasn't just offering the latest releases – that there were pirate tapes and hardcore pornography to be had. The *Speccy* could have investigated, but for its first few years the video business was like the Wild West: everything went, and nobody quite knew what the law was or, even if they did, who was supposed to enforce it. Richard played that fine line with a brilliant mixture of bravado and faux innocence.

Besides, the paper didn't want to take the risk of losing such a good customer, and he was bound to settle his account one day.

We also promoted his business for free. And when I say we, I mean I. I'd started up a video-review column and routinely toured Bangor's video stores picking up free movies for the weekend. Richard's was always the first stop because he somehow always had films the other clubs couldn't get.

He had rows and rows of *E.T.*s before it had even reached the cinema we no longer had. That *definitely* had to be illegal. But no, no, Richard insisted, it was a 'special import'. Then I can review it in the paper? Ahm, I'd rather you wouldn't – but you can borrow it. And thus, because I can be easily bought, I was sucked into being complicit in his pirate-video operation. On the plus side, I got to see *E.T.*

It became addictive. I was a huge movie buff and getting to see the latest cinema releases before they were officially available was glorious. I called into Richard's every Friday and, as well as the standard releases I could review in the paper, I'd ask for one of his 'special imports' and he'd slip me a copy of *Gandhi* or *Chariots of Fire* or *Porky's* and I'd go home with Marie-Louise and snuggle up.

One week I called in and Richard wasn't working, but the guy on duty, Tommy, seemed to know the routine. He gave me the videos for review, and then I asked about a 'special import' and he nodded and reached beneath the counter and handed me a cassette tape whose title I didn't recognise, nor indeed did I recognise the girl having explicit sex on the cover. It was just the hardest-core pornography you can imagine. Or you could have imagined then. A glimpse of pubic hair was still considered wildly unusual, so this was truly shocking. It was at last firm evidence that Richard had been running an illegal porn business. I could turn a blind eye to the pirate tapes, but not this. What I had in my hand was the Nazis I'd been seeking, it was my Watergate, and I would damn him for his perversions and be carried shoulder high around the town by clean-living Presbyterians singing 'Hosanna' as soon as my exclusive, my exposure appeared in the paper.

Or I would take it home and not walk for a week.

* * *

Things were starting to change at the *Speccy*. I'd been there for three-and-a-half years, which meant I was now a senior reporter. Traditionally, that was when you started to look for another job. Peter had already left to join Downtown Radio and Barry had become a government press officer. Joy was still there, and Maxine. Paul arrived, then Ann-Marie, and Chris – all graduates of a journalism course at the College of

Business in Belfast. I'd been the last to squeeze in under the wire without any kind of qualification.

With the previous generation of reporters, I'd always been the junior member and we never really socialised together; with this new intake, we were all roughly the same age and more inclined to head out to the pub together once our wages were handed over in little brown envelopes, cash rolled up in a payslip.

The working week was a relatively short one – a late night on Wednesday to finish most of the paper, then the rest of it done by Thursday lunchtime, then it was out on the town. Fridays were recovery days when very little was ever achieved. There was no clocking in or clocking out. It was easy and familiar.

Then Miss Roycroft dropped a bombshell. Miss Roycroft, who was essentially the *Speccy* in human form, the fount of all knowledge, our leader and inspiration, startled everyone by announcing that she was leaving; not only leaving, but getting married; not only getting married but marrying her cousin; not only marrying her cousin, but marrying her first cousin; not only marrying her first cousin, but moving to Cork.

This was, altogether, a *scandal*.

We didn't think you could marry your first cousin. In Newtownards you could marry your sister, but Newtownards has always had its own laws. But to marry your first cousin, that was shocking. Miss Roycroft taught Sunday School, for God's sake; she should have known that there was something somewhere in the Bible, some obscure Old Testament verse, that expressly forbade you from lying down with your first cousin – or, if there wasn't, there should have been. We didn't want to think about Miss Roycroft lying down with anyone, let alone her first cousin. Their children would have, like, six feet and three eyes, though, of course, they were well past childbearing years. That wasn't the point. Her first cousin! They were surely moving to Cork because of the shame of it. Although, it turned out her first cousin actually lived in Cork, so it made sense, if you forgot for the moment that they were FIRST COUSINS. We had no idea she even had a boyfriend. Miss Roycroft couldn't have a boyfriend. She was Miss Roycroft. Unless she was a dark horse. I'd heard about dark horses. She probably had a heroin habit as well, and a string of Arabian lovers, and now her family had had enough of her floozy ways and she was being forced into an arranged marriage with her first cousin.

We debated mounting an intervention, and the only thing that stopped us what that she seemed genuinely very happy. And to be clear, there's nothing illegal about marrying a first cousin.

We were powerless to stop it anyway. But when this unexpected event took place, when she actually left the building, it created a constitutional crisis. Miss Roycroft, the same age as the Queen, had been in power for decades, and the transition to the next monarch went smoothly because the *Speccy* operated on tradition. The next editor of the *Speccy* would be Joy, she with the nascent novel-writing career and large horses. That much was written in hot type. But it meant that her old position of deputy editor was now vacant.

Again, tradition dictated that it went to the next in line. That was Maxine. She wasn't only next in line, she was also clearly the most qualified and the best reporter we had. But

Maxine was pregnant. And that clearly wouldn't do. She surely couldn't devote sufficient time to the paper if she had a lovely wee baby to look after. She'd have to take time off for all kinds of reasons. And what about the school run? Maxine wasn't offered the job.

It was, of course, a scandal. It probably wouldn't have happened at a larger paper, where there were unions that actually worked, but the *Speccy*, in some ways so ahead of the curve – not one but *two* female editors when there were no others on the whole island – was also a family-run business subject to its own idiosyncrasies and unacknowledged prejudices.

Maxine left under a cloud, threatening legal action, while the rest of us muttered about insurrection or mass resignation. Of course, when it came to it, we did nothing. We needed our jobs. I'd already started looking for one on a Belfast paper, feeling that I should move on because it was the expected thing, but secretly relieved when it proved that there were none to be had, because I didn't really want to go anywhere. And, of course, with Maxine gone, the deputy-editor position would go to the next in line.

And that was me.

It wasn't quite *Et tu, Brute?* but it wasn't far off. Maxine was kind enough to say I should take it, although through gritted teeth.

A few days later I stepped into the office kitchen for something, and young Mr David followed me in. While making himself a coffee he casually asked if I'd had any thoughts about the vacant deputy-editor position, and I, not wishing to dance too enthusiastically on Maxine's grave, said I hadn't yet given it much consideration.

That turned out to be my job interview.

A few days later it was announced that Paul was to be the new deputy editor. He was a year older, but still junior to me. He had a journalism qualification and he was altogether more grown-up and presentable – whereas I was crushingly shy, still dressed like a punk, had infuriated the Kilcooley Strollers and caused a riot in Newtownards. They would have been mugs to give it to me; I just wasn't ready for it. But it was still supposed to be my job and it hurt to be passed over. This new generation of *Speccy* reporters had become such a tight-knit bunch, and now we were splintered.

The atmosphere wasn't the only thing that was different. Young Mr David was determined to move with the times. For the past eighty years the editorial office had reverberated to the steady clack-clack of manual typewriters. Now these were to be replaced with snazzy new IBM electric models.

When they arrived, sleek and beige, sitting there one morning where our dependable old mongrel mix of Olivettis and Smith Coronas had once ruled, we stared at them like they'd been beamed in from the set of *Star Trek*.

I nervously plugged mine in. *Plugged* it in.

I lifted a sheet of typing paper and tried to work out how to scroll it in, but there was nothing to crank it with. Instead, the IBM *sucked* it in. I stretched out a nervous finger and pressed one of the keys. CLACK! A letter miraculously appeared on the page before me. My muscles had been entirely built from the effort of bashing the old manual typewriters, and now there was my first letter with no effort whatsoever.

From behind, someone shouted, 'Judas!'

Soon we were all typing away, CLACK-CLACK-CLACK-

CLACKCLACK-CLACK-CLACK-CLACK-CLACK, a caco-phony which made it sound like we were working in a war-time munitions factory. The sound was annoying and, increasingly, so was the paper.

It was a bit like working in a goldfish bowl. The same stories came round again and again. The same courts, the same planning appeals, the same speech festivals, just more of the same, and I was starting to feel restless. I was getting blasé about it all – getting in free to gigs, the free records, books, pornographic videos – it had just become the norm. I was ambitious, but not so ambitious that I wanted to leave town. The unpleasantness surrounding the deputy-editor post didn't help.

Maxine and I met up for coffee to discuss our grievances and joked that the paper was so badly run that we could do better ourselves; and then it became less of a joke and we began to discuss setting up something of our own.

We didn't have the finances to set up a newspaper, but what if we launched something smaller? A magazine. A local magazine. We began to get quite excited about the idea. We could not only sell it through local newsagents, we could also do something altogether more revolutionary, we could recruit local people to sell it door to door, thus cutting out the middleman, or at least employing a much slimmer middleman, and in that way we'd keep more of the thousands of pounds that were sure to start rolling in.

The idea started to take on a life of its own. We looked at an office to rent. We approached the Local Enterprise Development Scheme, which was then offering start-up grants to small businesses. I was all set to hand in my notice at the paper when Maxine suddenly got cold feet. She'd been offered some shifts at the BBC and was going to pursue that instead.

I was pissed off. I didn't consider that she might have pulled out because it was a rubbish business idea, or because we had very little funding and no experience of the advertising world, which we would surely need to succeed; instead I concluded that she lacked vision, and that, when I was a press baron relaxing on my sunbed in the south of France, the sunbed being propped up by huge piles of cash, she would still be stuck in Donaghadee, where she lived, chasing fire engines and selling stories for handfuls of change. I was going to be the Robert Maxwell of Bangor and she was going to be no one.[2] Far from being deterred, I was newly determined. I was going to launch something entirely new and original, and it was all going to be mine. I was going to leave the *County Down Spectator* and publish the *County Down Magazine*. Yes, indeed, with startling imagination I called it the *County Down Magazine.* I imagine that my shortly-to-be-former employers were chortling into their coffees when I revealed my amazing plan, handed in my notice, took whatever holidays were owed to me and marched out of the door never to return.[3]

---

2   And I was right. She only ever became Ireland correspondent for Sky, then news editor for Reuters in Asia, then joined the BBC where she was the duty presenter in the early hours of 31 August 1997 when news broke of the fatal car crash of Lady Diana. She was a familiar face to international audiences for many years, when she could have been co-editor of our local magazine.

3   Er ...

9

Press Baron

HERE'S HOW BAD THE FIRST issue of the *County Down Magazine* was. I forgot to put any kind of a photo or illustration on the cover.

It didn't even enter my head that I needed one until the printer expressed his approval and surprise at my bold choice of choosing only to have headlines describing the stories inside instead of a proper cover. I had meant them only to act as a placeholder until I sorted something out, and then forgotten to do it. And by then it was too late to do anything about it, it was heading for the printing press and I was too embarrassed to put the process on hold. I had quit my job and within a matter of weeks was already well on the way to proving what an idiotic move it had been.

I was young, and had convinced myself that it would work, although there was always a nagging feeling. What I didn't know, or quite understand, was *me*. That I got enthusiasms that were never quite fulfilled. Being in a band, managing a band, being a promoter, setting up a record label – yes, did that, less said the better – they all had one thing in common: big dreams that were soon dashed on the shores of reality.

I wasn't a businessman. I wasn't a people person. My ambition to write the Great American Novel was just another one of those dreams, but, because I hadn't yet written anything, it still remained attainable – while simultaneously being unattainable because I hadn't yet written anything. It was the best, and worst, of both worlds. But you couldn't have told me any of this then – I was going to conquer the world, or at least Bangor, and nobody was going to stop me.

Five thousand copies of the *Country Down Magazine* duly arrived with the dullest cover in the history of publishing. They filled our garage. If I hadn't already knelt on my gerbil, it would have been flattened by the magazines or bored to death by the contents.

Inside there were half a dozen feature articles, all written by me. I didn't have the money to pay anyone else. They were all quite insipid – an interview with the mayor and profiles of local celebrities. I'd imagined it would be like a cross between *Punch* and *Private Eye*, funny and investigative, instead of the watered-down version of the *Ulster Tatler*, which was itself a watered-down version of the *Tatler*, which I ended up with.

I'd managed to secure a few small adverts. Two of them came from local banks – I had my business account with one, and the other had my personal account; I cannily played them off against each other, teasing them with the promise of the riches to come so that they'd take space in my first issue.

I placed my own advert in, of course, the *Speccy*, looking for people willing to sell the magazine from door to door and I got exactly what you might expect: applications from teens, layabouts and the obviously demented. After an exhaustive interview process,[1] I whittled down the applicants from twelve to twelve. The training programme consisted of me telling them to try and sell as many magazines as they could. They were, after all, investing in their own futures, though of course they weren't investing anything but their time and availing themselves of an opportunity to humiliate themselves. They were making ten pence per copy sold. Sell ten, therefore, and they'd have a whole pound. It doesn't sound like much now, and it didn't sound like much then, but it was something. Thus inspired, my intrepid band of door-steppers set out. They were bolstered by my dad with his bundle, and by Marie-Louise with hers. I would have helped, but I thought that might send out the wrong message. You didn't see Robert Maxwell[2] going from door to door selling the *Daily Mirror*. It was beneath him, and me. Instead, I would co-ordinate the operation from home and count the cash as it came rolling in.

That first issue sold relatively well. Or well to my relatives. One of the two. The team eventually managed to shift about half of them. It certainly sold well enough for me to begin planning future issues. The main problem was that I burned through the sellers very quickly. The older ones realised it wasn't quite the road to riches or redemption I'd sold them on. The teens just got bored. The demented just disappeared over the horizon with the magazines, like red setters called to heel, and were never seen again. Others, unable to face me, simply left them in a crumpled, damp pile outside their front

---

1   'Yes, you'll do.'
2   If he'd moored his yacht in our marina, he wouldn't have drowned when he fell overboard; he would have floated safely back to dock on a raft of discarded cider bottles.

doors and refused to answer even when I yelled abuse through their letter boxes.

A few actually did do sterling work,[3] but there just weren't enough of them. I began to realise that to get proper returns the magazine would have to scale up. Bangor was too small to sustain thousands of monthly door-to-door sales – for it to work I'd need a magazine that appealed to the whole of Northern Ireland, and then Ireland, and possibly the rest of the UK and the world. That would have meant recruiting hundreds more sellers, the staff to manage them, and advertising reps and journalists and all those cogs that go into running a well-oiled machine. And I wasn't capable of running such a machine. What I had done, once again, was let my enthusiasm run away with me; I liked the *idea* of running a magazine, but not the reality; but this time, instead of confining it to a hobby, or what today you'd call a side hustle, I'd jumped in with armbands on my feet, and now I was drowning, not necessarily in debt, but drowning all the same. The *County Down Magazine* limped along for half a dozen monthly issues and to diminishing returns, earning enough to keep me in Coke and Twix but not in a penthouse apartment. After a year I quietly closed it down, and I'm not sure if anyone noticed. There was no staff to fire, no office to close. It was just me.

Then Mum died.

Cancer.

It seemed like she'd always been sick – she was plagued with stomach problems and with migraines her whole life, so when she took to bed for what turned out to be the last time,

---

3   Future novelist Zane Radcliffe was very good.

I presumed she'd get better as she always did and would soon be up and about again, making cakes. But she lay there quietly reading her books for weeks on end, all the while slowly going downhill.

She was annoyed that I didn't own a suit. I had no idea why she wanted me to own a suit. No idea.

One day she said she was going into hospital. On the way out the door she said she didn't think she'd be coming home. I kind of laughed and told her not to be daft. She had a room in the Ulster. It overlooked a grass embankment where I'd take Patch for a play so she could see him. Mostly she lay there, looking poorly. Then one day she was sitting up in bed, make-up on, hair fixed, smiling and chatty like she hadn't been in months, and I thought, great, she'll be home soon, she can make some more buns. Then Dad went to visit the next day and phoned me from the hospital when I was at Marie-Louise's house to say that Mum had passed away. And then I knew why I needed that suit.

I didn't see her body. It still wasn't my policy. Dad and I came home after the funeral and didn't really know what to do. Our house had gone from five, a dog and several gerbils to two and a dog. Neither of us had ever really had to cook anything. Dad suggested I peel some potatoes. I'd no idea how. It took me ages. I peeled my hand more than I peeled a potato. We may have accidentally indulged in a little cannibalism.

Dad was a bit lost. He decided to go to England by himself to revisit some of his old haunts from when he was training to kill Hitler. He went to Aldershot to see his old barracks, but they'd been knocked down. He didn't seem to enjoy his trip very much.

I was adrift too. I was unemployed, and newly unengaged, as Marie-Louise, her eyes now opened fully to a life beyond Bangor, was embracing the student lifestyle, and other students. I couldn't blame her. I was nothing but a washed-up entrepreneur with no mum who had only a warm bed and a vicious Jack Russell to offer.

I don't know if I was heartbroken at getting dumped. I had that terrible feeling in the pit of the stomach you get when you suspect that someone is betraying you, like a depression in the form of a punch. It's not so much that you're totally in love, it's just the rejection. I had no job, no future, the Great American Novel was further away than ever, and now no girlfriend. For the first time in my life I began to feel like I needed to get out and start again somewhere else.

Marie-Louise announced she was off to America for the summer. Maybe it would be a good idea to go there too. I wasn't intending to stalk her, exactly, for I'd no idea where she was going, but if I'd managed to bump into Derek Larmour in London, then surely there was a chance I could bump into Marie-Louise too. I mean, how big could America be?

* * *

It turns out, quite big.

I wasn't a total lunatic. I didn't just take off without a plan. I wrote to about thirty newspapers looking for work. Then, you could do that. They smiled favourably on the Irish, and for economic purposes I was prepared to be Irish. The *I'm proud to be from the six counties of Northern Ireland that will always be British* approach wasn't going to get me very far in Irish America, even if it was true.

I wrote to *The New York Times*, *The Boston Globe*, the *Los Angeles Times* – you get the picture. As a back-up I surely wouldn't need I also wrote to some smaller papers I randomly plucked out of a directory I found in the library.

Of all the papers I contacted, the only one that wrote back was the *Addison County Independent* of Middlebury, Vermont. They offered me a summer job working as a reporter and free accommodation by way of babysitting the editor-owner's house while he went on vacation. This was without a single phone call or other investigation. I could have been a lunatic. He could have been a lunatic.

The *Addison County Independent* – it kind of reminded me of something. The only thing I knew about Vermont was that my boyhood pal Richard had moved there, but we hadn't been in touch for years. I'd heard that his dad had died from cancer not long after they moved, but beyond that, nothing. But even if I didn't bump into Marie-Louise, I was *bound* to bump into Richard, because Vermont, according to the Carnegie library's *Encyclopaedia Britannica*, was really small.

I flew to America full of excitement and nerves. I'd only ever been to London and Blackpool and the Isle of Man and Ballycastle. I'd certainly never been on a jumbo jet. But I felt like I already knew America – all my references were American: I loved the TV shows, the movies, Woody Allen was my God, *M*A*S*H* and newspaper drama *Lou Grant* were my favourite TV series; it was all bound to be exactly like I saw it on the big and small screens. I was done with Bangor, and I was done with the North. I loved practically nothing about what might be loosely described as Northern Irish culture. The only writer I had any time for was Graham Reid, author of TV's *Billy* plays, starring a very young Kenneth Branagh. Reid had actually taught English at Gransha Boys High School in Bangor but had left to pursue a writing career more or less as I joined the *Speccy*. I'd never met him. Even if I had, I wouldn't have known what to say to him. I have never known what to say to writers.[4]

I didn't love other Northern Irish writers because I wasn't aware there were any. Nor was I aware of any other playwrights or film-makers or poets. I wasn't generally aware of anything beyond punk rock and football. Punk was past its prime and I'd fallen out of love with footie because of my years in the Clandeboye Road garden shed. I was vaguely embarrassed by being Northern Irish. Our Troubles, our troubled sportsmen, our history, our hunger strikes. You couldn't help but carry it all around with you. The way people reacted to the accent. The way they rejected our banknotes. I was going to America. I was starting again. It was the land of opportunity. I told Dad I wasn't coming back. And Patch. I had a farewell party with my mates. I was going to work on a newspaper, I was going to meet a willowy American blonde, and then I was going to write my Great American Novel. Everything was going to work out.

Before I left, I had a letter from Marie-Louise. She was careful not to give away her location. She was playing hard to

---

4   I once saw Bernard MacLaverty, author and screenwriter of *Cal*, and many other great works, eating a hamburger in Jenny Watts pub in Bangor. I just watched him. He seemed to enjoy the burger. Many years later, at an awards ceremony in London, I stood beside him at a urinal and reminded him of this. He looked a little scared.

get. She did give me some advice for arriving in New York. I should stay at the YMCA. It was easy to find. You got the bus in from the airport, then when you exited the Port Authority Bus Terminal you turned left, and the hostel was a hundred yards up.

I stepped off the plane and immediately there was this muggy, oppressive heat; my clothes instantly stuck to me. My only other experience of summer holiday heat had been in Blackpool. This was of a different magnitude. It was hugely uncomfortable. I managed to get on a bus to the Port Authority and then stepped out onto 7th Avenue, ten o'clock at night, and turned left. The smells, the heat, the noise – it was New York, it was the '80s, it was a literal assault on the senses. Also, Marie-Louise had neglected to mention that there was more than one exit from the bus station, so within a few steps I'd turned the wrong way and was soon hopelessly lost. I was petrified of asking anyone for directions because every face seemed to be a black face and I'd never spoken to a single black person before and the only black people I knew were from TV cop shows and they were either violent muggers or jive-talking hipsters. I was exhausted from the flight and instantly dehydrated from the heat and paranoid that I was going to be murdered. I looked about twelve years old, I was sweating buckets, I was bug-eyed and wearing a bright-green Northern Ireland football top my friend Eddie had lent me. I may as well have been wearing a sign on my head that read NAIVE TOURIST, PLEASE MUG.

Eventually I went into a Chinese deli, dripped on their floor and asked for directions. Ten minutes later I saw the neon YMCA sign and stumbled through their doors, and they had a room I could have and I fell onto my bed, and the window was open and all I could hear were the police sirens and the clamour and the traffic and then, when I closed it, yells and shouts from the corridor outside my room – and it was exactly like that scene from *Big* where Tom Hanks finds himself alone in the big city for the first time, except he was much more mature than I was and that was a film and not real life (and also hadn't been made yet). I was terrified. I came from the tough cul-de-sacs of Bangor, and I was woefully unprepared for this. I was starving but didn't dare venture out. I wanted to go home. I wanted my dad. I wanted my *mum*. And Patch. What was I even thinking of, leaving Bangor? I got a rush of blood to the head every time I went to Belfast, and now I was in New York – New York in the '80s, when it was the murder capital of the world – and I didn't know anyone and there was just this wall of sound that would not allow me to sleep, until, of course, I closed my eyes and then I was out like a light and in the morning everything was okay.

* * *

I caught a Greyhound bus to Vermont. Once I left the city, the heat no longer felt so oppressive, or maybe I was starting to acclimatise. I had dreamed about crossing America by Greyhound bus, and there I was, crossing America by Greyhound bus. It was a bit like being on a bus for a very long time. America looked like I expected America to look, but the substance of it was slightly off. Their Mars bars tasted like Milky Ways, and their Milky Ways tasted like Mars bars. In New York I'd found an Irish bar and, already hankering after a taste of home, I ordered Irish stew for lunch. When it arrived it was full of *peppers*. Peppers! I'd never had a pepper in my life. There weren't supposed to be red things in Irish stew. It was *alien*. It was *wrong*. America was the same, but different.

I arrived in Middlebury, and saw that it was exactly like Bangor, except prettier. The Main Street wasn't blocked by security gates and they didn't search you when you went into a store. I queued up at a van where people were ordering sandwiches. I ordered a ham sandwich. The guy asked me what else I wanted in it. I said nothing. What else would you have in a ham sandwich? He seemed perplexed by this. He gave me a ham sandwich. A ham sandwich at home consisted of two pieces of bread, butter and a slither of ham. This ham sandwich contained three thickly sliced pigs and I could barely lift it. Americans were *nuts*.

I found the offices of the *Addison County Independent*. They looked exactly like the offices of the *County Down Spectator*. That was both disappointing and a huge relief. The owner was called Angelo S. Lynn. He was very friendly and showed me around the office. It was a family-owned paper that covered Middlebury itself and several smaller satellite towns. He took me home and I met his wife and kids and dogs. We sat around drinking cold bottles of Rolling Rock and they tasted fabulous. They asked questions about my tough life in Northern Ireland. I mentioned the tanks I had to avoid on the way to work. He and his wife were keen athletes and adventurers. In the winter that meant skiing. In the summer it was road running. They described how they had slept on an icy ledge thousands of feet up the Matterhorn. I described how I had slept under my car after three bottles of cider. They asked me if I wanted cider. I said of course. They gave me cider. It had no alcohol in it. I gave it back and explained that what they'd given me was apple juice and therefore of no use to man or beast.

My working brief couldn't have been simpler. Because I was a foreigner, and unused to how things worked, they didn't want to let me to do pure news stories. They put me on features. Or exactly what we would have done at the *Speccy* with someone on work experience – let them loose on the loonies.

The congressional elections were coming up, so they sent me to interview Morris Earle. Morris told me what he was standing against. He was against Big Agriculture, Big Arms Sales, Big Army, Big Business, Big Church, Big Cities, Big Corporate Takeovers, Big Government, Big Judgements in Lawsuits, Big Labour, Big Medicine, Big Pollution, Big Population, Big Real-Estate Development, Big Transportation and Big White House, but appeared flummoxed when I asked him what he was for. He was standing on a platform of 'Small is Beautiful', so I suppose the clue was in that. While it might have been aesthetically satisfying to discover that Mr Earle was, in fact, a midget, he was an average-sized gentleman of some sixty-nine years, a wonderfully entertaining ex-lawyer who had a snowball's chance in hell of getting elected, and knew it – and, in that regard, was exactly the same as every other fringe politician I'd met at home.

I wandered around the Robert Frost Memorial Park. I went to a county fair. I was asked two questions I will never forget. The first was, do you have TV in Ireland? The second was, when you look up at night in Ireland, can you see the stars? I told them we were so poor you didn't even have to go outside to see them, and they nodded like it might be the truth. The people I met in rural Vermont were less worldly than at home, and, conversely, happier for it.

The paper was indeed a carbon copy of the *Speccy*. The stories were the same, the photos the same, the family idiosyncrasies of the owners the same, the journalists had the same mix of provincial satisfaction and urban ambition. It was a country town and the surroundings were beautiful, and it reminded me so much of what I'd run away from that I was tempted to run home.

In my free time I tried to track down Richard. Eventually, through tireless investigative work only a trained journalist could undertake, I found Richard's mum. She was in the telephone directory. She lived a couple of towns away. She told me Richard had moved to Denver, Colorado. If I was on vacation, she said, I should go visit him. I explained that I wasn't on vacation, that I had a job and they'd told me I could stay as long as I wanted.

Next day I told them I was quitting. The paper was great, the town was great, the surroundings were great, but it was too much like Bangor. I would go to Colorado. That would be entirely different. That was The West. I loved The West. Custer of the West. I would get a job where the buffalo roamed and even if it was only on a small-town paper, that paper would be like that paper in *The Man Who Shot Liberty Valance*. I would create my own legend.

I flew to Denver. Richard met me at the airport. It was late at night. He was as friendly as ever, but also American. There weren't a lot of buffalo roaming around Denver. It was a big modern city. We went straight to a bar and got drunk.

He worked in a German restaurant. He helped with the food preparation but wasn't quite a chef. He lived in a one-bedroom apartment. I slept on the couch. On my first full day there I went to his restaurant, where he'd promised me a free meal. He brought me out a bowl of beef and pineapple soup. I took a spoonful. It was the single worst thing I've ever had in my mouth, and that includes a dentist's fist and the handful of soil my brother shovelled in after he promised me if I closed my eyes and opened my mouth, he'd put a sweet in it. I can still taste that beef and pineapple soup. Forty years and I can still taste it. Later, we went and got drunk, but everything still tasted of beef and pineapple. If that soup was popular in Germany, it explained why they were such sour krauts.[5]

I wrote a few letters to local newspapers offering my services. Nobody got back to me. I didn't press it. I was having too good a time getting drunk and hanging around in bars that were all old wood and bison heads and felt like they hadn't changed since cowboys hung out there, though they were probably just put together by interior designers.

I would get drunk and call home to talk to Dad and tell him what a great time I was having and avoid his questions about me getting a job. I'd earned a reasonable amount of money in Middlebury, but I was fast burning through it, what with having to get drunk every night and not working. We went up into the Rockies. I was used to the Mournes. The Rockies were mountains. The Mournes were hills. We went to the open-air amphitheatre at Red Rocks and saw 10,000 Maniacs, the band. We got drunk. We went to parties. We got

5   Sorry.

drunk. Richard worked most days. I went to the movies a lot. I loved the trailers as much as the movies. These were for films no one across the pond had ever heard of. I saw *Top Gun* and came out thinking maybe I'd be better off joining the navy and becoming a fighter pilot. Then we got drunk and I phoned home and told Dad I loved it there, and two days later I got a flight home because I didn't love it that much and because Richard's mum had been right, I was on vacation, and could no more live in Colorado or Middlebury than I could have lived in London; home was calling me.

I missed my dad. I missed Patch. I missed my friends. I missed where I was from. I could see that America was better in so many ways, but it wasn't home. I arrived back in Bangor to discover that my dad had sold our house and moved.

* * *

Eventually, through tireless investigative ...

Dad might have told me he was moving, but I was probably drunk. I don't think he was deliberately trying to lose me. He'd believed me when I said I was never, ever coming home, when he should have known that I had a history of not seeing things through. He'd gone from a fairly large bungalow to a small terrace house in Fairfield Park, which was close to Ward Park. I had the back bedroom and he had the front. There was also a small box room I could use as a study to write the Great American Novel. I'd now done all the research and would get started on it any day soon.

My friends didn't seem unduly surprised to see me. The only thing I'd brought home was a cassette tape of an exciting new American rap band called NWA. They had songs like 'Fuck the Police'. I played it for them and waited for their enthusiastic reaction. They told me to turn that crap off and I gave up plans to become a rapper.

Marie-Louise was already home and miserable. She'd fallen in love with the son of a Supreme Court judge, who'd dumped her at the end of her stay. It was hard to be sympathetic. She was leaving soon for London. She had a job. She was going to be an accountant. I was still unemployed.

In the move Dad had dumped a lot of my old things – my books and comics, my history. There was no garage, so nowhere to store anything. No driveway to park a car. It felt like we had gone down in the world.

I understood him downsizing. He didn't like being in the bungalow by himself. Probably there was too much of Mum in there. He never said though, and I never asked. I never asked how he felt about Mum dying. How he was coping. He never asked me about losing my mum. It's too much of a generalisation to say men don't talk about these things. But Bateman men don't. Or didn't. I think he was a bit lost, and lonely. So was I.

One day Dad was really thirsty. No matter what he drank, his thirst couldn't be slaked. He even went out and bought a bottle of my beloved cider, but it didn't help. It turned out he had become diabetic, so he had to sort out his diet. Then it became clear that being diabetic was just a symptom of something else, that his kidneys were failing. Cancer. He went into hospital and had one of those kidneys out and began radiotherapy. He lost a lot of weight, but they'd caught it just in time. He came out of hospital, went back to work for a brief spell but then took early retirement. He was still only in his early sixties.

We rubbed along okay together. Neither of us were big talkers. There is a comfort which comes with just having someone in the house; there doesn't always have to be engagement. Sometimes it seemed like we spoke to Patch more, or through him. Dad cooked most of the time. He placed his losing bets and I plugged away at my writing: short stories, radio plays, even scripts for comics – anything but what I knew I should be doing: the Great American Novel. Most of everything remained unfinished. Those few I sent off were returned, generally without comment.

I applied for jobs but didn't get anywhere until I spotted one at a charity in Belfast called Bryson House. It was an umbrella organisation for various small charities, and they needed an editor for their quarterly newsletter. I got the job. I'm not sure if anyone else applied. It was a government-supported post for the long-term unemployed. It had a minimum wage not much above the dole. I had to write the entire newsletter by myself, edit it and design it. There were exactly four tabloid pages in the newsletter and there was a tough publishing schedule of once every three months. To say that it was easy is an understatement. I still managed to be late with it. But at least it got me back to the routine of working and gave me my first experience of commuting.

It was strange, getting the train every morning and then home every night, seeing the hassled and harried faces. Belfast was only ten miles up the road, but the people there were different.

One morning I came into work very confused. I shared an office with a graphic designer, Susan. We got on great. She'd spent eight months designing a new logo for Bryson

House, which was housed in an old linen mill on Bedford Street. The chosen logo was the small blue flax flower used to make linen. It already existed in nature, but Susan spent the best part of a year drawing an improved version of it. She was more underemployed than I was. We mostly spent our time laughing at the sad cases reduced to working in Bryson House without realising that we were two of them. Every one of us had been chronically unemployed, and there was probably a reason for that. Susan asked why I was confused that morning, and I explained that every second person I'd passed on the way down Bedford Street had a dirty black mark on their faces. I thought that it might some kind of a sign so that aliens from *Invasion of the Body Snatchers* could recognise each other. She said no, it was the mark that priests daubed on worshippers' foreheads as part of their Ash Wednesday service, and I said what the fuck are you talking about, that's bonkers, but she didn't seem to think so. Catholics are weird. At least Protestants don't have any nutty traditions like that.

Some mornings it was a grind getting out of bed and running for the train. I usually left it very late. One morning I pulled on the first pair of socks I could find in the dark and was on the train before I realised I was wearing an old pair of my brother's Union Jack socks. Not ideal for central Belfast, but what was the worst that could happen?

When I got into work my boss called me in and said I had to go to a community centre in Andersonstown to cover the launch of a new European Community initiative to help its poverty-stricken tenants. Andersonstown was, and is, a staunchly republican area, and this was the height of the

Troubles in the '80s. If anyone had spotted my Union Jack socks, I would have been lynched.[6]

They all must have thought I was very weird refusing to take my hands out of my pockets all day. In reality I was forcing the bottoms of my slightly too-short trousers down over my shoes so that no hint of my socks would be visible. A saner person might just have taken the socks off, but it didn't occur to me. Later that week I published the latest Bryson House newsletter with the huge headline based on the EC plan to provide food parcels on the estate: 'Let Them Eat Cake'. I thought it was smart political commentary, but it was also extremely patronising, although that didn't occur to me then. It went to print before anyone noticed.

On a day out drinking in Bangor I bumped into my ex-workmate Chris, who had risen to become deputy editor of the *Speccy*. Joy had left to become a full-time author, and my old nemesis Paul was now the editor. Chris asked if I'd ever thought about going back. I said there was zero chance of that. I'd done my time there, and anyway, Paul and I had history. Chris said Paul would love to have you back, you should call in and see him. I said he'd stabbed me in the back. Anyway, I was writing a novel.

Next day, in the biggest shock since James Galway quit the 39th Old Boys Flute Band to go solo, I walked back into the *Speccy* and then back out with a job.

Truth was, I missed the bloody place. I missed having a platform. There is probably nothing worse than a shy person with a big ego, but that was me. I wanted people to come up

---

6   Metaphorically speaking. In reality I would have been kneecapped, or tarred and feathered.

to me and say they liked what I wrote, or even hated what I wrote – but I wanted them to come up, because I was too retiring to go up to them.

Local papers were dying off everywhere, but even though the *Speccy*'s circulation was also declining, it was still essential reading. Every week they sold nearly 16,000 copies. Every couple of years someone launched a free paper in the town, because free papers were the future, but they only ever lasted a matter of months. It was still pre-internet, pre-eBay – so if you wanted your local news, if you wanted to announce the death of a loved one, if you wanted to sell a lawnmower, if you wanted to be misinformed about how your favourite football team had performed, the *Speccy* was still the only place to go. It had a market penetration no daily paper could match, no radio station's listening figures could come close to. In the time I was away from it I had floundered and, despite that lingering sense of betrayal, I had only a few qualms about rejoining. About going home.

I was back in the ~~big~~ small time.

From the start, I had my own column. No particular brief to it, just the freedom to ramble on. I was back to covering the courts. Back to answering the phone to deranged women wanting a reporter to come out to their house because a cat had killed a bird. In a slower news week, we might have sent one. There was another new generation of reporters – Colette, Patricia, Fiona, Karen, Ruth; all quickly became good friends.

I also began to grow more comfortable in my new Fairfield Park surroundings. My friends Phil and Pauline moved in three doors up; my best friend Dave, Pauline's brother, moved in with them, and then he bought a house two doors up from them. My other friends, Gerry and Dawn, moved in across the road from Dave. You'd open the door and it would be like a scene from *Help!* with us all going to work at the same time.

I was older but not that much more responsible. At work I still enjoyed poking gentle fun at the town I loved so well. There was a shop on High Street called S&M Furniture. It sold mostly wicker chairs. They seemed not to be aware of the sexual connotations of the S&M moniker. I speculated in my column that there were bargains to be had there, but you'd probably have to submit to being tied to a chair and beaten with a bamboo stick before being offered them. The owners didn't seem to find this funny, and came into the office kicking up a stink and threatening to withdraw their advertising.

Still, lesson learned.

When summer rolled round again, Dave and I took off on holiday to America. I started writing a travel report when I got back. You always need a good intro to hook the readers in. Out of nowhere, or the dark recesses of my mind where I keep a huge list of grievances, I wrote that I was just back from America where I was buying guns for the Boys Brigade. That they intended to raise further funds by holding paramilitary coffee mornings, with an Armalite in one hand and a packet of Jaffa Cakes in the other. It was an adaptation of Danny Morrison's infamous phrase, first uttered at a Sinn Féin Ard-Fheis in 1981, that his party would fight the coming elections with 'an Armalite in one hand and a ballot box in the other'.

I thought it was an original way to open a travel report. I thought it would get a laugh. Paul was off on holiday that week, with Chris standing in, but he didn't see anything wrong with it and put it in the paper. We published as usual on a

Thursday afternoon then went to the pub, not suspecting for one moment what was to come.

We had forgotten one crucial thing.

Presbyterians have no sense of humour.

When we rolled into work the next morning, nursing hangovers and expecting a relaxing half-day, we found an ashen-faced Mr David, a stressed-out office staff and a telephone switchboard lit up like a Belisha beacon.[7]

Bangor boasted fourteen different companies of the Boys Brigade, and it seemed like every single member of every single one of them, their parents and their distant cousins, was calling to complain about the article. About the danger I'd put them all in by calling them paramilitaries and suggesting that they might be raising money to buy weapons. Not only members, and officials, and parents, and relatives, but also lawyers threatening legal action. And they weren't just on the phone. Parents descended on the office, shaking their fists in my general direction and looking for blood, although in a strictly non-paramilitary fashion.

Overnight the copious notes the different BB companies contributed every week to the paper, usually taking up an entire broadsheet page, disappeared, never to return. We lost hundreds of sales as a result. Shops and small companies withdrew their advertising. It wasn't just confined to Bangor either. My newly married brother, now living in Newtownards, was in church with the Duchess that first Sunday morning after the paper came out, and they both squirmed in their pews as I was denounced from the pulpit for my scurrilous comments.

---

7   Seymour Cocks would have been impressed.

The paper was used to dealing with legal threats. Every newspaper is. Usually, they amount to nothing. When push comes to shove, solicitors usually back down. But this time they were serious. The local BB companies took their complaints to their HQ in Belfast, and they employed serious lawyers to sue the paper for libel.

The problem is that once you start down the libel route, it gets very expensive, very quickly, and on both sides. Then it depends who has the deeper pockets and who can best hold their nerve. Even though my words might have been in dubious taste, there was nothing libellous about them – it was satire, and the BB did have a verifiable paramilitary past, so they wouldn't have won a court case in a thousand years. But for every day we continued to fight their claims, and barristers batted legal threats back and forth, the costs continued to grow.

Paul returned from holiday and attempted to put the fires out with diplomacy and common sense, but the BB wouldn't listen. Eventually the paper caved in. No fewer than three separate apologies were printed in the next edition. The letters page was also filled with angry complaints from offended parents and the outraged BB companies.

I was mortified by the capitulation, but it was out of my hands. At least it didn't look like I was apologising personally, and I never did. And the paper didn't fire me. These snowflake days, they probably would have.

Despite our rolling over, the heat didn't stop. I masterminded something of a rearguard action by recruiting friends to write in and protest about the BB's humourlessness; several letters even came in unprompted. But it didn't help. I was a marked man. If the prepubescent Kilcooley Strollers hadn't quite got to me, the much-better-drilled BB surely would. The Strollers were at least confined to Kilcooley, but the BB was everywhere, sure and steadfast in its determination to find me, cover me in black boot polish and drag me half-naked around the town.

I needed to get out of Dodge and lie low, somewhere they couldn't find me, somewhere they wouldn't even think to look – and Paul had the solution.

He sent me to Uganda.

Literally, to Uganda.

I became the *County Down Spectator*'s first foreign correspondent.

10

The Triangle

HE WAS THREE-AND-A-HALF YEARS OLD. His father had brought him on the back of a bike to the clinic on the steps of the battered old church at Kiwoko. He had large, ugly burns on his chest and legs. Boiling water had been accidentally spilt on him. Gudrun, the German nurse, said, 'Hold his leg, tight.' I took hold of it. His father held his other leg and right arm. Rosie, a nurse with the visiting Northern Irish work party, held his other arm.

At home they would have knocked him out to carry out the cleaning of the wound. Here they could only give him a Valium. Gudrun lifted a pair of scissors and began cutting away the burned skin. We gripped his limbs tightly as he flexed against us, screaming in agony; his father whispering reassuringly in his ear. He screamed on and on.

When it was over, and the blood was running down over the burns, they began applying antiseptic cream. The tube was nearly squeezed dry.

'What're we going to do when the tube is finished?' Rosie asked, for it was the last of them.

***

As a means of avoiding the fall-out from the BB debacle it might be considered an extreme overreaction to go all the way to the Luwero Triangle, in the heart of the Ugandan bush, but it was such an unlikely and unique opportunity for a local weekly newspaper to send someone there that it was impossible to say no.

Or, it was very possible to say no, and several of my fellow reporters did; but I said yes without thinking about it, without thinking that if covering a story outside of the council boundary seemed like an extraordinary adventure, Uganda was going to be fucking terrifying. I had freaked out during the 1976 earwig invasion of our bungalow in Ballymacormick Avenue; how much worse was Africa going to be when I knew or suspected or imagined it to be 90 per cent insect?

My assignment was to report on the activities of a Bangor-based charity called Love Uganda. I was to unmask their obscene jungle cult which ... well, no, actually, as they were paying for it my job was to give a glowing report of the sterling work they were doing bringing healthcare and Christ to the Third World. And actually, they weren't really bringing Christ because he was already there, and mostly He was all that they had, besides many bananas and kids with extended stomachs.

They really had a lot of bananas. It was the basis of their diet the way potatoes were and are for us. And they had a lot of extended stomachs because the kids kept getting parasitic infections because they had no sanitation, and they had no sanitation because ... well, because that's Africa. We had plenty of extended stomachs at home, due to our habit of stuffing our fucking faces.

I rolled up to the airport looking like I was going to a punk gig when I should at least have been wearing a safari suit and a pith helmet. That was because my general knowledge of Africa then was entirely based on TV's *Daktari*, which featured Clarence the cross-eyed lion, and William Boot's journalistic adventures in Ishmaelia in *Scoop*.

To be fair, I was a *little* acquainted with Uganda. It had featured in the news for several years because of the psychotic ravages of President Idi Amin, the subsequent famous raid on Entebbe to rescue Israeli hostages, and the recently concluded civil war, which had left a quarter of a million people dead. They didn't all die on the battlefield. Most died as a result of murder, rape and torture. The Luwero Triangle had been one of the worst-affected areas, so of course that's where I was going. I *should* have been fucking terrified. And if all that wasn't bad enough, I was going with *Christians*.

On the plus side, they weren't Presbyterians and had no obvious affiliations to the BB. But they were potentially something worse. They were happy-clappy Born-Again do-gooders prone to speaking in tongues. Throughout the trip they referred to me as 'the heathen'.

There were half a dozen of us – nurses and general volunteers, all but me Church-connected – going out to stay with Dr Ian Clarke, a Bangor GP who'd given up his cosy life here to go and live and work in the bush. He'd been there with his wife, Roberta, and two children for just over eight months by the time I joined them. When they picked us up at the airport, they were anxious for news from home. I told them The Co-ordinates had split up.

Outside the airport we were stopped at a checkpoint by

soldiers. We were well used to this at home, but these ones were all about thirteen years old and carrying Kalashnikovs. They searched everything we had, and then wanted to know what we were going to bribe them with. Ian offered to give them a Bible. That didn't go down well. They finally settled for a bottle of Roberta's Johnson's baby powder. They weren't going to get rich, but their skin was going to be very soft.

We swung into Mulago Hospital, the main hospital in Kampala, for Ian to pick up medical supplies. Then to a private house where his doctor friend lived. It had the last plumbed toilet I'd see for a while. A guard with an Uzi watched over us.

The roads surrounding Kampala were pretty good, but as we headed for Luwero, they became more than 50 per cent pothole. Ian said there was an expression in Uganda: 'If you drive in a straight line you must be drunk.'

Many bone-shaking miles later we rolled into Kabubu, a cluster of houses with corrugated roofs. Inside, papyrus walls divided the boys' quarters from the girls'. I met Gudrun, who could talk nonsense in two languages and had a pet monkey everyone hated called Bobby. There were half a dozen Americans already there. They were more upfront about their religion than my other travelling companions. They indulged in a lot of spontaneous praisin' of the Lord. There was no electricity. Oil lamps and candles. We had a guard posted outside our dorm. He was more than seventy, partially blind, and armed with a bow and arrow. This was not reassuring. Theoretically there was nothing to worry about, because Uganda was at peace again, but the pyramid of skulls at a crossroads on the way there and the burned-out tank were a gentle reminder of how things had been in the very recent past and could quickly be again.

Ian and his family lived in a small bungalow close by. They had electricity from a small generator and Ian conducted a morning surgery on the bungalow steps. On the first morning a middle-aged man turned up with blood streaming out of his head. He'd had a falling out with his girlfriend and she had whacked him with a machete. He'd wandered around the bush all night before turning up at Ian's. Luckily, he hadn't indulged in the local tradition of packing a wound with cow dung. It does stop the bleeding, but also kills you. I helpfully swatted away flies as Ian stitched him up. I am not without talents.

It was then also the height of the Aids epidemic. At home a doctor might not even have seen a single Aids sufferer; there they saw thirty in a morning. It was known locally as Slim, because of the rapid weight loss. Overweight women were particularly popular with men because they clearly couldn't have Aids. It didn't help when rumours circulated that you could catch Slim from eating fish from the Nile river. The theory was that Aids victims got dumped in the river, the fish ate their bodies, and then passed the disease on when caught and consumed. Fish sales fell off the scales.[1]

It was all eye-opening and overwhelming, and I was hugely impressed by the work of Ian and his team, by the enthusiasm and commitment of the volunteers, and the Christian charity they were showing – even if that was all based on a load of superstitious mumbo-jumbo. It certainly put our Troubles into perspective. They'd experienced more violence in one day than we'd then endured in twenty-five years of our nonsense. Poverty in Northern Ireland was not being able to afford a

---

1   Sorry. It's like an illness.

Sky satellite dish. The health care, the disease, the Aids – I flew back determined to do something to help. Not just the articles I would write, but something bigger.

I had no practical skills to offer, but there was my journalism. To this end I decided to collect the best of my columns in the *Speccy*, publish them in a book and donate all the profits to Love Uganda. It would be a good thing. I might also get some kind of an award for raising awareness. I might be considered for sainthood. Saint Colin of Ballyholme. Saint Colin of the Wellington Boot. My main priority was the little children, not self-aggrandisement, obviously.

And I did it.

I published it.

I called it *Bar Stool Boy*. Susan from Bryson House designed the cover. The *Speccy* printed it. We had a launch party. We all got very drunk.

Everyone agreed I was a grand fellow. The book was released into the wild.

And, of course, it *lost* money.

Family bought it, friends bought it, but those dozen copies weren't enough to cover the thousands owed for the printing. I was almost literally taking food out of the mouths of the little African children.

I couldn't even do something good for charity without fucking it up. To my long list of failures, I could add Failed Saint.

* * *

Dad started to lose weight again. He was sleeping a lot, often in the armchair in front of the telly. He had medicine from the doctor. But we never sat down and discussed how he was or exactly what it was for. He never complained, never seemed in obvious distress. He just went slowly downhill. He began to stay in bed. I should have recognised the signs from Mum's illness, but I was too busy going out to work, too intent on having a good time when I went out with my mates. One day he asked me to call the doctor and she arrived with some extra medicine and went upstairs to see him. When she came back down, she said, 'You do know he's dying?' in a kind of off-hand way that shocked me.

I don't know how much pain he was in. I don't remember there being any morphine or drips or any suggestion that he go into hospital, yet it was also now clear that he was indeed dying.

I'd been alone with him for a few days when my brother came over to give me a few hours off. I went with Dave and another friend, Jill, to the pictures. We saw *Rain Man* with Dustin Hoffman and Tom Cruise. It was hard to concentrate. My brother went home. I said goodnight to Dad and went to bed.

A few hours later I heard him shouting. He'd had a nightmare, but the only coherent thing he could say was, 'Tumbling into the darkness.'

He needed to pee, but no longer had the strength to get to the bathroom. I got him up and he leaned on my shoulder, with my arm around him, but he was perilously weak. I held him up as he peed. Then he fell forward onto the cistern and then back, and the weight of him brought us both down until I was lying on the floor with my naked dad on top of me and I could hardly shift him. He was, almost literally, a dead weight. When I did get out from under him, I couldn't get him up again, and ended up dragging him back to bed and pulling him into it after me and then getting out the other side and throwing the quilt back over him. I retreated to my bedroom. I was terrified, but not as terrified as my dad. Maybe things would be better in the morning.

They weren't.

I called the doctor and said, I think my dad needs to go into hospital. She sent an ambulance. I followed it over to Ards Hospital. Dad was taken into a private room and the doctors went in to see him. My brother arrived. A nurse took us into a small waiting room. There was a man in a wheelchair already in there who kept nodding his head. After a while the nurse came in and said she was sorry to tell us that our dad had passed away. It was no more than an hour after they'd brought him in.

My brother and I hugged.

The man in the wheelchair yelled, 'Why don't you give him a kiss, you bastard?'

The nurse apologised and wheeled him away.

Dad was gone. Dad, who'd fought Hitler, stolen broken paving stones, rejected advances from men in bushes, and made me. So many questions I hadn't asked and never would.

David went in to see him, lying there. I was maintaining my strict no-bodies rule.

I drove home. I phoned Uncle Andrew, one of the twins who'd helped build the US cavalry fort with my dad on Christmas Eve back in Wellington, and probably my dad's closest friend. I started to tell him that Dad had died, but I couldn't speak. He understood and came round.

After a while Pauline called over, already wearing black, and gave me a hug. Her brother Dave came home from work. We started drinking. What else was there to do? There weren't any visits from my dad's relatives because there weren't any that he still spoke to. There was no raucous Irish wake, no anything really. Mum and Dad had maintained only a tiny circle of friends, and after Dad went I didn't really see any of them again. I was twenty-eight years old, too old to be considered an orphan in anyone's eyes but my own.

Dave and I got very drunk. It was too weird to have our gang round to mine, with the detritus of our interrupted lives still everywhere – the dishes Dad would never use again, the dog's hairs he would never have to brush off the sofa – so we drank across the road in his house. But I kept disappearing off home to play records, loud, and Dave kept coming over to bring me back so that I wouldn't be alone. But I was alone, of course I was.

The next day my brother and I registered the death at the council offices and then went to a funeral home on Hamilton Road. We were shown into a waiting room where a young undertaker joined us. She looked about eighteen years old. She might have been on a Job Training Scheme. She was appropriately dressed in dark clothes, but her skin was very white. Too white. It suited her occupation, but it was still unsettling. She spoke very quietly, very respectfully. We discussed the various arrangements. Then she said, 'I'll just book the cremation,' and lifted the phone and dialled. When it was answered she said, 'Hello, good morning, I'd like to book a cremation for Wednesday morning, please.' She listened for a moment, then nodded, and said, 'I'm sorry, I must have a wrong number.'

David and I nearly wet ourselves. It was awful for her, but also the best thing that could have happened for us.

From five to four to three to two to just me and an angry Jack Russell. Six years, *Three Funerals and a Wedding*. An empty house. Even if you're not the world's best communicators, it's often enough just to have another presence in the house to take comfort from it. With Dad gone, it was all eerily quiet.

* * *

The Speccy had long since shifted from electric typewriters and we were now using new-fangled Amstrad word processors. I would often bring one of them home to make false starts on the Great American Novel. Anyone passing by might have seen the green glow from the computer screen as I typed away at all hours of the day and night; except nobody did pass by because Fairfield Park was a dead end, literally and metaphorically.

Chris left the paper to join the BBC, and this time the right of succession was honoured. I became deputy editor. It meant an extra ten pounds a week. I invested it in Harp and Pedigree Chum. There wasn't really any extra responsibility with the job, save that when Paul was on holiday, I was in charge of editing the paper.

At weekends, and indeed during the week, our Fairfield homes would become drinking dens, and we would migrate between them. It was a game of Russian roulette for the neighbours over who would get the music blasting until all hours. They were generally very good. Or they were cowed into silence.

I had Bert next door. He lived with his sister. They were both in their sixties, which seemed incredibly old back then.

I wouldn't say he was simple, but the elevator didn't go quite the whole way to the top. He had a terrible stutter. We knew him as Bbbbbert. You couldn't say that these days, and he couldn't say it then.

Bbbbbert worked as a security guard at a building site. He rode a motorbike with an L-plate that stayed attached to it for years. When I returned to work at the *Speccy*, I dropped off a free copy of the paper through his door on a Thursday afternoon, just as a nice neighbourly gesture. I did it for a few weeks and then forgot about it. Then Bbbbbert came into the office and complained to young Mr David that I'd stopped leaving him his free paper.

Bbbbbert's life wasn't easy, mostly because of the music he had to endure in the wee small hours. The walls were paper thin. Nobody needs to hear The Clash blasted out at that time, apart from me. I kept promising to mend my ways but never did. Relations eventually got so bad that it was easier to get an intermediary, so Bbbbbbbert got the police to call and ask me to turn it down. When they said they couldn't keep doing that, the council got involved and sent someone out to measure the sound levels. I toed the line for a few weeks, and then resumed normal service.

Bbbbbbbbbbbbbert wasn't the only neighbour upset by our partying. One who was only ever known as Pig in a Wig was constantly on at us. There was one set of neighbours, situated between Phil's and Dave's who had a particularly bad time of it: the Andersons. They got it from both sides. Mr and Mrs Anderson were a big, friendly couple who never, ever complained. Everyone should have neighbours like the Andersons.

Once the police came to my house and found me lying drunk under my car. I had no idea what I was doing there apart from preparing it for the MOT. They were going to cart me away until Phil came and rescued me. I didn't have a drinking problem. I mean, I *did* have a drinking problem, but so did everyone; it was what we did. We partied. We listened to music. We didn't do drugs – though if they'd been generally available, we might have. A couple of our friends smoked 'the weed', but most of us never got into it. Cider was our drug of choice, and then we grew up and Harp became our preferred opiate. But we could be tempted. Once at the Matinee, an after-hours drinking club by Bangor Train Station, someone offered Dave and I speed, and we were keen to try it. We bought a *wrap*, took it outside to snort, opened the silver paper, and the wind blew it all away. That was the sum total of our dealings with the drugs business.

When we weren't partying in Fairfield, we were out at the Windsor Bar on the seafront. Most of our friends were coupled up by this stage, so it was often just me and Dave heading out, usually on a Thursday night and a Friday night, oh, and on a Saturday night. We drank downstairs, then moved up to their middle bar, and from there across to their disco. It was like a one-stop shop for rejection.

The owner, Paul Donegan, knew me from the *Speccy*, and he always let us in for nothing, which was great, though he knew he'd get it back in spades. The resident DJ was Jon Anthony, who, like Richard Morrow, had flirted with celebrity in the '60s and '70s but now found himself peddling a schtick long past its sell-by date. Records were 'rations of passion'. Like Terri Hooley, he only had one eye. It was very fashionable.

There's a famous photograph of Thin Lizzy when they played in Bangor in their early days. They're walking along outside the Royal Hotel, next door to the Windsor, and scholars of their history have long pondered over the one member of the band they've been unable to identify, for the simple reason that Jon Anthony was never a member of the band, it just makes him look like he was. Jon later died after slipping on ice and cracking his head. Irony would have had it that it was dry ice, but no.

For many years, Paul Donegan's dad would patrol the dance floor like a 1940s priest making sure that the rations of passion didn't actually translate into true passion, angrily parting couples who got too close. There wasn't much danger of Dave and I falling under his watchful eye. We were hopeless.

Dave had played guitar in a local band, Carpenter Joe, who had enjoyed a modicum of success despite the disadvantage of not being managed by me. With his pop-star pedigree and my rock'n'roll journo persona we should have been laughing, but our strike rate was atrocious. We went on endless tours of the Windsor and other bars. We called these our *touralouras*, and they were remarkable for the fact that we were in perpetual motion – like sharks, never stopping long enough to engage with any girls, even if they'd been that way inclined. We were crap sharks.

Once, downstairs in the Windsor, enduring another fruitless night, we confided our frustrations in Ken, a hairdresser who always seemed to have a different girl on his arm. Ken sagely pointed out that we were naively waiting for the girls to notice us, to approach us. That's never going to happen, he said, you have to make the first move. Watch me, he said. Three young, attractive women were just entering the bar. Ken gave us a wink and turned to these complete strangers with all his charm and smile and bravado and said, 'Hiya girls,' and they said, as one, 'Fuck off,' and brushed on past him.

It seemed that even for those who were good at it, getting a girl wasn't always easy.

On those extremely rare nights when I did meet someone, it didn't always end well. I managed to persuade one girl to come back to Fairfield. She thought Patch was lovely. I told her he wasn't that lovely. She said dogs loved her and bent to give him a kiss. Patch bit her on the lip. There was no ration of passion that night.

Dave and I usually ended up walking home together – or, indeed, staggering. Frequently we'd stop at the chip shop at the top of High Street to try and repair some of the damage, particularly if there was work the next day. Invariably, as we walked, Dave would drunkenly drop his fish and, in trying to pick it up, would spill his chips, and all done with smooth, balletic poise.

We always laughed a lot. Our theme tune as we walked was a modified version of The Temptations' 'My Girl', which we called 'What Girl?' Then it would be into his house to cook yet more food. Our speciality was fish-finger sandwiches, with the fish fingers burned on one side and frozen on the other.

Dave and I never had an argument, never a cross word. Best man at each other's weddings, eventually. Well, we had one argument, on the way home from the Windsor. Neither of us can remember what it was about, but it was something trivial. We were walking back down Fairfield Park; our disagreement wasn't so serious that I wasn't still going in for fish-finger sandwiches. But as we approached his house Dave suddenly took off ahead of me. He reached his front door just as I turned in at his gate. He put his key in the door, but then stood back for a moment and turned his face upwards, before shouting at the top of his voice, 'Mrs Anderson is a big fat bitch!' and then he went on in and shut the door behind him, leaving me stranded halfway down his path as Mrs Anderson appeared at the window to find out who was doing the shouting, and our eyes locked.

11

The Gilded Spires

I HAD NO OBVIOUS REACTION to the death of my father. Or my mother. Or my auntie. Or the gerbil I had knelt upon. This was stoicism or, more likely, denial. But it came out in different ways, and not until at least six months after Dad had gone. I burst into tears at inexplicable moments. A series of panic attacks led me to spend several nights sleeping on my brother's couch in case I suffered a stroke during the night. Odd to think of anyone going to Newtownards for comfort, it being one of the world's largest open prisons. Then there was the Gransha Stores Incident, which people in the *Speccy* still talk about.

Gransha Stores was the corner shop. It was owned by a middle-aged couple – he a bit stand-offish, tall with glasses, and she a bottle-blonde but friendly enough; they also employed a constantly rotating rota of schoolgirls to work the till. Since I'd moved to Fairfield, I'd probably been in their shop every single day, sometimes two or three times a day. It was a convenience store. It was very convenient. They knew my face very well and they knew that I worked for the *Speccy*.

One Sunday I called in to buy a loaf of bread. I didn't open it until the next day when I popped home for lunch and went to make a sandwich, only to discover that it was all blue-moulded inside.

I wandered back down to the shop and the woman owner was behind the counter. I said to her that I'd bought a loaf yesterday but look, it's all blue-moulded; would she mind if I swapped it for a fresh one? She asked for the receipt. I said I didn't have the receipt and repeated that I'd only bought it the day before. She said she couldn't change it without a receipt. I kind of laughed and said, ach, come on, you know me, I'm in here every day, I'm not trying to rip you off, you sold me a blue loaf, can I not just change it? She said not without a receipt. *Oh, for fuck sake.* It's only a loaf. She told me not to swear. I said, well, what do you expect, I'm in here every day and you won't even change a poisonous loaf you just sold me. And she said not without a receipt. At that point I may have lost it. Her husband, alerted to the growing row, entered from the back. I explained the situation to him. He said I'd need a receipt. I said I'm in here every fucking day, this is ridiculous. He said I'd need a receipt. I threw the loaf at him. As he ducked, I grabbed another and made for the door. The woman cut me off, so I veered right, and the husband began to chase me around the shop. It was like a scene from the Keystone Cops. Eventually, with another flurry of fucks, I threw the second loaf at them and stormed out.

The next day, June, one of the *Speccy*'s advertising reps, called in to discuss their regular advert and had to endure a ten-minute lecture from the shocked owners. They told her they'd never heard such language in their whole lives. June returned to the office ashen-faced and with another account lost. I was barred from the shop for life, making it a rather inconvenient convenience store.

There was definitely something off with me. Working on a newspaper means that you routinely have to suffer fools gladly, but I was slowly becoming less inclined to do so. I didn't even have time for King Om.

There are weird, memorable characters in every town, and inevitably they find their way to the local paper, because a love of publicity seems to go hand in hand with their eccentricities; they're usually very self-aware.

When King Om came into the paper, we threw ourselves under our desks; it was a game of non-musical chairs and the last journo standing had to deal with him. Usually I didn't mind, but my patience was beginning to wear thin. He would talk and talk and talk. It became increasingly like that scene in *Airplane!* where the hero is explaining his troubles to the little old lady sitting beside him, and by the time he's finished she's hung herself.

The thing about King Om was that he always started out quite sensibly. There was always the kernel of a true story, but inevitably it quickly spiralled into another dimension. He claimed that he was Julia Roberts' first boyfriend. Now, that might sound ridiculous, but he had lived in California, he spoke with a slight American twang and the dates kind of fitted. The problem was that the whole of America was also living in America then, so he had competition. He had apparently moved in quasi-celebrity circles, so perhaps that reduced the odds. When he told me about Julia, she was just then experiencing her first rush of global success with *Pretty Woman*, but he said they'd been together before splitting up when she took off to New York to follow her acting dream.

Broken-hearted, he returned to live in Bangor and painted a series of ninety-nine paintings in tribute to his lost love.

Yes, ninety-nine.

King Om didn't do things by half.

Another time he told me he was making a TV documentary about his life and work. He was an artist, a surrealist who in the 1960s had been described as Northern Ireland's answer to Andy Warhol. King Om's real name was Cecil McCartney. It is fairly safe to assume that at some point in his life some mind-altering drugs were taken, or not enough prescription ones. But he definitely moved in interesting circles. He was verifiably a close friend of Van Morrison when Van was just coming up. According to legend, when Van visited him at his home in Bangor he spotted some paintings themed around astral projection, and they gave him the idea for his acclaimed solo album *Astral Weeks*.

You could see that there might be a documentary in all that. But Cecil couldn't leave it there. He told me Steven Spielberg was going to pay for it. I thought, well, it's not impossible. But he followed that up with the news that it was going to be a *fifty*-part series. And at that point you knew that it had gone from unlikely to not in a million years.

The Van story alone should have been enough for Cecil to dine out on for the rest of his life. The problem was that it soon morphed into him also having written 'Layla', either with or for Eric Clapton, and his having contributed strongly to the song-writing of The Beatles. He claimed to be a distant cousin of Paul McCartney. He also said he had sold his paintings to Roger Daltrey, to Robin Williams and Bono, and there may be some truth in that, though it's just as likely he gave them to the stars and could thus claim that they owned them.

Cecil lived just beside the Bryansburn Inn, in a house absolutely crammed full of his paintings. During the '60s he also found time to record several psychedelic LPs, at least several tracks from which can still be heard on Spotify or on YouTube. King Om, ruler of the universe, was his stage persona, though I don't know if he was ever actually on a stage. King Om was Ziggy Stardust, before *Ziggy Stardust* was Ziggy Stardust. The only thing that stopped him being a huge star was his inability to sing well or write good songs.

Cecil could definitely paint. In 1967 the Floral Hall, which was situated in the grounds of Belfast Zoo, was the scene of Pink Floyd's first ever show in Northern Ireland – it included 35mm slides of abstract paintings by Cecil being projected over the band.

His connection with Van Morrison lasted until the late 1980s when they had a falling out. Morrison was then living at least part of the time in a house at Crawfordsburn, a small village just outside Bangor. When he wanted to rehearse before a tour, he would take his band down to the Windsor Bar and set up in their disco. Owner Paul would take his morning coffee in and sit and listen to Van play his set. But Van's preferred watering hole was the Crawfordsburn Inn, and it was here that the famously curmudgeonly singer finally lost it with Cecil – arguing not over music, not over art, but rather more prosaically over whether Myra Hindley, the Moors Murderer, should be forgiven for her sins.

Cecil was always hopeful of a reconciliation with the great man, but it wasn't to be. His cause wasn't helped by his spilling the beans on his friendship with Van in a controversial biography.

All of this could be, and perhaps was, a goldmine that could have been exploited by an ambitious young reporter looking for a story with international appeal, but the truth is, I couldn't be annoyed with him. Increasingly, I didn't want to be writing about other people. I just wanted to be writing. But there was also always a good reason not to. I spent more time concocting stories at the mahogany ridge[1] than applying myself to the Great American Novel.

My house was full of memories of my dad and unsold copies of *Bar Stool Boy* staring accusingly at me. I thought perhaps that if I hadn't been able to help the poor children of Africa, I could at least exploit them further.

I entered a version of what I'd got up to in Uganda in a travel-writing competition in *The Observer* and became one of six finalists. We all got sent off to South Korea to compete to be the Young Travel Writer of the Year. I didn't win, but I started going out with the winner, Rosie, which in my book was better than winning.

We stayed on and went to China; it was before they caught capitalism and the roads were still full of bikes instead of luxury cars. We hired two and got caught up in a rush-hour frenzy, which was like competing in the final stage of the Tour de France. We went early one day to the local zoo and locked our bikes up; when we emerged a few hours later there were about ten thousand bikes outside. If you've ever thought forgetting where your car is in a large car park and

---

1   Journalistic term for stories filed from a public bar.

then trying to find it was hard, you should try bikes; we were there for days.

Rosie was from London, and we continued a kind of holiday romance. She introduced me to the mystery novels of Robert B. Parker, and I got addicted. But it ended the way holiday romances usually do. We travelled back and forth for a while, but I think she sensed that I was never really going to leave Bangor – because that's what I told her.

The Young Travel Writer of the Year Competition came round again. I figured it was my best chance of ever having sex again, so I re-entered, this time under a pseudonym, on the presumption that they wouldn't select the same finalist twice. I got selected. And then disqualified for being deceitful.

I was a contradiction – wanting to travel, desperate to do something away from Bangor, but always, always, inexplicably drawn back.

I wasn't finished with exploiting the children of Uganda, either.

Every week the *Speccy* got the *UK Press Gazette*, the trade paper for journalists. I noticed an advert for a Journalism Fellowship at Oxford University. They were looking for journalists to spend three months amongst the dreaming spires working on a specific project. It was mainly designed for foreign reporters. For their blinkered purposes, Northern Ireland was considered foreign. I would have put them right, but I was too busy taking them up on their offer. They would even provide a stipend to live on, and free accommodation in a comfy house in Jericho (the suburb of Oxford, not the ancient Biblical city, which was no longer considered fit for purpose due to trumpets being played too loudly. Bbbbbert up to no good again). Paul was good enough to give me the unpaid time off, and Patch was good enough to go into kennels.

Oxford! It was going to be fabulous. I'd never been to university; no Bateman ever had. This was the top university in the country, possibly the world. This was my big chance. I was going to make the connections that would set me up for the rest of my life. I would dine with future prime ministers. I would debate urgent matters in the Oxford Union. I would go punting on whatever they called their river. I would fall in love and marry someone who played the cello.

Amongst the Fellows there were a couple of Indian reporters, one from Peru, an Australian and three from the US. I immediately struck up a friendship with my housemate, Chris Fox, the only other British reporter. He had qualified because he mainly wrote about oil fields and gas pipelines in places like Kazakhstan. He later went on to become chairman of the Liberal Democrats, and then a lord. But I knew him when he was reporting on gas pipelines and trying to drink me under the table, sometimes successfully.

I also immediately zeroed in on a willowy American called Danielle. She was everything I wanted in a woman. That is, female. She was tall and blonde and funny, and we got on extremely well. She wasn't a big drinker, but we palled around together. I was determined that she should be my girlfriend and possibly my wife, even though she lacked a cello. We would live in New York where I would write my Great American Novel actually in America. She would be my muse and make sure I wrote sidewalk instead of footpath. Then we would move to Hollywood to make the film version, though by then I'd be saying movie version, and our path would be smoothed by her brother Steve, who already worked there with Robert Zemeckis, director of *Back to the Future*. My career and love life would be sorted, if only I could win her heart. I tried to achieve this by gazing into her eyes and getting her drunk. She was unconvinced by this approach.

I knew I had to amp things up.

So we got the bus to London to go and see Margaret Thatcher.

At least, we tried to see her, using our press credentials to get into the viewing gallery at the Houses of Parliament. I hoped that this access to our prime minister, to power and the historic setting, would somehow stir something up in Danielle. She breezed past the security guard, but he wouldn't let me in because I was Northern Irish, although he disguised his obvious racism by saying it was because I wasn't wearing a tie. I said I didn't wear ties. He said then I couldn't come in. We stared each other down and eventually agreed on a compromise, which involved him going to get a cardboard box full of grubby ties people had thrown away in disgust and me agreeing to put one of them on. I asked Danielle to tie the knot. It was quite a romantic thing to suggest, although I only did it because I didn't know how to tie one.

Once inside we watched Maggie Thatcher, then in her final year of power, doing a very good Maggie Thatcher impression during Prime Minister's Questions. Afterwards we adjourned for drinks and something to eat. Danielle's blood was not running as hot as I might have hoped following her exposure to the Milk Snatcher, and she seemed more interested in, and appalled by, the way I was eating my hamburger – that is, with a knife and fork. I said only savages ate with their hands, which did not help me in my pursuit of her undergarments. We got the night bus back to Oxford, and we remained chaste, and she remained chased.

The three months in Oxford flew by. I was supposed to be working on a paper about the work of the charity Love Uganda. I had even done some new research, which involved flying to Kampala for a second visit. Ian Clarke and his family were thriving. He'd gone from treating patients on the steps of his house in the Luwero Triangle to building a large state-of-the-art hospital in the capital. He had also begun writing a weekly column in Uganda's biggest daily paper, the *New Vision*. He later opened new medical facilities in Sudan and Tanzania, as well as twelve other clinics in Uganda. He opened a boutique hotel in Zanzibar. Not having enough to keep him busy, he entered politics and got elected mayor of one of the five municipal districts of Kampala. His private medical group is now worth some $15m. He is a classic overachiever, when he would clearly have been better off staying in Bangor, being a GP.

Although some of his achievements were still in the future, there was plenty for me to write about. Instead, I wrote a radio play about drinking in The Blues. Or part of one. I never finished it. Mostly, instead of doing what I was supposed to be doing, instead of writing a scholarly paper, I skived off, and instead of building bridges, I burned them. I crammed three years of student drinking into three months. From day one I'd known that academia wasn't for me; in fact, I'd always known it.

I had gone to Oxford to have a great time, not to garland my CV, and it was all building towards a terrific climax, hopefully with Danielle.

I was betting everything on the last-night house party, when all of the Fellows would gather to say their fond farewells. I was hoping mine with Danielle would be fonder than with the others. This was my moment, my time, my destiny. For immoral support I invited my friend Eddie up from London. He'd moved over from Bangor to work at the Ministry of Defence. I made a couple of trips up to see him, which involved a lot of drinking, although we also went to see Wimbledon play Liverpool, which also involved a lot of drinking. He paid several visits to Oxford. When I walked him back to the train station the next morning, we'd stop off for a pint while he waited to board. The pint always turned into several, and before we knew it several days had also passed.

Eddie didn't know anyone at the last-night party, but he soon did. He was a charmer of the old school. I worked steadily on my alcohol intake to ensure I was in the proper condition to take the plunge, or indeed, lunge, with Danielle. I found myself sitting on one side of her on a sofa, with Eddie on the other. When I determined the time was right, I made my move, slipping my arm around her and my lips towards her, and she expertly avoided both and stood up to find someone more interesting to talk to.

I retreated to the bathroom to regroup. I determined that my move had been too public. All of the other Fellows were there; we couldn't just suddenly start going at it in front of them, we would have to find some dark corner or adjourn to the garden where I could lay my coat down and we would have at it on the cool grass in the sultry moonlight. Yes, absolutely, that was how it was going to play out. Definitely. Definitely until I returned to the living room to find Danielle snogging the face off Eddie. She had known him for twenty minutes. TWENTY MINUTES. It made no sense, and every kind of sense.

Oxford ended not so much with a bang as a whimper, which was what Patch was doing when I finally saw him after so long away. In my absence my friends had broken into my house. Once in, they cleaned and tidied it. It seemed I wasn't quite capable of looking after myself. I was an untrained, ageing orphan.

I settled back into the routine of work, drinking, and not working on the novel. I had started at the *Speccy* as a callow teenager, and now I was turning thirty and all I had to show for it was a string of broken bright ideas and some mediocre provincial journalism. I couldn't get started on my book.

One of our reporters, Colette, was being sent just over the border to County Monaghan to write a feature about the Tyrone Guthrie Centre. Guthrie was a famous but dead Shakespearean actor whose huge house had been turned into an artists' retreat. Colette had the leaflet for it on her desk. I studied it obsessively. If you were a writer, you could go there for a week, or a month, or a year, just to work. That was my *dream*. That was what I really needed to be able to write my book, to get away from all the distractions (drink, *Coronation Street*, football, drink). I should have gone to write the article myself, but I hadn't let on to anyone that I had ambitions to write a novel. *Anyone*. Not family, not friends, not colleagues; only Patch had his suspicions. I didn't want to show my hand in case they all laughed at me. No, Colette was set for County Monaghan. She drove down and pulled into the beautiful grounds, with their picturesque lake and stunning main house. She parked her *Spectator* van in front of a window. The director of the centre immediately appeared out of the front door, waving enthusiastically as he hurried in her direction. But as he drew closer, Colette realised he wasn't waving, but angrily gesticulating. Baffled, she began to climb out, but he stopped her in her tracks with, 'No! You have to move the van! The poets have to be able to see the lake!'

When she related this on her return, my obvious reaction was, what a bunch of wankers. But it didn't put me off. I continued to nurse dreams of one day retreating there.[2] But it wasn't for complete novices. You had to have some kind of pedigree, and I had nothing.

I decided that actually physically *writing* might be the problem. I'd read that some famous authors actually dictated their books, so I bought a Dictaphone, and sat on the stairs at home and began to compose my Great American Novel out of thin air, letting my mind wander and the words spill out. I brought every character to expressive life and lived every twist and turn of a nascent plot, and that worked right up to the point where Bbbbbbbbert banged on the wall and yelled at me to shut up.

So I did.

The book was not only never going to be written, it wasn't even going to be spoken.

* * * *

---

2 Ten years later I went there for a week. I got some work done. But there wasn't a single TV in the entire house. They were such philistines. When I found myself sitting in my car on the second night, listening to a Liverpool match on the radio in complete darkness, I decided it wasn't for me and did a moonlight flit.

Occasionally in the summer months the gang would hold a barbecue at Ballymacormick Point. It was beautifully scenic, full of gorse and hidden nooks sheltered from the sea breeze. We called it a barbecue, but nobody ever brought any food. What it was, was a campfire, though nobody ever camped. What it really was, was a fire. We brought loads of drink and a ghetto blaster, and if it was a good night we sat there until the sun was coming up, and then we'd wander home with the first faint stirrings of our hangovers. They were always good fun, but this time I wasn't looking forward to it so much. Everyone had coupled up. Even Dave, my *touraloura* partner, was going steady. I was, literally, the odd man out. I refused to go. I wanted to go into Bangor, around the pubs, in that endless, fruitless quest to meet someone. I was on Bob Dylan's Never Ending Tour, and I was just as out of tune with what the public wanted as he was. I just thought, fuck it, I'm going out by myself. I'd never done that before. It smacked of desperation, and I was. I don't know what I expected to happen, but I certainly didn't expect to meet someone I'd eventually marry.

I got pretty drunk before I went out. I went to Jenny Watts in High Street. I drank a couple of pints. Two girls approached. Of course *they* approached *me*. Debbie and Andrea. They liked what I wrote in the *Speccy*. It was soon clear they also liked *me*, and had done for a while, but I'd never stopped still long enough before for them to approach.

It was getting towards closing time. I said there was a brilliant barbecue happening around the Point. They were game. We got a carry-out from behind the bar and walked there.

My friends took the piss out of me for turning up with two girls. We all sat around the fire talking and listening to the music. As the sun came up the three of us began to walk home along the beach. Debbie, sensing something was up, picked up her pace and soon disappeared. Andrea and I walked up Ballyholme Road and on to Hamilton Road. We stopped for a kiss. Andrea would later say our hearts were on fire, but the truth is it was the Tonic cinema that was on fire.

It was 5 a.m., it was broad daylight, there was no one else around, and the massive Tonic cinema, where I'd spent so many happy times, was burning down.

We could hear fire engines in the distance.

And our clothes already stank of smoke from the non-barbecue barbecue.

Fearing that we would be fingered for setting the fire, I suggested that we immediately go to my house and take our clothes off. Andrea, not wishing to go to prison, responded positively.[3]

When we woke a few hours later, Patch was curled up at the bottom of the bed. Patch *never* did that. He didn't growl at Andrea, or attack. These were *signs*.

It was Patch saying, 'My job here is done.'

He collapsed the next day. I took him to the vet. He told me Patch's time was up. I stroked him as the lethal injection was administered. And Patch was gone. When I came out of

---

3   Nobody was ever 'done' for the Tonic burning down. It had lain vacant for several years. Some suspicious types later suggested that because the unique art deco building was covered by a preservation order the fire was an inside job, staged for both the insurance money and so that the site could be sold. As if.

the surgery and went up to pay, I couldn't speak. They waved me away, which was a world first for a vet. I went out to the car and burst into tears. Patch had been my best buddy for sixteen years. He had protected me even when I didn't need it, and he knew all my secrets. He had bitten and attacked other dogs, rabbits, horses and humans, but never once growled at me. He had terrified everyone. The Duchess wouldn't enter my house unless he, or she, was sedated.

I don't know what it says about dogs, or me, that I shed tears over Patch, but not my auntie, or my mum, or my dad. Maybe there in the car I was crying for all of them, I was at last getting it out. Or perhaps it was because I hadn't had to hold either of my parents down while they were euthanised.

Either way, it was five, four, three, two, and now one.

The empty house had become emptier.

There might have been something developing with Andrea. It was early days. She saw my distress over Patch and tried to help. She went to the USPCA kennels and got me another dog. She meant well, but it was a bit like going to the hospital after Dad died and getting me another parent. I freaked out when she arrived back, because she'd chosen a dog who was the spitting image of Patch, except his legs were twice as long. It was Patch on stilts. I felt sorry for the poor mutt, but I had to tell her to take him back. It was too soon. And thirty years on, it's still too soon.

* * *

It only happened a few times a year. Paul would go off on holiday, and for those weeks I was the editor of the *Speccy*. It wasn't particularly stressful, and I enjoyed the responsibility and the papers I produced were exactly the same as the ones Paul produced. They were dependable, traditional and uncontroversial. I was maturing nicely. But also beginning to realise that this was becoming a job for life, that I would never leave the *Speccy* and that I might never become editor, because Paul was only a year older than me and he had no interest in going anywhere either.[4]

It began to eat away at me. It meant I would remain on a fairly low wage for the rest of my life, because I had travelled enough to know I was never leaving Bangor. I was already bored by my weekly column and had stopped writing it. The only challenge in work was tracking down and excising the outrageous libels our freelance contributors tried to sneak into their junior-football reports. There was no excitement on the horizon. The fantasies that had launched me into journalism, of tracking down Nazis, of toppling a president, were exactly that. The most you could say about my journalistic career – from young punk rocker to, er, older punk rocker – was that I had been granted considerable licence to annoy a lot of people, but as enjoyable as that was, it was all ultimately rather insignificant – controversial only because the events had occurred on a very small stage, in a very small town and they had already been forgotten. The Strollers had grown up and the Boys' Brigade still marched up and down. Punk rock had been about nihilism and anarchy, but also youth – and even while still relatively young I was slipping into conformity, and my sad pipe-and-slippers years were already looming. The

---

4   He would remain editor for the best part of thirty years.

punk cry had been 'No future', and I was beginning to embody it.

Here's the date when it all started to change: 22 October 1992.

Paul was off on holiday. I was in charge of the paper. That week had been unremarkable, the same as almost any week dating back to 1904. We put the paper together as we normally did, with most of the heavy lifting taking place on the Wednesday. We worked through that day and into the evening, writing and editing the final copy, then all taking turns to proofread the stories before they were corrected and finally pasted onto their pages.

As the night wore on, I gradually let the reporters go home, until I was the last one left on the editorial side. All that really remained to be done was to decide on our lead story, which we would do the next morning, so that when the paper finally appeared on the streets it would be as up to date as possible.

I went home to Fairfield, tired from the long day, had something to eat and went to bed. I quickly fell asleep. And then woke at 2.45 a.m. when a sonic boom rattled the windows.

I knew instantly it was a bomb.

It was a 200-pounder set off by an IRA unit from the lower Ormeau Road in Belfast. There was no warning given. It devastated our Main Street, badly damaging more than thirty shops. The late-night bars, luckily, were already closed. Four part-time reserve police officers walking up Main Street were seriously injured when the bomb detonated.

I raced down to the scene. There was pandemonium. Fire engines and ambulances and the police and the army and people running about in panic. There was glass everywhere and acrid smoke, and the relentless sound of shop and car alarms filled the air.

Nobody wants a massive bomb in their home town.

Nobody wants to see anyone injured by the IRA.

But if there *has* to be a bomb, if a bomb is inevitable, if you can do nothing about a bomb, then please God let it happen on a Wednesday night, because it is *perfect* timing for a weekly paper.

As long as our premises weren't damaged too badly our paper would come out the next morning with our biggest story in – with our biggest story *ever*.

If it had happened on a Monday, or a Friday, or any other day, it would still have been a huge story, but it would already be old news, it would be second-hand news because it would already have been covered by all of the other outlets, by TV and radio and the daily papers. People would still buy our paper, but our coverage would be retrospective, not of the moment. This bomb in the early hours of Thursday morning was different: it was current; it was now.

And I was in charge.

Captain of the ship.

This was my moment.

My Nazis, my Nixon.

The provincial journalist's dream, local story with international appeal.

I was *there*, it was all happening in front of me, the immediate aftermath of a bombing, and I …

… absolutely froze.

I was 90 per cent adrenaline, but still I froze.

I couldn't make myself do anything.

I knew should be interviewing people. Making calls. I should be marshalling my journalistic troops to cover every possible angle – this is it guys, this is our time – but I couldn't move. The windows had all blown in at the front of the *Speccy*, but I could have got in the back and put everything in motion, begun reporting the greatest story we would ever report.

Instead, I drove home.

I lay down in bed and pulled the quilt over my head.

It was at that moment – my brain pounding, my soul full of confusion and despair, my nostrils still full of smoke and fire – that I realised fully for the first time that I wasn't a journalist, that I'd *never* been a journalist. I enjoyed writing, but I didn't enjoy reporting. I had no interest in, and no capacity for, interviewing people in their moments of crisis. I had no empathy, no urgent curiosity. And it wasn't just about the bomb: I had *never* really had that interest, and it had been amply illustrated by the diversions I had embraced, from band manager to rock promoter to a Diet Coke version of Bob Geldof. I'd failed at all of them because what I really wanted to be doing, but had successfully avoided for years and years, was to be writing that fucking book.

By morning I had regained my faculties. I hurried somewhat fearfully into work, expecting to be taken to task for disappearing, to be quizzed suspiciously about where I'd been and what I'd done, but no – my absence hadn't even been noticed, because everyone else *had* known what to do, had adapted to the conditions and done their job. The reporters had interviewed, the photographers had taken their pictures and they had presumed that I was off somewhere pulling the strings, when in reality I was hiding in bed.

They were all did their jobs brilliantly, and in the end we put together a great paper. My biggest decision was to clear the front page of all news and just run a huge photograph, with a headline superimposed over it: 'DEVASTATED'.

The IRA wrecked our town. But we recovered. We always recovered. Nobody died. The glass was swept away. It was the talk of the town, and then after a while it was no longer the talk of the town. We went back to reporting on council business. In the chamber a councillor said he was caught in a 'Catch-2 situation'. The magistrate continued to chastise and punish shoplifters and careless drivers and drinkers with poor bladder control. We no longer sent reporters to cover Bangor FC's football matches. Instead, they wrote the reports themselves. It was dereliction of duty, but a blessed relief, At least they were able to give everything a positive spin. And it seemed to work, because the following May, fifty-five years after their last appearance in an Irish Cup Final, The Seasiders qualified again, and after two replays they actually won it. It was made all the sweeter because they beat local rivals Ards.

The *Speccy* continued to appear week after week after week, loved and derided in equal parts, but always essential.

After we published our paper in that week of the bomb, we went out and got very drunk. High Street, where most of our pubs are, was mercifully unscathed. We ended up back at my house. They found my kettle covered in cobwebs and took the piss. I'd not had a cup of tea since accidentally drinking my mum's cold tea leaves back when I was four, so the kettle was never used. Instead of making tea, we drank some more.

Bbbbbbbert banged on the wall, but we ignored him and cranked it up. I came out of the bathroom upstairs and found one of the reporters studying the books in my study. When I asked her what she was looking for she turned and kissed me. We were still caught in an embrace when her boyfriend appeared behind us. It all started to kick off. It was a lovely kiss, so worth it. I wouldn't say she was that drunk, although when she went to go home she tried to leave via the airing cupboard.

The next morning I lay in the bath,[5] steaming off my hangover and listening to a replay of *Desert Island Discs* on the radio. One of the selected tracks was a classical piece which I vaguely recognised. I know little about classical music and rarely listen to it. At the end the presenter said it was the *New World Symphony* by Dvořák.

There was something about the name, Dvořák, that stuck with me.

I started repeating it – Dvořák, Dvořák, Dvořák – and then laughing to myself because I'd always pronounced it Dvor-*Jack*. Then I was repeating Dvor-Jack, and playing with it, slowly turning it as it rolled off my tongue into Divorce Jack. It sounded a little bit like a Harrison Ford movie I'd seen recently, *Regarding Henry*. I adjusted it a little to *Divorcing Jack,* and then said it out loud again, deepening my voice like it was the title of a Hollywood movie, the way they did it in the trailers. *Divorcing Jack*, coming soon. It did sound like a movie. Or maybe a book. It could be a good title for a book. All it needed was a plot and characters. I sighed at the thought of making another attempt on the Great American Novel. That was clearly never going to be written. I wasn't capable of it,

---

5   Try not to picture this, it will disturb your sleep patterns.

any more than I was capable of writing the Great Irish novel. Or even the Great Northern Irish Novel. I couldn't even write the Great *Bangor* Novel.

Or could I?

Maybe that had been the problem. I'd set the bar really high. What if instead I set it really low?

The Great Bangor Novel.

That had to be achievable. There would be no competition. My former editor, Joy, was English *and* lived in Groomsport. I could have the title of Great Bangor Novel all to myself.

All I had to do was write it.

But what to write about?

The obvious place to start was with what was freshest in my mind.

The bomb.

And the oldest cliché in the writing handbook is to write about what you know. I would do that. I would write about a journalist, because I was a journalist. A columnist who was a big drinker. Because …

A necessarily fictional element would be that he would be a big hit with the girls. He would be a good-looking charmer, but also a total shit magnet. He would need a name: something short and sharp and memorable, like Bond, or Spade, or even Strummer. I thought back to my wife-not-to-be, Danielle. Her surname was Starkey. That had a certain ring to it. He could be Starkey, Dan Starkey.

The story would be about here, about the bomb, or the impact of a bomb. Who it killed, and why. There were dozens of novels already out there about the Troubles, and I'd read most of them. Invariably they got *here* wrong. They generally got their facts right, but they never understood how we spoke, our gloriously black sense of humour, our dark sarcasm; that was how I would write *Divorcing Jack*. I didn't know who Jack was, or how to work Dvořák into the plot, but I would surely get there. I'd now read all of Robert B. Parker's books, and there was a style of writing ready-made for me to copy: short sentences, not much description, but funny dialogue. I could surely have a crack at that.

I would start it all at a party, with Dan Starkey being caught in an illicit kiss, and that would set off a train of events that ...

I got into a bath to cure a hangover, and got out ready to cure a need, a desire, that had been gnawing at me since I was a teenager. For the first time I knew what I wanted to write, what I *needed* to write, and I also knew that it wasn't going to be done overnight, that there was a long road ahead of me; but in that moment I was convinced that if I parked my arse for long enough, I would get there, I would write what would ultimately become the Greatest Bangor Novel ever written.[6]

---

6   Or certainly in the Top Ten.